HP Technology Series

Cloud Computing: Beyond the Hype

Second Edition

Paul McFedries

HP Press
660 4th Street, #802
San Francisco, CA 94107

CLOUD COMPUTING: BEYOND THE HYPE
Paul McFedries

WARNING AND DISCLAIMER

This book is designed to provide information about Cloud Computing. Every effort has been made to make this book as complete and as accurate as possible, but no warranty or fitness is implied.

The information is provided on an "as is" basis. The author, HP Press, and Hewlett-Packard Development Company, L.P., shall have neither liability nor responsibility to any person or entity with respect to any loss or damages arising from the information contained in this book or from the use of the discs or programs that may accompany it.

The opinions expressed in this book belong to the author and are not necessarily those of Hewlett-Packard Development Company, L.P.

Readers should be aware that Internet Web Sites offered as citations and/or sources for further information may have changed or disappeared between the time this is written and when it is read.

TRADEMARK ACKNOWLEDGEMENTS

All terms mentioned in this book that are known to be trademarks or service marks have been appropriately capitalized. HP Press or Hewlett-Packard Inc. cannot attest to the accuracy of this information. Use of a term in this book should not be regarded as affecting the validity of any trademark or service mark.

GOVERNMENT AND EDUCATION SALES

This publisher offers discounts on this book when ordered in quantity for bulk purchases, which may include electronic versions. For more information; please contact U.S. Government and Education Sales 1-855-4HPBOOK (1-855-447-2665) or email sales@hppressbooks.com.

FEEDBACK INFORMATION

At HP Press, our goal is to create in-depth technical books of the best quality and value. Each book is crafted with care and precision, undergoing rigorous development that involves the expertise of members from the professional technical community.

Readers' feedback is a continuation of the process. If you have any comments regarding how we could improve the quality of this book, or otherwise alter it to better suit your needs, you can contact us through email at feedback@hppressbooks.com. Please make sure to include the book title and ISBN in your message.

We appreciate your feedback.

Publisher: HP Press

HP Contributors: Christian Verstraete and Richard Hykel

HP Press Program Manager: Michael Bishop

HP Headquarters

Hewlett-Packard Company
3000 Hanover Street
Palo Alto, CA
94304-1185
USA

Phone: (+1) 650-857-1501
Fax: (+1) 650-857-5518

Contents

Chapter 5 The Pros and Cons of Cloud Computing 87

Introduction

In a famous Dilbert comic strip from 2011 (see http://dilbert.com/strips/comic/2011-01-07/), the Pointy-Haired Boss tells his assembled team that he has "hired a consultant to help us evolve our products to cloud computing." That consultant (played by Dogbert) then repeats the phrase, "Blah blah cloud" four times. The Boss, his eyes wide in amazement, exclaims, "It's as if you're a technologist and a philosopher all in one!" To which the consultant replies, "Blah blah platform."

This strip hits home because if you listen to cloud mavens, talk to cloud experts, and read cloud pundits, "Blah blah cloud" is a pretty good approximation of what they seem to be saying. Cloud computing papers, articles, books, podcasts, and talks are all-too often an impenetrable mix of IT jargon, business buzzwords, and bad metaphors. (If one more cloud wordsmith tells me that "not every cloud has a silver lining" or warns me that "a storm is brewing in cloud computing" or describes an overview as being "above the clouds," I think I might scream.)

How bad is it? A well-known cloud computing analyst was asked to define cloud computing and, as part of his answer, said the following:

> Put simply cloud computing is the infrastructural paradigm shift that enables the ascension of SaaS.

It is hard to know where to begin here! Perhaps it is the head-scratchingly opaque text that follows the "Put simply..." opening; or perhaps it is the use of the phrase "paradigm shift," a guaranteed eye-glazer (for the record, other than what you have just read, you will not find the phrase *paradigm shift* anywhere else in this book); or, finally, it might be the sheer incomprehensibleness of the phrase "the ascension of SaaS" for anyone who does not know what on earth *SaaS* might be (good news: you will learn all about SaaS in this book!).

Even worse, much of what passes for cloud computing journalism out there is misguided, confused, or just plain wrong. For the latter, I can think of no better example than the official (who shall remain nameless) who claimed that, "Cloud computing is unreliable in a storm; if it rains, the data might get washed away." (And, no, I do not believe this person had his tongue in his cheek; would that it was so!)

The tragedy of all this inscrutable and inaccurate cloud info is that it prevents the rest of us from learning about what is turning out to be one of the most important IT trends of the young century. Your company must deal with megatrends such as globalization, speed-of-light information exchange, and increasingly intense competition, and we are beginning to see that cloud computing is an ideal tool for handling these trends and even turning them to your advantage.

That may be why the people who work with you or for you are clamoring for cloud—whether it is the IT department, which sees cloud computing as a way to turn IT into a center of innovation for the company, or a business unit that needs the cloud because they are tired of waiting forever to get their technology projects up and running. Your people are asking you to make the move to cloud computing, but how can you evaluate such a move when you do not know what cloud computing is all about, and the available resources range from esoteric to erroneous?

Welcome, therefore, to *Cloud Computing: Beyond the Hype*. In this book, I explain cloud computing, using the assumption that you are not an IT professional. Instead, this book looks at cloud computing from the point of view of a business manager who needs to know the cloud's basic ideas and characteristics, who needs to be sold on the cloud's merits, who needs to be warned about its pitfalls, and who needs to know the basic steps for getting from here to cloud. I take you on a complete cloud journey, from the very basics, to the most important cloud components, to making the business case for cloud, and to getting your company to the cloud efficiently, economically, and safely.

Even better, I do all of that without relying on IT jargon and cloud buzzwords, and without getting into the arcane and abstruse technical details that underlie even the simplest cloud implementation. (That is what your IT department is for.)

I had a great time researching and writing this book, and I believe you will find it the best and easiest-to-understand introduction to cloud computing. I hope you enjoy the book!

1 Introducing Cloud Computing

We are used to seeing fads come and go, particularly in the fickle realm of popular culture: hula hoops, Pet Rocks, CB radio, the Atkins Diet, and Crocs, to name but a very few. You would think that technology would not be buffeted by such changeable winds, but a quick look at some technologies in even recent history belies that hope: PointCast, flash mobs, Tamagotchis, Second Life, Friendster, and LOLcats, to name a few. So the to-the-point question is this: "Is cloud computing just another technological fad?" If you talk to people in IT or read the business press, you'd be forgiven for thinking the answer is a resounding "Yes!" After all, the word cloud seems to be on every speaker's lips and every writer's fingertips.

One of this book's goals is to convince you that cloud computing resolutely is not a fad. It may be overhyped at the moment (more on that later), but it is definitely not some passing technical fancy that you can turn a blind eye to and move on with your business life. Why am I so sure that cloud computing won't end up in the dustbin of technological history, alongside virtual reality and (soon) MySpace? Because, at its heart, cloud computing is not based on the appeal of whimsy or the pull of marketing. Instead, it is a reaction to a world that is undergoing drastic changes economically, culturally, and socially.

For example, Christian Verstraete, HP's Chief Technologist for Cloud Strategy, recently identified five key megatrends that are helping to fuel the cloud computing fire[1]: *urbanization* and the subsequent rise in buying power of an ever-growing urban middle class, particularly in the cities of developing nations; *globalization*, which increases competition and puts pressure on businesses to lower costs; the *rise of social media*, which generates unprecedented amounts of data that businesses can take advantage of for marketing, product development, and more; the *mainstreaming of mobility*, where almost everyone has a mobile phone or tablet and, therefore, expects to be able to access data, make purchases, and perform many other traditional desktop chores while nowhere near a desk; and *sustainability*, where the movement to greener technologies and smaller carbon footprints means companies must change how they do business.

Combine a dynamic business environment, the current uncertain economic situation, and the inevitable cost limitations imposed on any company that watches the bottom line, and the result is that businesses today must be fast, flexible, and frugal.

Combine the *consumerization* of IT (IT end users increasingly make their own computing choices); the coming tsunami of *big data* (massive amounts of often unstructured data generated by server logs, social networking, and the *data exhaust* of customers, suppliers, and employees); and the rise of a new workforce of *digital natives* (people who have grown up using digital technologies); and the result is that businesses today must be inclusive, intelligent, and innovative.

Yes, every business still needs strong leadership, good products and services, and talented people to implement a well-defined business strategy, but it also needs the help of the IT department. However, traditional IT requires big-budget hardware, extensive end-user training, and a team of engineers and developers that act as go-betweens for that hardware and those users. It's powerful, to be sure, but it's neither nimble nor quick, and neither agile nor frugal.

It's an Instant-On World

Welcome, therefore, to the brave new world of the *instant-on* business. To understand what I mean, consider what happens when you enter a darkened room. No doubt your first act is to locate and then flick on the nearest light switch, instantly lighting the room. That is how electricity works: it is always available, it can be delivered with a mere flip of a switch, and you never have to give a single thought to where it comes from.

It was not always so. Even long after it was shown that electricity could be harnessed to power devices and machines, and even long after Thomas Edison had shown that it was possible to use a central generating station to supply electricity to remote buildings, most businesses generated their own electrical power. In fact, according to Nicholas Carr in his book *The Big Switch*, by the year 1900 there were a whopping 50,000 private electric plants running in the United States[2].

However, thanks to the discovery of alternating current, the invention of sophisticated usage meters, and the advent of variable pricing models, it soon became more efficient and more cost effective for businesses to purchase electrical power from a utility rather than generating it themselves. By 1930, utilities were supplying 80 percent of the electrical power used in the United States, and not long after that only a few diehard factories still generated their own power[4]. But that switch to utilities wasn't just about saving money. As Carr says:

> Manufacturers came to find that the benefits of buying electricity from a utility went far beyond cheaper kilowatts. By avoiding the purchase of pricey equipment, they reduced their own fixed costs and freed up capital for more productive purposes. They were also able to trim their corporate staffs, temper the risk of technology obsolescence and malfunction, and relieve their managers of a major distraction.[5]

As you will see throughout this book, the benefits that came from moving electrical power generation from an internal plant to an external utility mirror quite precisely the benefits of adopting cloud computing. As Amazon CEO Jeff Bezos once said, "You don't generate your own electricity, why generate your own computing?"[6]

> "Factory owners, having always supplied their own power, were loath to entrust such a critical function to an outsider. They knew that a glitch in power supply would bring their operations to a halt—and that lots of glitches might well mean bankruptcy."[3]
> —Nicholas Carr

So *instant-on* describes computing services that are available immediately (or, at least, extremely quickly), just like electrical power or other utilities, such as water and natural gas. Do you have instant-on IT in your business? Probably not. It's more likely that your IT products are "eventually on" where they go through the same interminable process over and over: identifying a business need; applying for a new IT product to meet that need; planning meetings; approval meetings; ordering new IT assets (such as hardware and software); installing the new assets when they finally arrive; developing the application; testing the application; and, at long last, deploying the application.

In a typical IT department, it can easily take weeks or, more likely, months to go from idea to deployment, a timeframe that is anything but nimble. Moreover, these newly provisioned IT assets will almost certainly be designed, configured, and optimized to solve only the original business need. Such assets are said to be *siloed* since other departments or lines of business have no access to the new assets, a situation that is anything but flexible. Put simply, if a bit starkly, a business that is neither nimble nor flexible lacks the overall agility to compete successfully in the modern marketplace.

In a globalized, accelerated, wired world, the *eventually on, siloed* way of doing things no longer delivers what business needs, when it needs it. Today's companies must be agile, on-demand entities that can quickly, effectively, and proactively respond to competitive threats, macroeconomic shifts, business opportunities, and technological trends. Becoming an instant-on business means giving your IT department the technological equivalent of a gym membership that transforms IT into a lean, mean, computing machine that offers the following:

- **Speed** Like flipping a light switch or turning on a tap, you need business solutions *now*, not months from now.

- **Flexibility** New IT assets should deliver value to the entire company, not just a single department or line of business.

- **Leanness** The era of overspending and underutilizing IT assets is over; the instant-on enterprise utilizes smart pricing strategies that match actual needs.

> "There was a time when every household, town, farm or village had its own water well. Today, shared public utilities give us access to clean water by simply turning on the tap; cloud computing works in a similar fashion. Just like water from the tap in your kitchen, cloud computing services can be turned on or off quickly as needed." [7]
> —Vivek Kundra

- **Agility** The instant-on enterprise implements an overall IT model that provides the right solution, at the right time, for the right price.

This book's thesis is that cloud computing is the IT makeover you need to transform your company into an instant-on enterprise. To that end, let's take a closer look at cloud computing to help you understand what you're getting into.

What is Cloud Computing?

In many network diagrams, the designer is most interested in the devices that connect to the network, not the network itself. After all, the details of what happens inside the network to shunt signals from source to destination is often extremely complex and convoluted, so all that minutiae would serve only to detract from the network diagram's larger message of showing which devices can connect to the network, how they connect, and their network entry and exit points.

When the designer of a network flowchart wants to show the network but not any of its details, he or she almost always abstracts the network by displaying it as a *cloud* icon. (It is, if you will, the "yadda yadda yadda" of network diagrams.) This practice began with the telephone network, and Figure 1-1 shows a typical example.

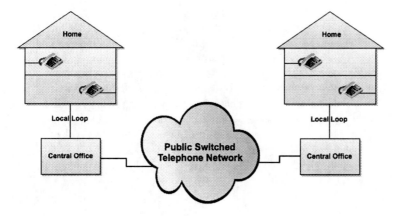

Figure 1-1 In telephone network diagrams, the network portion is often represented by a cloud. Source: www.sellsbrothers.com[8]

Computer network engineers took naturally to the cloud concept, and for several decades network designers have been using the cloud symbol to abstract the complexities of network routers, switches, relays, and protocols. At first the cloud symbol represented the workings of a single network, but in recent years it has come to represent the Internet, as you can see in the example diagram in Figure 1-2.

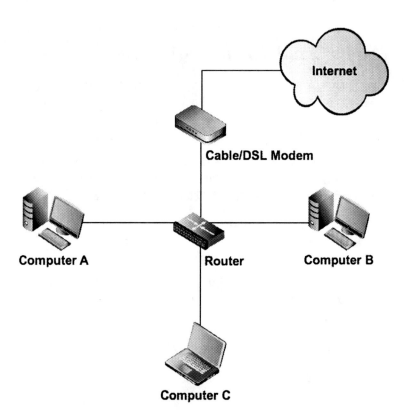

Figure 1-2 The cloud symbol is now most often seen as an abstraction for that network of networks, the Internet.

In the 1990s, when Sun Microsystems made their famous declaration that "the network is the computer," scientists and engineers began giving serious thought to the idea that computing could happen remotely, as part of a network process, instead of locally, as part of a computer process. Somewhat inevitably, this came to be known as *cloud computing*, and the first known use of the term comes from Ramnath Chellappa, now an Associate Professor at Emory University, at the INFORMS meeting in Dallas in 1997. In a talk titled *"Intermediaries in Cloud-Computing: A New Computing Paradigm,"* professor Chellappa introduced the world to a new phrase:

> Computing has evolved from a main-frame-based structure to a network-based architecture. While many terms have appeared to describe these new forms, the advent of electronic commerce has led to the emergence of *cloud computing*.[9]

The NetCentric Corporation actually tried to trademark the phrase *cloud computing* back in 1997, but they prudently abandoned the attempt in 1999.[10]

The phrase was later popularized by Google's then-CEO Eric Schmidt who, in an interview at the Search Engine Strategies Conference on August 9, 2006, said:

> It starts with the premise that the data services and architecture should be on servers. We call it cloud computing — they should be in a "cloud" somewhere. And that if you have the right kind of browser or the right kind of access, it doesn't matter whether you have a PC or a Mac or a mobile phone or a BlackBerry or what have you — or new devices still to be developed — you can get access to the cloud.[11]

Figure 1-3 shows a Google Ngram plot for *cloud computing*, where you can see how the phrase has taken off in recent years (as I write this, 2008 is the latest year available in the Google Ngram Viewer).[12]

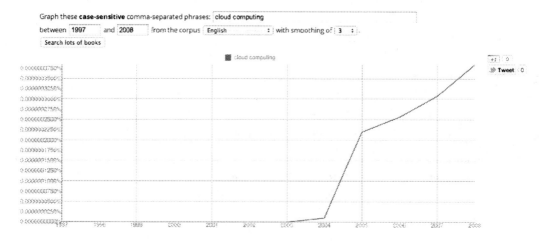

Figure 1-3 A Google Ngram plot that shows the frequency of references to the phrase "cloud computing" within the Google Books collection.

Defining Cloud Computing

So just what exactly *is* cloud computing, anyway? You would think that the world's cloud geeks and gurus would have gotten together ages ago to nail down a pithy and precise definition of cloud computing, but I am afraid that is not the case. Ask 25 cloud mavens to define cloud computing, and you will get 25 different answers in return. That is not good enough for our purposes, so I will provide you with the most generally accepted definition shortly. In the meantime, let's get a feel for things by looking at some alternative definitions:

- **Barebones** The best computer is no computer.

- **Casual** The *cloud* refers to the amorphous, out-of-sight, out-of-mind mess of computer tasks that happen on someone else's equipment.[13]

- **Forrester Research** A standardized IT capability (services, software, or infrastructure) delivered via Internet technologies in a pay-per-use, self-service way.[14]

- **Gartner** A style of Computing where scalable and elastic IT capabilities are provided as a service to multiple customers using Internet technologies. [15]

- **IDC** An emerging IT development, deployment and delivery model, enabling real-time delivery of products, services and solutions over the Internet (i.e., enabling cloud services). [16]

- **Wikipedia** Cloud computing is the delivery of computing as a service rather than a product, whereby shared resources, software, and information are provided to computers and other devices as a metered service over a network (typically the Internet). [17]

For our purposes in this book, I am going to refer to two key definitions of cloud computing throughout. The first is the *standard* definition used by many cloud professionals and pundits, and it is supplied by the National Institute of Standards and Technology (NIST):

> Cloud computing is a model for enabling convenient, on-demand network access to a shared pool of configurable computing resources (e.g., networks, servers, storage, applications, and services) that can be rapidly provisioned and released with minimal management effort or service provider interaction. [18]

The second is the HP definition, which hews closely to the NIST text, albeit with some useful additions and emendations:

> Cloud computing is a delivery model for technology-enabled services that provides on-demand access via a network to an elastic pool of shared computing assets (e.g. services, applications, servers, storage, and networks) that can be rapidly provisioned and released with minimal service provider interaction. The entire value can be bi-directionally scaled as needed to enable pay-per-use.

Cloud Computing: Key Terms and Features

To help you understand these definitions, let's break out some key terms and features and expand upon them a bit:

- **Model** It is important to remember that cloud computing isn't a step-by-step, one-size-fits-all technique for doings things in the cloud. There are many paths to the cloud and many destinations once you get there, and this is reflected in the use of the word *model* in these definitions.

- **Delivery model** The inclusion of the word *delivery* in HP's definition is to remind you that the main purpose of the cloud is to provide solutions to business problems.

- **Technology-enabled services** From a cloud perspective, a *service* is a set of software functions that are related in some way. For example, a customer relationship management service would have functions for adding contacts, editing contacts, recording customer interactions, and so on. These services are generated by a cloud provider and accessed through an online or network interface, so they are *technology-enabled*.

- **On-demand access** Cloud providers give you direct access to resources, so they provide an *on-demand* service.

- **Shared/elastic pool** A traditional IT resource is configured as a silo, making it available only to a narrow subset of users, and preventing it from being used by other parts of the business. By contrast, similar cloud resources are combined together into a *pool* that can be *shared* by many other users, and can be provisioned and released as needed, making it *elastic*.

- **Configurable** Cloud resources often come with some sort of management interface that enables the user to configure the resource to suit the user's needs.

- **Computing resources/assets** These are the items that the cloud delivers, and they are either hardware-related, such as servers, storage, and networks, or software-related, such as services and applications.

- **Rapidly** Cloud providers give you access to resources within seconds or minutes, not weeks or months.

- **Provisioned and released** Once you have requested (*provisioned*) a new cloud asset, you need only use it for as long as it is required, at which time you then return (*release*) the asset back to the pools.

- **Minimal management effort** Cloud providers give you access to resources without you having to jump through the hoops involved in the traditional request/create/deploy process.

- **Minimal service provider interaction** In most cases, you can provision a cloud asset without dealing directly or indirectly with a cloud provider employee.

- **Bi-directionally scaled** The cloud enables you to adjust the amount of resources you are using—that is, to *scale* those resources—in two directions: It can provision resources when you need extra assets, for example, during your company's busy season; and it can release resources when you no longer need them, for example, when business slows.

- **Pay-per-use** With the cloud, you pay for assets only when you use them.

Characteristics of Cloud Computing

From the NIST and HP definitions of cloud computing, and my explanations of the key terms in those definitions, a few important cloud-computing characteristics are starting to bubble up to the surface. In *The NIST Definition of Cloud Computing*, the authors list five such characteristics:[19]

On-demand self-service

Broad network access

Resource pooling

Rapid elasticity

Measured service

You'll see that these characteristics form the core of cloud computing, but if you want to develop a more sophisticated and more nuanced appreciation of the cloud, then we need to extend and emend these ideas. With that goal in mind, here are four more traits of cloud computing that you need to know:

Abstraction of resources

Virtualization of resources

Automation

Service-based, not product based

The next few sections describe each of these characteristics.

On-Demand Self-Service

NIST: A consumer can unilaterally provision computing capabilities, such as server time and network storage, as needed, automatically, without requiring human interaction with each service's provider.

Broad Network Access

According to the NIST, capabilities are available over the network and accessed through standard mechanisms that promote use by heterogeneous thin or thick client platforms (e.g., mobile phones, laptops, and PDAs).

Resource Pooling

According to the NIST, the provider's computing resources are pooled to serve multiple consumers using a multi-tenant model, with different physical and virtual resources dynamically assigned and reassigned according to consumer demand. There is a sense of location independence, in that the customer generally has no control or knowledge over the exact location of the provided resources but may be able to specify location at a higher level of abstraction (e.g., country, state, or data center). Examples of resources include storage, processing, memory, network bandwidth, and virtual machines.

Note

Here, the *network* refers to either an internal network or the Internet, and *standard mechanisms* generally refers to the protocols that enable network communication, such as TCP/IP. Although not specifically mentioned here, you can also interpret the word "broad" to mean "from any location."

Note

Any cloud service offers a particular *tenancy model* that determines who has access to the resources. A *shared tenancy* (more often called *multi-tenant*) model refers to a cloud service that enables multiple, diverse customers to share resources; a *dedicated tenancy* model refers to a cloud service that allows only a single customer to use its resources.

Rapid Elasticity

According to the NIST, capabilities can be rapidly and elastically provisioned, in some cases automatically, to quickly scale out, and then rapidly released to quickly scale in. To the consumer, the capabilities available for provisioning often appear to be unlimited and can be purchased in any quantity at any time.

Measured Service

According to the NIST, cloud systems automatically control and optimize resource use by leveraging a metering capability, at some level of abstraction appropriate to the type of service (e.g., storage, processing, bandwidth, and active user accounts). Resource usage can be monitored, controlled, and reported, providing transparency for both the provider and consumer of the utilized service.

 Note

Measured (more often called *metered*) service means that cloud spending becomes an operational expense rather than a capital expense, a change that can have a huge effect come budgeting time. See "Chapter 6: The Business Case for Cloud Computing," for more information about this.

Abstraction of Resources

In the cloud, hardware resources—particularly servers, storage, and networking—are abstracted from the software and data resources. The NIST document refers to this obliquely by talking about *location independence* (see the *Resource Pooling* paragraph, above), which means that where resources are located is opaque to the customer (the resources could be across the building or across the country). But abstraction goes beyond that, where whatever physical mechanism is used to store and process data in the cloud, as well as to transmit data to and from the cloud, is also opaque to the consumer. The amalgamation of resources into a shared pool is also a form of abstraction, since it no longer matters to the customer which server or hard drive gets provisioned.

Virtualization of Resources

To *virtualize* a resource means to create a simulation of that resource, using software. The most common example of virtualization is a *virtual machine*, which is a simulation of a computer that is a fully functioning device in the sense that it can have its own operating system

Note

Although virtualization is a feature in almost every cloud offering these days, the absence of the term from both the NIST and HP definitions (indeed, from all of the definitions I provided earlier) tells you that it's not a necessary feature of cloud computing. Cloud providers could just as easily (although not as quickly) provision "bare metal" resources, such as physical servers and hard drives.

and run its own applications. In the cloud, these virtual machines are servers, but other cloud resources are also virtualized, including storage and networking infrastructure. This enables a cloud service provider to offer huge pools of resources, because instead of purchasing, say, thousands or tens of thousands of physical computers, it can operate a much smaller number of servers and have each one run dozens of virtual machines. Virtualization also contributes to the "rapid elasticity" of the cloud, because a virtual resource can be provisioned and released extremely quickly compared to a physical resource that might take hours or days to add or remove. Finally, virtualization also means that any updates to a resource—such as more memory, a faster processor, or an operating system patch—are streamed to the customer automatically.

Automation

In the *On-demand self-service* characteristic I mentioned earlier, the NIST authors talk about consumers provisioning resources "automatically without requiring human interaction with each service's provider."[20] This is part of the concept of cloud *automation*, but the idea goes further than that. In many cases, cloud applications *themselves* (that is, without operator intervention on the customer side) can provision new cloud resources as needed, during periods of high demand. When demand slows, these applications can also de-provision resources to reduce costs.

Service-Based

The offerings of cloud providers are not products, in the traditional sense of the term. A product is (usually) a physical object with certain characteristics that can be configured and customized based on interaction between the customer and the seller. By contrast, cloud offerings are virtual objects (the details of which have been abstracted to be opaque to the consumer), which can be provisioned and configured automatically. Therefore, cloud offerings are services, not products.

What Is Not Cloud Computing?

In IT circles, *cloudwashing* refers to renaming or rebranding an existing non-cloud product or service to make it appear (most often innocently, but sometimes deceptively) as though the product is cloud-related. This is also called *cloud envy*, because some companies are so envious of other vendors' cloud offerings that they assuage this feeling by rebranding an existing product as a cloud tool.

When you're shopping for a cloud provider or cloud services, how can you avoid getting duped by cloudwashing? The easiest way is to take the cloud computing characteristics from the previous section and apply them to the provider or service. In particular, watch out for the following non-cloud *features*:

- The vendor wants to charge you a license fee for the use of a service. In the true cloud, you only pay for what you use.

- Along similar lines, the vendor charges a minimum amount per month (or whatever). In the true cloud, if you don't use a service, then your monthly minimum becomes zero.

- The vendor requires that you use a particular resource for a minimum amount of time. In the true cloud, you can immediately provision resources and, just as importantly, you can immediately release those resources when you no longer need them.

- The process for provisioning or releasing computing resources is complex and must be handled by someone at the provider end, such as a sales rep. In the true cloud, resources are scaled automatically and are self-provisioned.

- The vendor brags that its cloud services are based on technologies from a particular company. In the real cloud, abstraction means that it doesn't matter where the underlying technologies come from, and virtualization means that multiple technologies are (or can be) supported.

Cloud Computing Service Models

> "You can find 100 reasons not to move to the cloud. But you're going to look up one day and all you will be doing is managing the systems that connect all your printers."[21]
> —Carl Ryden

At its heart, cloud computing is a variation on the classic client/server networking model, where a client—which might be a dumb terminal or similar *thin client* that offers only limited computing resources, or a notebook or desktop computer—connects to and uses a server computer's resources, which might be applications, documents, storage, or even peripheral devices such as printers.

In cloud computing, the client side may still refer to thin clients, particularly modern devices such as smartphones and tablets, but it can also refer to end-users, developers, IT personnel, and even software that require access to cloud services. The server side refers to hardware or software that has been specifically designed to deliver cloud services, but abstracted and almost always virtualized.

Between the cloud client and the cloud server there are various categories of services that can be accessed within the cloud. These are known as the cloud service models, and The NIST Definition of Cloud Computing lists the following three:[22]

- **Cloud Software as a Service (SaaS).** The capability provided to the consumer is to use the provider's applications running on a cloud infrastructure. The applications are accessible from various client devices through a thin client interface such as a web browser (e.g., web-based email). The consumer does not manage or control the underlying cloud infrastructure, including network, servers, operating systems, storage, or even individual application capabilities, with the possible exception of limited user-specific application configuration settings.

- **Cloud Platform as a Service (PaaS)** The capability provided to the consumer is to deploy onto the cloud infrastructure consumer-created or acquired applications created using programming languages and tools supported by the provider. The consumer does not manage or control the underlying cloud infrastructure including network, servers, operating systems, or storage, but has control over the deployed applications and, possibly, application hosting environment configurations.

- **Cloud Infrastructure as a Service (IaaS)** The capability provided to the consumer is to provision processing, storage, networks, and other fundamental computing resources where the consumer is able to deploy and run arbitrary software, which can include operating systems and applications. The consumer does not manage or control the underlying cloud infrastructure, but has control over operating systems, storage, deployed applications, and, possibly, limited control of select networking components (e.g., host firewalls).

See "Chapter 3: Cloud Service Models," to learn more about these and other service models.

Cloud Computing Deployment Models

A second way of looking at cloud computing is through its *deployment models*, which reference the location of the cloud's infrastructure and how it is managed. The NIST Definition of Cloud Computing lists the following four deployment models:[23]

- **Private cloud** The cloud infrastructure is operated solely for an organization. It may be managed by the organization or a third party and may exist on premise or off premise.

- **Community cloud** The cloud infrastructure is shared by several organizations and supports a specific community that has shared concerns (e.g., mission, security requirements, policy, and compliance considerations). It may be managed by the organizations or a third party and may exist on premise or off premise.

- **Public cloud** The cloud infrastructure is made available to the general public or a large industry group and is owned by an organization selling cloud services.

- **Hybrid cloud** The cloud infrastructure is a composition of two or more clouds (private, community, or public) that remain unique entities but are bound together by standardized or proprietary technology that enables data and application portability (e.g., cloud bursting for load-balancing between clouds).

See "Chapter 4: Cloud Deployment Models," for a more detailed look at these deployment models.

Some Problems Solved By Cloud Computing

In "Chapter 5: The Pros and Cons of Cloud Computing," I take you through some of the major advantages of moving to the cloud (and, to keep things balanced, I also work through some of the not insignificant disadvantages of cloud life). You'll see that cloud brings many good things to the IT table, but it can also help solve a few problems that are probably plaguing your IT department right now: IT silos, IT sprawl, and shadow IT.

IT Silos

Although the modern business world is characterized by its fevered rate of change and the ferocity of its competition, companies have always had to adapt and compete to survive. Any organization that merely treaded water for any length of time was doomed to sink without a trace.

From an IT point of view, adapting and competing usually means coming up with new infrastructure, technologies, and applications to handle burgeoning data requirements, solve business problems, and support new and changing lines of business. In a traditional IT environment, however, these new resources are budgeted, planned, and provisioned for a particular department, business application, or line of business. This means that the resources "belong" to a single entity within the company, and that the resources are, therefore, supported by a single set of requirements, processes, and governance that are configured and optimized for that entity.

All this means that it is impossible to share these resources with any other part of the business, and it is extremely difficult for these resources to communicate with other technologies within the company (for example, to share data). Such resources are known as *silos* because they are effectively isolated from the rest of the business. There are two main problems associated with silos:

- **Overprovisioning** Since a silo technology is provisioned for a single entity within the business, it must have enough capacity—such as processing power, memory, or storage—to handle peak demands expected by the consumer of the technology. This almost always means that the technology runs well under capacity most of the time, so it is said to *overprovisioned*. It's bad enough that provisioning dedicated hardware or software is a slow and cumbersome process, but overprovisioning adds cost injury to process insult by forcing the business to pay more just to support a hypothetical peak demand that might arise rarely, if at all.

- **Inefficiency** Since a silo technology cannot communicate with other resources within the business, developers must build or purchase applications—known as *middleware*—that bridge the gap between the silo and any other system where a connection is required. This is inefficient not only because IT personnel almost always have better things to do than write or configure middleware applications (particularly, middleware that only works for a single case), but also because these applications often degrade performance.

> "Organizations still taking a siloed approach to addressing organizational challenges need to reconsider their strategy or risk becoming obsolete in a market that is rapidly adopting cloud and virtualized technologies to support their business needs with our without IT."[24]
> —Christian Verstraete

Cloud computing solves the IT silo problem. First, because provisioning is on-demand and elastic, an application can ask the cloud for more resources during peak demands, and then de-provision those resources when demand ebbs. Second, since cloud resources are abstracted, virtualized, and pooled, they can be shared with multiple departments or lines of business.

IT Sprawl

If you were to take a cold, hard, dispassionate look at your IT department, what would you see? If your company is like most today, chances are you would see an infrastructure being held together with the digital equivalents of duct tape and chewing gum. Despite years of massive capital expenditures, you would see long-in-the-tooth hardware, ancient legacy applications, archaic storage technologies, and formidably complex network architectures.

How did this happen? The main culprits are those IT silos I talked about in the previous section. A single silo does not amount to much in a large IT infrastructure, but today's businesses are saddled with an exploding number of silos in every corner of the organization. Inherently rigid, expensive, and inefficient, these silos drag down the

> "In the long run, though, the greatest IT risk facing most companies is more prosaic than a catastrophe. It is, simply, overspending."[25]
> —Nicholas Carr

IT department, forcing them to spend most of their time and budget maintaining and patching these silos and "just keeping the lights on." This is known as *IT sprawl* (or sometimes *data center sprawl*).

As a result of sprawl, IT spends a sobering 70 percent of its time on operations and maintenance and just 30 percent of its time on innovation.[26] In a dynamic, competitive, innovate-or-die world, your goal should be to reverse those percentages. Cloud computing can help you do that by eliminating technology silos, reducing IT capital expenditures, and giving your business a nimble, agile way to handle IT resources for the benefit of the business.

Shadow IT

> "A number of years ago we asked a line of business people what percentage of their business processes changed more than once a year, and they came back with 40-45%. We then asked CIO's how many of their applications were changed more than once a year and they came up with 5-10%. Business people are tired by IT's inability to address their changing needs. They have to use Excel and other tools to bridge the gap."[27]
> —Christian Verstraete

Back in the 1980s, I worked for a publishing company with a traditional IT department. By "traditional" I mean that if you needed to analyze or query some data, you had to submit a request to IT, which then reviewed the request, approved it (hopefully!), and then ran the report. That sounds reasonable enough, but the time between the initial request and receiving the printout (yes, it was hard copy-only) could be weeks or months. I'd been programming most of my life, and took lots of computing courses at university, so I knew this was an inefficient process, and as a manager I knew that there had to be a faster way. So I started taking matters into my own hands. Without IT's knowledge, I installed the Lotus 1-2-3 spreadsheet program and the dBASE database program on my work PC, loaded the raw data by hand, and started doing my own data analysis, querying, and reporting.

This is an example of what's now known as *shadow IT* (or sometimes *stealth IT* or *rogue IT*), the use of technologies, devices, services, and applications outside of the IT infrastructure and without IT's approval or knowledge. Shadow IT is a big problem because it means that enterprise data and knowledge ends up scattered around the organization rather than consolidated in one place. It opens security holes because employees can unwittingly expose enterprise data to outsiders and allow unauthorized users access to the corporate network. It can impose extra burdens on IT because if a department's stealth technology suddenly fails (for example, if it was provided by a startup that goes out of business), the department manager might demand that IT replicates the technology, which is now essential because it solves some customer need.

Another aspect of shadow IT is the *consumerization*, because it involves consumers—that is, end-users—circumventing IT not only by wanting to access both internal (IT) and external (Internet) resources using their own devices (a phenomenon known as bring you own device (BYOD)), but also by installing their own software and signing up for their own external services, particularly social networks.

Cloud computing can help solve shadow IT because it offers on-demand self-service, which means that business units can provision infrastructure and applications as needed and without IT involvement. Also, a well-designed cloud strategy can help mitigate the effects of consumerization, because the cloud is inherently friendly to mobile devices such as smartphones and tablets. Not only that, but IT can then offer both internal *and* external cloud services that meet end-user needs, thus turning the IT department into a kind of strategic service broker.

> "What technologies precisely are those in the empowered employees' quiver? There are five: mobile devices, cloud computing services, social technology, exploratory analytics, and specialty apps (that is, apps for the user's specific job, from presentation software to engineering calculators)."[28]
> —Galen Gruman

What Can You Do in the Cloud?

Just how popular is cloud computing? Let's look at some numbers:

- According to the research firm Gartner, cloud computing will be a $149 billion industry by 2015.[29]

- The global cloud-computing market is expected to reach $241 billion by 2020, according to Forrester Research.[30]

- According to IDC, in 2012, 80% of new commercial enterprise applications will be deployed on cloud platforms.[31]

- Cicso IBSG estimates that 12% of enterprise workloads are expected to be in public clouds by 2013.[32]

There are many reasons for the increasing popularity of cloud computing (see "Chapter 5: The Pros and Cons of Cloud Computing"), but one of the biggest is that the cloud is a very welcoming place to do business. I'll get into this in more detail when I discuss the cloud service models in "Chapter 3: Cloud Service Models." But for now it's enough to know that IaaS enables the provisioning of processing power, servers, storage, networking, and more; PaaS gives developers an easy way to build prototypes, run proof-of-concept projects, and serve web apps; and SaaS offers a wide variety of services, including the following:

> Customer relationship management
>
> Human resources and human capital management
>
> Finance and accounting
>
> Content management
>
> Marketing analytics
>
> Business intelligence
>
> Email
>
> Data management (including contacts, schedules, and projects)
>
> Collaboration

Cloud Computing and the Hype Cycle

According to Gartner Group analyst Jackie Fenn, a *hype cycle* is a sequence of events experienced by an overly-hyped product or technology, including a peak of unrealistic expectations followed by a valley of disappointment when those expectations aren't met.

Gartner's hype cycle is actually a five-part sequence, as you can see in Figure 1-4:[33]

- **Technology Trigger** A potential technology breakthrough kicks things off. Early proof-of-concept stories and media interest trigger significant publicity. Often no usable products exist and commercial viability is unproven.

- **Peak of Inflated Expectations** Early publicity produces a number of success stories—often accompanied by scores of failures. Some companies take action; many do not.

- **Trough of Disillusionment** Interest wanes as experiments and implementations fail to deliver. Producers of the technology shake
  out or fail. Investments continue only if the surviving providers
  improve their products to the satisfaction of early adopters.

- **Slope of Enlightenment** More instances of how the technology can
  benefit the enterprise start to crystallize and become more widely
  understood. Second-and third-generation products appear from
  technology providers. More enterprises fund pilots; conservative
  companies remain cautious.

- **Plateau of Productivity** Mainstream adoption starts to take off.
  Criteria for assessing provider viability are more clearly defined.
  The technology's broad market applicability and relevance are
  clearly paying off.

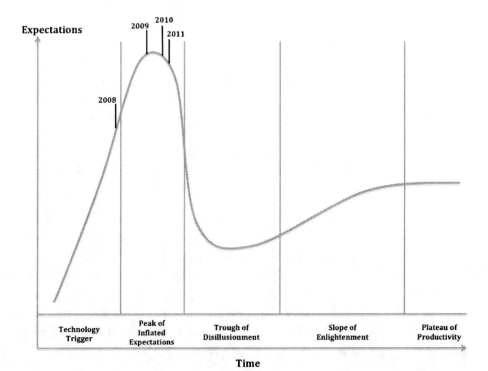

Figure 1-4 The hype cycle. Source: Gartner Group

How does cloud computing fit into the hype cycle? It first appeared in 2008 at the high end of the Technology Trigger phase (see Figure 1-4). By 2009, it had migrated to the very top of the Peak of Inflated Expectations, in 2010 it appeared just below that peak, and in 2011 it had moved a tiny bit further down the curve.[34] In other words, Gartner feels that there's still a whiff of hype to cloud computing, but its steady (albeit slow) movement downward along the hype cycle curve means that it's well on its way to becoming a mainstream technology (which Gartner foresees happening in two to five years).

Dispelling Some Cloud Computing Myths

The hype that still attends many discussions of cloud computing means that you will often come across many misleading, or downright false, cloud-related claims. Many of these are easily dismissed as greatest-thing-since-sliced-bread boosterism, or cloudwashing (see "What Is *Not* Cloud Computing?" earlier in this chapter). However, some of these claims are more subtle because, although they're wrong, broadly speaking, they contain kernels of truth, making them both easier to believe and harder to refute. I will close this chapter by looking at five of these cloud computing "myths."

MYTH 1 Cloud Computing is All about Saving Money

As you'll see in "Chapter 6: The Business Case for Cloud Computing," the study of *cloudonomics* is complex, and the conclusions you can draw about the costs of cloud computing are not always straightforward or cut and dried. However, I can broadly say that making the move to cloud computing does lead to cost savings for most businesses, mostly because it involves exchanging expensive, provisioned-for-peak-demand capital expenses (CapEx) for relatively cheap, pay-per-use operating expenses (OpEx).

However, if you listen to some cloud computing pundits, the move from CapEx to OpEx and its resulting improvement to the company's bottom line is the *only* reason to shack up in the cloud. It is an important reason, to be sure, but if you go into this thinking only of saving money, then your cloud computing adventure will be off to a wrong start from which it may never recover.

The true goal of any cloud computing effort is to reallocate IT resources to allow the business to focus on projects that differentiate it from its competitors, and to react with nimbleness and agility to changing market, macroeconomic, or technological conditions.

MYTH 2 Slow and Steady is the Right Pace to the Cloud

Cloud computing is a relatively new technology, so its principles and best practices are not yet set in stone. The conventional wisdom is that when you want to make a move to the cloud, baby steps are the way to go. For example, if you want to implement a private cloud, you begin by virtualizing a few IT resources, particularly servers. From there, you slowly virtualize more resources, not just servers but also networking, storage, and so on. Once a critical mass of virtualization is reached, you then implement *infrastructure convergence*, which creates a pool of all your virtualized resources so that they can be allocated dynamically and efficiently. From there, you create or install automation technologies that enable resources to be provisioned automatically. Finally, using your converged infrastructure as a foundation, you install private cloud software and run a few proof-of-concept test deployments. Once you have things shaken out, you deploy the full private cloud.

That is called "taking the stairs" to the cloud, and there's nothing wrong with that approach, particularly if you want to leverage your existing hardware. Remember, however, that it is not the *only* approach. You can also "take the elevator" to the cloud by implementing a private cloud right off the bat. In this approach, you virtualize your resources, converge and automate your infrastructure, and set up the private cloud all at the same time. Instead of taking months to get a cloud up and floating, you can do it in weeks. For example, HP's CloudStart[35] turnkey private cloud solution claims it can get your cloud off the ground in just 30 days.

MYTH 3 There is One and Only One Path to the Cloud

You have seen in this chapter that cloud computing is a complex bit of business, with multiple service models (IaaS, PaaS, and SaaS) and multiple deployment models (private, public, community, and hybrid). Despite this, many cloud experts will tell you that there is only one way to get your business involved in cloud computing. Some swear that only a private cloud is necessary, while others counsel a dive into the deep end of a public cloud. Some pundits say in no uncertain terms that the only way to go is an IaaS cloud that enables you to construct your own platform and build your own apps. Others declaim in equally confident tones that all anyone needs these days is a good collection of SaaS providers.

So, which path is the right one? All of them. And none of them. In reality, the "right" path is the one that's best for your enterprise, based on your resources and business needs. As you'll see in "Chapter 7: Setting Up a Cloud Strategy," your first step towards cloud computing should always be to assess your company's needs and goals, and then choose a cloud path that satisfies those needs and supports those goals.

MYTH 4 Mission-Critical Applications are Too Important for the Cloud

Your mission-critical applications are the lifeblood of your enterprise, and they are probably the most expensive and complex applications you run, and the most hardware-dependent. Whether it is Microsoft Exchange Server, SAP BusinessObjects, or SAS Enterprise BI, how can these behemoth and critical applications run in the cloud? Many pundits will tell you these apps should *not* go near the cloud because they are simply too important and too complex.

For many businesses, these pundits are right, and those businesses should concentrate on other types of cloud deployments. However, that does not mean that mission-critical applications can *never* be deployed in the cloud. Many tools are available to help migrate applications to the cloud, such as HP Cloud Maps,[36] which offers workflows, deployment scripts, and best practice templates for some of the most popular enterprise software packages.

MYTH 5 Private Clouds are Secure, Public Clouds are Insecure

Cloud security is a huge and important topic, so I devote an entire chapter to it later in the book (see "Chapter 13: Understanding Cloud Security Issues"). However, the received wisdom on cloud security goes like this: Public clouds are inherently insecure, so you should protect sensitive data by storing it in a private cloud, which is inherently secure.

It's certainly true to say that, generally speaking, public clouds are less secure than private ones. After all, private clouds are located on the business premises and so, reside behind the corporate firewall, while public clouds are "out there" on the Internet where, theoretically, anyone can access them. That is fine as far as it goes, but it is not the whole story.

First, consider that most public clouds are operated by computing giants such as Amazon and Google. These colossi have the wherewithal (and incentive) to hire the most talented, knowledgeable, and experienced cloud security personnel, and the resources to install the most advanced cloud security hardware and software. This does not mean that public clouds will never be compromised. The world's dark-side hackers are simply much too smart and determined for that claim to ever be made with full certainty. It does mean, though, that public clouds are much more secure than you may have been led to believe.

However, your company's governance, risk, privacy, and compliance regulations may mean that you have not-to-be-trifled-with rules concerning the storage and handling of sensitive data. Those rules might then force you to store your data locally, in a private cloud. Does that make your data 100% safe? No, unfortunately, not. Those same nefarious hackers have been known to penetrate corporate firewalls, and of course there is always the risk of insider attacks, employee data theft or loss, or inadvertent non-authorized access to the network, due to consumerization and shadow IT vulnerabilities.

REFERENCES

1   **Christian Verstraete**, *The business aspects of Cloud: Part 1 – Responding to Megatrends*, Cloud Source Blog, http://h30507.www3.hp.com/t5/Cloud-Source-Blog/The-business-aspects-of-Cloud-Part-1-Responding-to-Megatrends/ba-p/104861 (December 28, 2011)

2   **Nicholas Carr**, *The Big Switch* (New York: W. W. Norton & Company, 2008), p.37.

3   **Carr** p. 37.

4   **Carr** pp. 38-44.

5   **Carr** 43-44.

6   **Jeff Bezos,** as quoted in Spencer Reiss, *Cloud Computing. Available at Amazon.com Today*, Wired, http://www.wired.com/techbiz/it/magazine/16-05/mf_amazon (April 21, 2008).

7   **Vivek Kundra**, *The Economic Gains of Cloud Computing*, CIO.gov, http://www.cio.gov/pages.cfm/page/Vivek-Kundra-Speech-at-Brookings-Institution (November 4, 2011).

8   *Windows Telephony Overview*, http://www.sellsbrothers.com/content/poststuff/writing/intro2tapi/pstn.htm

9   **Ramnath Chellappa**, *Intermediaries in Cloud-Computing: A New Computing Paradigm*, INFORMS Dallas 1997, http://meetings2.informs.org/Dallas97/TALKS/MD19.html, October 29, 1997

10 http://tarr.uspto.gov/servlet/tarr?regser=serial&entry=75291765

11 **Eric Schmidt**, *Conversation with Eric Schmidt hosted by Danny Sullivan*, Search Engine Strategies Conference, http://www.google.com/press/podium/ses2006.html (August 9, 2006)

12 http://books.google.com/ngrams/graph?content=cloud+computing&year_start=1997&year_end=2008&corpus=0&smoothing=3

13 **Ashlee Vance**, *The Cloud: Battle of the Tech Titans*, Bloomberg Businessweek, http://www.businessweek.com/magazine/content/11_11/b4219052599182.htm (March 3, 2011).

14 **James Staten**, *Cloud Is Defined, Now Stop the Cloudwashing*, Forrester, http://blogs.forrester.com/james_staten/09-10-14-cloud_defined_now_stop_cloudwashing (October 14, 2009).

15 **Daryl Plummer**, *Experts Define Cloud Computing: Can we get a Little Definition in our definitions*, Gartner, http://blogs.gartner.com/daryl_plummer/2009/01/27/experts-define-cloud-computing-can-we-get-a-little-definition-in-our-definitions/ (January 27, 2009).

16 **Frank Gens**, *Defining "Cloud Service" and "Cloud Computing"*, IDC, http://blogs.idc.com/ie/?p=190 (September 23, 2008).

17 http://en.wikipedia.org/wiki/Cloud_computing

18 **Peter Nell and Tim Grance**, *The NIST Definition of Cloud Computing*, National Institute of Standards and Technology, Information Technology Laboratory, http://www.nist.gov/itl/cloud/upload/cloud-def-v15.pdf (October 7, 2009).

19 *The NIST Definition of Cloud Computing* 1.

20 *The NIST Definition of Cloud Computing* 1.

21 **Carl Ryden**, quoted in Ashlee Vance, *The Cloud: Battle of the Tech Titans*, Bloomberg Businessweek, http://www.businessweek.com/magazine/content/11_11/b4219052599182_page_7.htm (March 3, 2011).

22 *The NIST Definition of Cloud Computing* 2.

23 *The NIST Definition of Cloud Computing* 2.

24 **Christian Verstraete**, *Cloud computing no longer just a CIO issue as it grabs attention of the C-Suite*, Cloud Source Blog, http://h30507.www3.hp.com/t5/Cloud-Source-Blog/Cloud-computing-no-longer-just-a-CIO-issue-as-it-grabs-attention/ba-p/102757 (November 30, 2011).

25 **Nicholas Carr**, *IT Doesn't Matter, Rough Type*, http://www.roughtype.com/archives/2007/01/it_doesnt_matte_6.php (January 11, 2007).

26 *HP Converged Infrastructure: Solution Brief*, http://h20195.www2.hp.com/V2/GetPDF.aspx/4AA3-2922ENW.pdf.

27 **Christian Verstraete**, *Cloud is not just another form of Outsourcing*, Supply Chain Management Blog, http://h30507.www3.hp.com/t5/Supply-Chain-Management-Blog/Cloud-is-not-just-another-form-of-Outsourcing/ba-p/83285 (November 14, 2010).

28 **Galen Gruman**, *Hands off, IT: 5 key technologies users must own*, InfoWorld, https://www.infoworld.com/t/consumerization-it/hands-it-5-key-technologies-users-must-own-181200 (December 23, 2011).

29 http://www.nytimes.com/2011/08/31/opinion/tight-budget-look-to-the-cloud.html

30 http://www.informationweek.in/Cloud_Computing/11-04-26/Forrester_forecasts_USD_241_billion_cloud_computing_market_by_2020.aspx

31 http://www.businesswire.com/news/home/20111201005201/en/IDC-Predicts-2012-Year-Mobile-Cloud-Platform

32 http://www.cisco.com/web/about/ac79/docs/wp/sp/Service_Providers_as_Cloud_Providers_IBSG.pdf

33 *Hype Cycles*, Gartner, http://www.gartner.com/technology/research/methodologies/hype-cycle.jsp

34 http://www.gartner.com/it/page.jsp?id=1763814

35 http://www8.hp.com/us/en/business-services/it-services.html?compURI=1077482

36 http://h71028.www7.hp.com/enterprise/us/en/partners/cloudmaps.html

2 A Review of Cloud Computing Architecture

One way to explore a new land is the *boots on the ground* technique, where you wander the territory and note its features and formations. However, that approach is time-consuming and almost always provides only a sketchy view of the terrain. An often better way to get a feel for a fresh landscape is the *bird in the air* technique, where you survey the area from on high. This big-picture approach lets you see the ecosystem in its entirety, which allows you to orient yourself when you are finally ready to explore the new land in detail.

Cloud computing has only been around in any sort of significant form for a few years. As such, it is new territory even for many people in IT, and it is almost completely unknown terrain for most folks on the business side of the enterprise. In this chapter, you take to the air, so to speak, as I offer you a bird's-eye view of the cloud computing landscape. You learn about various cloud computing architectures, which are models that provide a forest-instead-of-the-trees view of cloud computing. This will help you get comfortable with the lay of the cloud computing land, and give you a mental map to use as we explore the cloud in more detail in the chapters to come.

The NIST Cloud Computing Reference Architecture

In "Chapter 1: Introducing Cloud Computing," I presented several cloud computing definitions, but I focused mainly on the *NIST Definition of Cloud Computing*[1] (as well as the closely-related HP definition). The NIST definition offers the twin advantages of being both widely cited and respected, and vendor- and technology-neutral. As such, it represents the best starting point for explaining cloud computing concepts and terminology.

In this chapter, I return to the hard-working folks at NIST's Information Technology Laboratory. Here, I will use the NIST Cloud Computing Reference Architecture[2] as the starting point for a big-picture discussion of the cloud computing ecosystem. Once again, NIST is an ideal place to begin because this reference architecture is vendor- and technology-neutral, and is widely cited within the cloud community. However, this architecture is not without its critics, and I will examine those as well to help provide you with a more complete and more nuanced overview of cloud computing.

Without further ado, Figure 2-1 shows a model that offers a high level view of the NIST reference architecture.

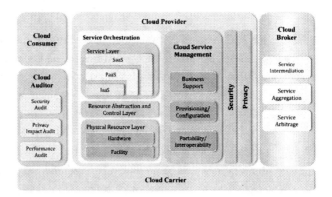

Figure 2-1 An overview of the NIST Cloud Computing Reference Architecture. Source: NIST[3].

The purpose of the model in Figure 2-1 is to identify the major entities involved in cloud computing, and to describe what these entities do and what their functions are. In this chapter, I discuss the five main cloud computing entities: providers, consumers, brokers, auditors, and carriers. In "Chapter 3: Cloud Service Models," I offer you a detailed look at the IaaS, PaaS, and SaaS service models, and then in "Chapter 4: Cloud Deployment Models," I complete this architecture discussion with a rundown of the public, private, community, and hybrid deployment models.

Cloud Provider

A *cloud provider* (also called *a cloud service provider* or *CSP*) is an organization that makes cloud computing services available to others, particularly to cloud consumers and cloud brokers. The cloud provider is responsible for acquiring, configuring, and managing whatever hardware and software is required to provide these services, as well for arranging the delivery of these services through the network to cloud consumers and brokers.

The details of this vary depending on the service model used by the cloud provider. At one extreme, you have a full IaaS provider who must acquire and manage the physical servers, storage, networks, and other computing infrastructure required to offer end-users virtualized computing resources, such as virtual servers. At the other extreme, you have a SaaS provider that merely hosts its application on a platform offered by another PaaS provider, and so has no infrastructure responsibilities at all.

In Figure 2-1, you can see that the cloud provider's duties fall into four broad categories:

- Service orchestration
- Cloud service management
- Security
- Privacy

Service Orchestration

This category refers to the array of resources that the cloud provider uses to build, support, and deliver its services. The NIST Cloud Reference Architecture represents this category as a three-layer stack.

The lowest of these is the *physical resource layer* where the actual hardware—that is, the physical data center components—that serves as the cloud computing infrastructure resides. This includes the physical computing hardware such as servers, network components (including routers, cables, and firewalls), and storage devices (hard drives), as well as the data center facility resources, such as lights, power, and air conditioning.

The middle section is the *resource abstraction and control layer*. Resource abstraction refers to the virtualizing of computing resources, including virtual servers, virtual hard drives, and virtual networks, and the pooling of those resources to allow for rapid provisioning and de-provisioning. The control layer refers to the software programs and interfaces that are responsible for abstracting, pooling, allocating, and metering these resources.

The topmost component is the *service layer*, which defines the categories of service the provider needs to implement whatever offerings it presents to the consumer. Note that a cloud provider need not (and, indeed, most do not) implement all three service models. For example, there are cloud providers who are just IaaS, PaaS, or SaaS vendors. Moving up to the next level of complexity, a cloud platform provider who wants maximum control over the underlying infrastructure would build its PaaS offering on its own IaaS components. Similarly, an app vendor that requires more control over the platform on which it builds and tests its applications would construct its own PaaS layer and use it to develop and deploy its SaaS applications. At the top of the complexity heap would be a SaaS provider that maintains its own PaaS development layer running on its own IaaS infrastructure.

⚡ Note

Although it is not obvious from the reference architecture model shown earlier in Figure 2-1, it is important to note that the cloud consumer (and the cloud broker) only interact with the Service Orchestration category via the service layer—the IaaS, PaaS, or SaaS offerings. Only the data center operator has access to the physical resource layer and resource abstraction and control layer.

Cloud Service Management

This category refers to the functions that the cloud provider uses to manage its services and the interactions between those services and the cloud consumers (and brokers). The NIST Cloud Reference Architecture breaks down this category into three subcategories.

The first subcategory is *business support*, which includes all the business-related processes that the cloud provider must implement for provider-client interactions. These include managing accounts, customer support and service, managing contracts, billing, pricing, and reporting. A major aspect of this subcategory is the creation and management of the *service catalog,* which is a list of the services that the provider makes available to the client.

The second subcategory is *provisioning and configuration*, which covers the processes that enable the client to choose and manage the provider's services. These include provisioning and de-provisioning of resources, configuring resources, monitoring resource use, metering resource use, and monitoring and enforcing service level agreements (SLAs).

The third subcategory is *portability and interoperability*. *Portability* refers to the ability to move information from one cloud environment to another. Specifically, *data portability* means being able to copy data from one cloud to another, and *system portability* means being able to migrate a full virtual machine from one provider to another. *Interoperability* refers to the ability to use cloud data and services across two or more cloud environments.

Security and Privacy

No matter what type of cloud deployment model is used—public, private, or hybrid—the cloud provider is responsible for keeping important data safe and sensitive data away from unauthorized users. This is such an important topic that I devote an entire chapter to it later in this book. See "Chapter 13: Cloud Security Issues."

Cloud Consumer

The *cloud consumer* is an end-user or organization that uses one or more services offered by a cloud provider. At the retail level, the cloud consumer is an individual who uses public SaaS offerings, such as Google Docs and Microsoft Office Web Apps; at the enterprise level, the cloud consumer is an employee, IT department, or business unit that requires private or public SaaS, PaaS, or IaaS resources for a business need.

After establishing an initial relationship with the provider, the cloud consumer peruses the provider's service catalog, chooses a service, and then arranges for payment (if any). The consumer will also have to agree to the terms of service offered by the provider, particularly an SLA that stipulates the minimum levels of performance, uptime, and security.

Figure 2-2 shows a few example services that cloud consumers can choose.

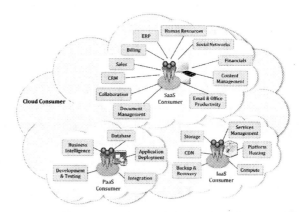

Figure 2-2 Some services that a cloud consumer can choose from a cloud provider's service catalog. Source: NIST.[4]

SaaS consumers can be individuals who use applications directly; organizations that provide access to an application for some or all of their users; or administrators that use the cloud providers' interfaces to configure applications for their users. Many SaaS offerings are free, but most often payment depends on factors such as storage, bandwidth, time used, or the number of users.

PaaS consumers are almost always software developers, testers, deployers, or administrators. PaaS consumers are billed based on storage, bandwidth, or computing resources used by the application.

IaaS consumers are usually IT managers, system administrators, software developers, and, increasingly, business managers who require access to infrastructure resources, particularly, virtual computers and storage. IaaS consumers are billed based on usage, such as per-hour charges for use of a virtual machine, and per-gigabyte charges for use of a virtual hard drive.

Cloud Broker

A *cloud broker* is an organization that acts as an intermediary between a cloud consumer and one or more cloud providers. In much the same way that an insurance broker simplifies the procurement and management of multiple lines of insurance—such as home, auto, and life—a cloud broker simplifies the procurement and management of multiple cloud computing services. Given guidelines and priorities set by the consumer, the cloud broker can research cloud providers, negotiate terms and contracts, and manage the relationship between the provider and the consumer.

The NIST reference architecture breaks down the cloud broker's duties into the following three categories:

- **Service Intermediation** The cloud broker injects some value-added service between the cloud provider and the cloud consumer. For example, the cloud broker might offer enhanced security or sophisticated monitoring and reporting.

- **Service Aggregation** The cloud broker combines two or more cloud provider services into a new service that satisfies a consumer need or simplifies consumer-provider interactions. For example, the broker might offer both data cleansing and data integration in a single service.

- **Service Arbitrage** The cloud broker aggregates multiple services into a single service, but is also given the flexibility to choose from a variety of providers within a set of specified parameters, such as pricing or performance.

> "In the post-modern business, we'll witness the emergence of cloud brokerages, which will act as specialist intermediaries between customers and cloud service providers. Cloud brokerages aggregate, integrate, govern and customize cloud services to make those services more specific to the needs of the customers. IT leaders must engage cloud brokers to make it easier to trade in a world of specialists."[5]
> —Daryl Plummer

Cloud Auditor

A *cloud auditor* is a third-party individual or organization that examines a cloud provider's services from one or more of the following perspectives:

- **Security Audit** This type of audit determines whether the cloud provider service implements safeguards and measures that protect against accidental loss of data or unauthorized access to the system.

- **Privacy Impact Audit** This type of audit determines whether the cloud provider service conforms with applicable laws and regulations or enterprise guidelines and rules concerning the confidentiality and integrity of personal information.

- **Performance Audit** This type of audit determines whether the service meets the minimum performance guarantees spelled out in the cloud provider's SLA.

Cloud Carrier

A *cloud carrier* is an organization that builds and maintains the infrastructure that enables the connection between a cloud provider and cloud consumer, and that transports the provider's services to the consumer.

The HP Functional Cloud Reference Architecture

The NIST model for a cloud reference architecture is useful for understanding many important cloud concepts, including the interactions between a cloud provider and a cloud consumer, service orchestration, and service management. However, this model is not without its problems. In particular, the NIST model places a great deal of emphasis on the SaaS/PaaS/IaaS stack, but fails to place these service models within the context of the cloud platform on which they run.

That is because the NIST model is somewhat consumer-centric, and the consumers of services generally do not care where those services come from or how they are delivered.

However, our goal here is to understand how cloud computing works, so we need to go beyond the NIST model and view cloud computing from a different, more holistic angle. This new viewpoint is provided by the *HP Functional Cloud Reference Architecture*[6], which is summarized by the diagram shown in Figure 2-3.

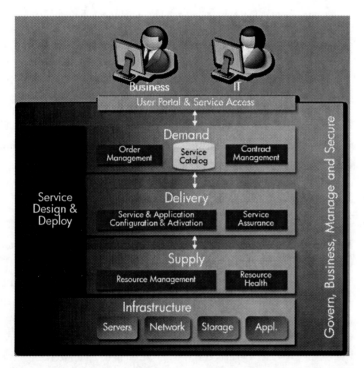

Figure 2-3 A diagram for the HP Functional Cloud Reference Architecture.

This model divides IT's responsibilities into functions that apply only to the cloud, and functions that apply to both cloud and non-cloud environments.

The common cloud and non-cloud functionality is depicted as the background of the diagram shown in Figure 2-3, and it comprises four main functions:

- **Governance** IT must support enterprise policies and standards, as well as rules and guidelines for things like compliance and risk.

- **Business needs** IT must enable business functionality, including things like accounting, finance, strategy, procurement, and client relationships.

- **Management** IT must manage its own services, including the design, deployment, and operations of those services.

- **Security** IT must ensure the security of the enterprise through functions such as identity management, network monitoring, and the protection of information, applications, and infrastructure.

The rest of the architecture diagram applies to the cloud side of IT's responsibilities, which is represented as a four-layer stack: demand, delivery, supply, and infrastructure.

Demand Layer

The demand layer is where the end-user (that is, the cloud consumer) interacts with the cloud. The user can be an individual accessing the cloud through a portal (for example, a website), or an application accessing the cloud through the cloud provider's application programming interface (API). In either case, the purpose of this layer is to allow the user to browse, provision, and configure services from the cloud provider (which could be an internal IT department or an external cloud vendor).

The demand layer works by first having the user log on to the provider's system. An individual logs on through a *self-service portal* set up by the provider, which is often a website running on the Internet (if the provider is external) or an intranet (if the provider is internal), but it can also be an interface from an application running on the user's PC (or similar device); an application logs on by including credentials as part of its initial API calls. The provider then uses identity management functionality to verify the user and determine which services she is allowed to access.

> "By 2016, no one will be using the term cloud. This isn't because it is a fad that will fade, but because it will actually be the new normal."[7]
>
> — Ric Telford

An individual user is then presented with a *service catalog*, which is a collection of services that the cloud provider offers, although the user only sees those services that are allowed based on her security credentials. For each service, the catalog lists components such as the infrastructure and applications that make up the service, the resource pools from which service components can be provisioned, and service information such as the cost, current discounts, and SLAs.

After perusing the catalog, the user chooses an appropriate service. At this point, the demand layer's *order management* function takes over and initiates the provisioning of the service. (Note, too, that the user may also request to configure or de-provision an existing service.)

If the user is interacting with an external cloud provider, that request first travels to the provider's own demand layer, where the provider verifies the user and its *contract management* function takes care of billing, usage stats, and SLA issues.

Delivery Layer

Once the user makes the service request, it is passed to the delivery layer, which is responsible for provisioning and configuring services and their components. In the delivery layer, the *service and application configuration and activation* function takes care of the request. This function is responsible for determining which components comprise the service, and then provisioning, configuring, and activating those components. For example, a business team might need a collaboration solution, in which case the provider might offer the following components as part of the service: a virtual server, a server OS such as Windows Server 2008 R2, a collaboration application such as SharePoint, and collaboration-related components within the application, such as a calendar, contact list, discussion forum, and group blog. The delivery layer only makes the service available to the user once each component has been provisioned and activated for use.

The delivery layer also determines (from the supply layer) whether the requested resources are available. If there are not enough resources available, the delivery layer has the option of requesting additional resources from an external provider—this is called *cloudbursting*—to meet the request. In this case, the delivery layer contacts the demand layer (via API calls) of the external provider, which then verifies the request and passes it along to its own delivery layer.

Alternatively, the delivery layer has the option of moving one or more existing workloads to an external provider, so that the new request can be run internally. The latter strategy is required if security, compliance, or performance issues dictate that the new request not run outside the enterprise firewall.

Finally, the delivery layer's *service assurance* function is responsible for ensuring that the service meets the minimum levels of quality, uptime, and performance spelled out in the SLA, as well as ensuring that resources are fully patched and upgraded.

Supply Layer

The supply layer is the home of the resources that deliver the service to the user. These are generally virtualized resources and can include servers, networking, storage, applications, IP addresses, and more. The supply layer's *resource management* function takes care of the resource pool, including creating, configuring, and monitoring the resources. A separate *resource health* function monitors resources for problems.

Infrastructure Layer

The infrastructure layer is the physical underpinning to the entire model. This layer holds the servers that run the virtual resources, the hypervisors that manage those resources, the hard disks that store everything, the networking hardware that ties everything together, and the data center support resources, such as main power, backup power, air conditioning, lights, and so on.

The Cloud Cube Model

As a final take on cloud computing architecture, you should also know about the *Cloud Cube Model,* created by the Jericho Forum. This is a framework for understanding different types of cloud configurations based on how they are provisioned. Figure 2-4 shows the model.

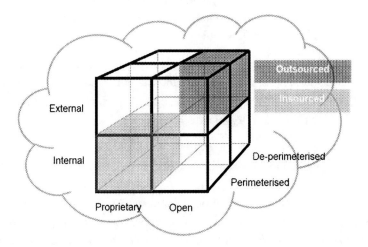

Figure 2-4 The Cloud Cube Model. Source: Jericho Forum.[8]

The Cloud Cube Model looks at cloud architecture along the following four dimensions:

- **Internal/External** This dimension refers to the relative physical location of the cloud environment. An *internal* cloud resides within the physical boundary of the enterprise (for example, in the company data center), while an *external* cloud resides outside the enterprise (for example, in a data center operated by a third party).

- **Proprietary/Open** This dimension refers to the ownership of the technology that underlies the cloud environment. *Proprietary* cloud technology is owned by the company that built or developed the technology, while *open* cloud technology is not owned by any entity and so may be freely shared or used by multiple cloud providers. In general, proprietary systems are more innovative, but data and system portability and interoperability are problematic, while open systems are more generic, but data and systems are much easier to move and interoperate.

- **Perimeterized/De-perimeterized** This dimension refers to whether the cloud services operate within the IT security boundaries. A *perimeterized* operation keeps all cloud services within the IT security firewall, while a *de-perimeterized* operation allows some cloud services outside the firewall (albeit with security precautions in place to protect the data).

- **Insourced/Outsourced** This dimension refers to who provides the cloud service. An *insourced* cloud is built and operated by the enterprise IT staff, while an *outsourced* cloud is built and managed by a third party organization.

These four dimensions create a cloud continuum of sorts. At one extreme, a cloud environment that is internal, open, perimeterized, and insourced will give you the most control over the cloud, its data and applications, portability, interoperability, performance, quality of service, and security. The other extreme is an external, proprietary, de-perimeterized, outsourced cloud, which offers minimal control. Understanding where a cloud provider resides within the Cloud Cube Model can help you decide whether that provider is a good fit, based on the type of service you need, the sensitivity of the data involved, and any compliance issues that surround the service and its data.

Note

The perimeterized/de-perimeterized dimension is not the same as the internal/external dimension, since a perimeterized cloud service could run in an external cloud environment by extending the IT domain to the remote location using virtual private networking to include the virtual server in the internal network.

REFERENCES

1 See http://www.nist.gov/itl/cloud/upload/cloud-def-v15.pdf.

2 **Fang Liu, et al.**, *NIST Cloud Computing Reference Architecture*, National Institute of Standards and Technology, Information Technology Laboratory, http://www.nist.gov/customcf/get_pdf.cfm?pub_id=909505 (September 8, 2011)

3 *NIST Cloud Computing Reference Architecture*, 10

4 *NIST Cloud Computing Reference Architecture*, 13

5 **Daryl Plummer**, *Gartner Says EMEA Enterprise IT Spending in Euros Will Decline 1.4 Percent in 2011 and Grow Only 2.3 Percent in 2012*, Gartner, http://www.gartner.com/it/page.jsp?id=1841115 (November 7, 2011)

6 See http://h30499.www3.hp.com/t5/Grounded-in-the-Cloud/ The-Strategic-Service-Broker-and-the-Cloud-Architecture/ba-p/2407053.

7 **Ric Telford**, *Don't settle for the check mark. Embrace cloud strategically, not tactically.* Wired Cloudline, http://www.wired.com/cloudline/2011/12/ don't-settle-for-the-check-mark-embrace-cloud-strategically-not-tactically/ (December 20, 2011)

8 *Cloud Cube Model: Selecting Cloud Formations for Secure Collaboration*, Jericho Forum, http://www.opengroup.org/jericho/cloud_cube_model_v1.0.pdf (April 2009)

3   Cloud Service Models

I t is not a stretch to say that cloud computing is all about services. Or, more accurately, cloud computing is all about scalable, virtualized services delivered rapidly, elastically, and on-demand, with minimal provider interaction, easy network access, and pay-per-use billing. But the key term remains *services*, not products or systems or any similar consumable computing resource.

So, it is no wonder that the *NIST Definition of Cloud Computing* that you learned about in Chapter 1 has as one of its main components a list of cloud service models that includes Software as a Service (SaaS), Platform as a Service (PaaS), and Infrastructure as a Service (IaaS). These service models form the foundation of all cloud computing interactions between cloud providers and consumers, so if you understand these models, you are well on your way to understanding cloud computing itself.

With that laudable goal in mind, this chapter gives you a more detailed look at these service models, including how they work, how they are used, and examples of what is available.

Review of the SPI Model

The combination of SaaS, PaaS, and IaaS is sometimes called the *SPI model*, and it is an instructive way to look at cloud computing. When it comes to modeling technologies, technologists often turn to the metaphor of the *stack*, a vertical, hierarchical, serially-dependent arrangement of the technology's components. Here, *serially-dependent* means that each component in the stack can only interact with the components above and below it in the hierarchy.

For example, a stack model of a PC (see Figure 3-1) would show the computer hardware at the bottom, the operating system above the hardware, the applications above the OS, and the user at the top. The user can only interact with the applications (including any interfaces presented by the OS, which are de facto applications), the applications can also interact with the OS, and the OS can also interact with the hardware. However, the user can't interact directly with the OS, and neither the user not the applications can interact directly with the hardware.

Figure 3-1 A simplified stack model of the PC.

Stepping back a bit, you can create a similar stack model for the old way of providing computing resources. That is, you have the IT infrastructure at the bottom, a development platform running on top of the infrastructure, the resulting applications above that, and finally, at the top, the user and the devices with which they access these applications. Figure 3-2 shows this stack and, again, the relationships between the layers are serially independent, with each layer interacting only with the layers above and below.

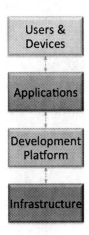

Figure 3-2 A simplified stack model of the old way of delivering IT resources.

To get a cloud computing stack, you might think we could just plug IaaS into the Infrastructure layer, PaaS into the Development Platform layer, and SaaS into the Applications layer (with cloud consumers populating the Users & Devices layer). However, that is not going to give us a complete view of how cloud computing works. Why not? Because, in the cloud, the layers no longer have to interact only with their neighboring layers. For example, a cloud consumer can be a business user provisioning a SaaS application, a developer provisioning a PaaS platform, or an IT manager provisioning an IaaS server.

Nico Poop, of VeriSign, calls this new IT landscape the *cloudscape,*[1] where he envisions the single landmass of the old IT stack broken apart into multiple continents, surrounded by seas of interaction. Figure 3-3 shows his model of the cloudscape.

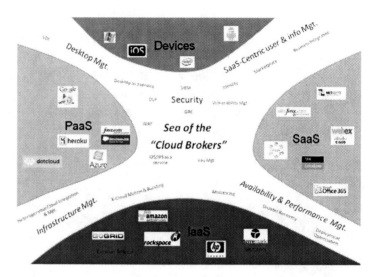

Figure 3-3 The new cloud paradigm uses the SPI model to envision a cloudscape of interacting services.

Keep this cloudscape in mind as I take you through the specifics of the SPI models in the rest of this chapter.

Infrastructure as a Service (IaaS)

IaaS (pronounced *EYE.az*) is the provisioning of virtual, remote computing resources—servers, storage, memory, and networking—that the consumer can use as though they were physical, local resources. Most commonly, consumers provision virtual servers on which they can install and configure whatever operating system and software they require.

So you could say that IaaS is the most fundamental of the service models because, in a simplified sense, it is the *computing* in cloud computing.

How IaaS Works

The IaaS provider purchases, installs, configures, and connects the physical computing hardware that is used to generate the IaaS resources. These physical components include servers, storage, and networking hardware. Not that long ago, all or most IaaS providers ran their own in-house data centers, which meant they also had to configure and manage facility hardware such as lights, cooling systems, power, and backup systems. Nowadays, however, many public IaaS providers are opting to share an existing data center with other IaaS vendors (this is called *co-location*).

The IaaS provider also installs and configures the software that enables it to virtualize, abstract, and automate the resources it offers to consumers. These resources include virtual servers, virtual storage, and virtual networking. The PaaS provider also installs and manages cloud software that offers consumers an interface to provision, configure, and de-provision virtual resources.

The responsibility for configuring, controlling, and managing the physical IaaS infrastructure and the cloud software lies entirely with the provider. The IaaS consumer has near full control over the virtualized resources, allowing the consumer to, for example, install any type of operating system and software on a virtual server.

IaaS virtual server resources are typically priced per hour, and the consumer is charged only for the time spent using the resource. Virtual storage is usually charged per gigabyte per month, while virtual networking costs are based on the amount of upstream and downstream bandwidth consumed.

> "Fundamentally, operating a public IaaS cloud is a networking and software management/development task. Whereas, conversely, running a data center is a utility operation akin to operating a power station! They require a very different focus, skill set and staff." [2]
> —Patrick Baillie

IaaS Use Cases

Since IaaS is really just the provisioning of computing resources on an as-needed basis, the use cases for IaaS are theoretically as varied as the use cases for computing in general. However, there are a few situations and tasks where renting data center resources is particularly useful. Here is a list of the most useful ways that businesses are using IaaS:

- **Computing** Provisioning virtual machines whenever they need raw computing power.

- **Websites** Provisioning virtual servers configured with web server software (and perhaps middleware such as a database management system and web development platform) to offer a website for public (Internet) or private (intranet) use.

- **High-performance computing** Provisioning multiple virtual machines networked as a grid and running software that enables the VMs to work together to solve a complex problem or perform some other task that requires massive amounts of computing power.

- **Storage** Provisioning virtual hard drives to hold massive data stores, such as applications, file archives, and databases.

- **Backup and recovery** Provisioning virtualized storage to use for backups of data or even full system images from network servers and PCs. Those backups can then be used to recover data and systems in the event of a hardware failure.

- **Content delivery network (CDN)** Provisioning virtual machines and networking to store and deliver a CDN, which is a system of networked computers that stores copies of a large data store, such as streaming video, website text and images, or a database.

- **Batch processing** Provisioning multiple virtual machines and networking to partition large batch processing jobs (such as billing) among all the machines.

IaaS Providers

There are dozens of IaaS providers offering computing, storage, and other infrastructure services, so the proverbial (albeit very real) space limitations prevent me from listing all of them. Instead, Table 3-1 lists the most popular IaaS providers of virtual infrastructure resources.

Table 3-1 Some popular IaaS providers.

Company	IaaS Type	Product
Amazon	Computing	Elastic Compute Cloud (EC2)[3]
Amazon	Storage	Elastic Block Store (EBS)[4]
Amazon	Storage	Simple Storage Service (S3)[5]
AT&T	Computing	Synaptic Compute as a Service[6]
AT&T	Storage	Synaptic Storage as a Service[7]
GoGrid	Computing	Cloud Servers[8]
Google	Storage	Cloud Storage[9]
HP	Computing	Cloud Compute[10]
HP	Storage	Cloud Storage[11]
Joyent	Computing	SmartMachines[12]
Microsoft	Computing	Windows Azure Compute[13]
Rackspace	Computing	Cloud Servers[14]
Rackspace	Storage	Cloud Files[15]
Savvis	Computing	Symphony[16]
Terremark	Computing	vCloud Express[17]
Verizon	Computing	Computing as a Service[18]

 Note

For a more complete and constantly growing listing of IaaS providers, see the Infrastructure as a Service section of OpenCrowd's *Cloud Taxonomy*.[19]

Platform as a Service (PaaS)

PaaS (it's pronounced *paz*) is the provisioning of a virtual, remote cloud platform, which is an environment for developing, testing, and deploying applications using tools provided by the PaaS vendor.

How PaaS Works

A PaaS provider installs, configures, and operates the cloud software that offers a platform for consumers to build, test, and deploy applications. The platform components usually include an integrated development environment (IDE) to enable the consumer to code, debug, and test applications; one or more software development kits (SDKs) to enable the developer to code for the platform; and tools to deploy and manage the applications.

The PaaS provider also provisions and manages the infrastructure (servers, storage, operating systems, and so on) that supports the platform. The provider might run its own data center, but it is not uncommon for PaaS providers to lease virtual infrastructure from an IaaS provider.

Finally, the PaaS provider also installs and manages the middleware and other components required by the platform, which might include one or more database systems and a software runtime module to enable the execution of compiled applications.

The responsibility for configuring, controlling, and managing the PaaS infrastructure lies almost entirely with the provider. The PaaS consumer has full control over the application being developed, and also usually has some leeway to configure or customize the development environment provided by the PaaS vendor.

It is also important to understand that different PaaS providers offer different approaches to deploying applications. There are three broad types to consider[20]:

- **Instance PaaS** The provider deploys a single instance of an application for each virtual machine. This is best suited for moving existing applications to the cloud, because the developer can tailor the virtual machine to match the requirements of the application.

- **Framework PaaS** The provider deploys multiple instances of an application as required by demand. To do this, each app must conform to the runtime constraints (that is, the software framework) associated with the virtual environment, so this approach is best suited for new applications.

> **Note**
>
> Some PaaS providers (for example, Amazon Elastic Beanstalk) only provide application deployment services and support for runtime services (such as load balancing and application health monitoring). In these cases, the developer uses its own resources (such as an IDE) to code and test the application, and then uploads the completed application to the PaaS provider.

- **Metadata PaaS** The provider offers a graphical development environment that enables the developer to build the application based on data structures, business rules, forms, and so on.

Whatever type of PaaS provider you use, moving your development team to the cloud offers significant advantages. For example, you never have to worry about configuring middleware components, such as the web server or database management system, and you never have to concern yourself with provisioning virtual machines when demand increases. The PaaS provider handles all that. You also don't have to install or configure the runtime modules, and deploying applications usually takes but a few clicks or a single command-line instruction.

PaaS Use Cases

Here is a list of the most common ways that independent software vendors (ISVs) and IT departments are using PaaS:

- **Development and testing** PaaS consumers can provision development platforms that offer the infrastructure and tools to develop, debug, and test new applications. This is often more convenient than trying to develop and test applications using an in-house platform.

- **Application deployment** PaaS consumers can provision the platform components (runtime modules, database systems, and so on) that enable them to deploy SaaS applications.

- **Database** PaaS consumers can provision platform components that enable them to operate scalable database services, either relational SQL-based systems or non-SQL data stores.

- **Business intelligence** PaaS consumers can provision platforms that enable them to create and deploy business intelligence applications for areas such as data analysis, reporting, and monitoring.

PaaS Providers

There are many existing PaaS providers, and new vendors are putting up PaaS shingles with alarming regularity. Table 3-2 lists the most popular PaaS providers of virtual development platform tools.

Table 3-2. Some popular PaaS providers.

Company	Product	PaaS Type	Language(s)
Amazon	Elastic Beanstalk[21]	Instance	Java
AppFog	AppFog[22]	Framework	Java, .NET, Perl, PHP, Python, Ruby
Engine Yard	Engine Yard[23]	Instance	Ruby
Google	App Engine[24]	Framework	Java, Python
Microsoft	Azure[25]	Instance	Java, .NET, Node. js, PHP
OrangeScape	Visual PaaS[26]	Metadata	N/A
Salesforce.com	Force.com[27]	Metadata	Apex
Salesforce.com	Heroku[28]	Framework	Clojure, Java, Node. js, Play, Python, Ruby, Scala
VMware	Cloud Foundry[29]	Framework	Java, Node.js, Ruby, Scala
WOLF Frame works	WOLF[30]	Metadata	N/A

Note

For more PaaS providers, see the Platform as a Service section of OpenCrowd's *Cloud Taxonomy*.[31]

"The near-infinite scalability of many IT functions, when combined with technical standardization, dooms most proprietary applications to economic obsolescence. Why write your own application for word processing or e-mail or, for that matter, supply-chain management when you can buy a ready-made, state-of-the-art application for a fraction of the cost?"[32]
—Nicholas Carr

Software as a Service (SaaS)

SaaS (pronounced *saz*) is software that is hosted on a provider's cloud platform and is accessible to the consumer using a web browser or similar interface (such as an app running on a smartphone). SaaS is designed to replace many types of retail applications—that is, ready-made programs purchased individually or in bulk via licensing—as well as custom applications coded by an enterprise IT department.

SaaS is the 800-pound gorilla in the cloud computing market, with its share compared to IaaS and PaaS estimated as high as 80 percent. When most consumers think of cloud computing (if they think of it at all; does anyone actually say "Oh, look, I'm cloud computing" when checking Gmail?), they think of web applications such as Google Docs or the Microsoft Office Web Apps, or Apple's iCloud service. They think, in short, of SaaS. This makes SaaS the real domain of the end-user: the person at home, the freelancer, the employee. Yes, IaaS and PaaS have *consumers*, but they tend to be overwhelmingly IT-related: administrators, project leaders, developers.

How SaaS Works

A SaaS provider is responsible for developing, deploying, updating, and configuring one or more applications using a cloud infrastructure that enables the consumer to provision an application. The provider might run its own data center to support the cloud infrastructure, but most often nowadays (particularly with software startups), SaaS providers rent virtual infrastructure from an IaaS vendor (such as Amazon Web Services), or virtual deployment platforms from a PaaS vendor.

The responsibility for configuring, controlling, and managing the applications falls almost entirely with the SaaS provider. In some cases, SaaS consumers can do no more than provision the application, but most SaaS products do offer the end-user some degree of configuration.

SaaS Use Cases

SaaS is the largest cloud computing market for the simple reason that consumers require applications, and they realize that it is often cheaper to use web-based software, and it is often far more convenient, because SaaS apps can be accessed anywhere, anytime, and with just about any device. Also, thanks to technologies such as AJAX and HTML5, it is becoming increasingly feasible to replicate just about any type of application interface and experience over the web (or over an intranet). With the exception of applications that require extreme amounts of computing resources (such as movie editing and animation rendering, although even these are showing signs of moving to the cloud), this means that most common types of software are portable to a SaaS cloud.

> "Forrester reckons SaaS accounts for 80% of the cloud market revenue and dwarfs those revenues from IaaS and PaaS. So when we talk about the cloud market, we are actually beginning to talk about two markets—the enterprise IT department (IaaS/PaaS) and verticals and line-of-business (SaaS)." [33]
> —Steve Hughes

> "Where open-source computing gave us a 90-percent reduction in our software, Amazon [Web Services] gave us a 90-percent reduction in our total operating costs. Amazon allowed 22-year-old tech developers to launch companies without even raising capital." [34]
> —Mark Suster

With all this in mind, here's a list of the most common use cases for SaaS applications:

- **Email** Applications that enable receiving, sending, and maintenance of email messages. This is the most popular SaaS category, with hundreds of millions of users accessing accounts on Google Gmail, Windows Live Hotmail, Yahoo! Mail, iCloud, and many others.

- **Office productivity** Applications that enable the user to perform standard office tasks, such as writing and editing word processing documents, building spreadsheets, and creating presentations.

- **Customer relationship management (CRM)** Applications that enable business users to manage interactions with customers, clients, and sales prospects.

- **Content management** Services that enable the user to produce, organize, and access content for web-based applications.

- **Document management** Applications for creating, organizing, and managing documents, including the use of document workflows and document workspaces.

- **Project management** Applications that enable project leaders to create and maintain project workflows, and enable project members to track project progress.

- **Collaboration** Software tools that enable multiple users to work together to create, edit, and review documents or other types of creative content.

- **Billing** Applications that enable the online management of customer billing and invoicing.

- **Financials** Applications for managing finances, including accounting, expense management, budgeting, payroll, and taxes.

- **Human resources** Software that enables human resource personnel to manage employees, process new hires, and perform other human resources functions.

- **Sales** Applications that enable sales professionals to manage functions such as pricing, promotions, contracts, and commissions.

- **Enterprise resource planning (ERP)** Enterprise-wide systems that manage internal and external business resources, including capital assets, financial resources, materials, IT assets, and human resources.

SaaS Providers

SaaS is the largest and fastest-growing segment of cloud computing, so it boasts hundreds of providers, from tiny, niche startups to globe-straddling corporations. To give you a flavor of what is available, Table 13-3 lists a few SaaS providers in the various categories that you learned about in the previous section.

Table 3-3 Some popular SaaS providers.

Company	SaaS Type	Product
37signals	Project management	Basecamp[35]
37signals	Collaboration	Campfire[36]
37signals	CRM	Highrise[37]
Aria Systems	Billing	Recurring Billing[38]
Dropbox	Collaboration	Dropbox[39]
egnyte	Collaboration	HybridCloud[40]
firLab	Human resources	staffRostering P.R.A.G.A.[41]
Google	Office productivity	Docs[42]
Intuit	Financials	QuickBooks Online[43]
KnowledgeTree Inc.	Document management	KnowledgeTree[44]
Limelight Networks	Content management	Dynamic Site Platform[45]
Microsoft	Collaboration	Office 365[46]
Microsoft	Office productivity	Office Web Apps[47]
NetSuite	ERP	NetSuite ERP[48]
Oracle	CRM	CRM On Demand[49]
Qvidian	Sales	Various[50]
Salesforce.com	CRM	Sales Cloud[51]
Taleo	Human resources	Taleo[52]
Tata Communications	Content management	Mosaic[53]

 Note

For more SaaS providers, see the Software as a Service section of OpenCrowd's Cloud Taxonomy.[54]

More Cloud Services (XaaS)

The *as-a-service* portion of the cloud computing definition is covered completely by the SPI model. However, when people want to discuss all these services as a whole, you won't often see people use the phrase *SPI model* in articles and posts. Instead, they will most often use *XaaS* (pronounced *zaz*), which is short for *Everything as a Service* (often seen as the alternative acronym EaaS, or sometimes *Anything as a Service*—AaaS).

Also, cloud vendors and pundits often find it convenient to break out aspects of the SPI model to focus on more specific service areas. In IaaS, for example, you will often see people focusing on areas such as storage and networking to discuss how these types of virtual hardware can be accessed as a service. So, of course, we need new acronyms to cover the sub-services—such as STaaS for Storage as a Service and NaaS for Network as a Service—and the XaaS ecosystem grows accordingly.

To give you a sense of how large this ecosystem has become (and, therefore, how specific many cloud computing ventures have become), here is a not-even-close-to-complete list of XaaS services (along with their acronyms, if they are popular enough):

- **Backup as a Service (BaaS)** Provisioning cloud-based storage to use for system and data backups.

- **Business Process as a Service (BPaaS)** Cloud services that implement business processes.

- **Communications as a Service (CaaS)** Cloud-based services that enable consumers to communicate using multiple devices via multiple channels (voice, text, and so on).

- **Data as a Service (DaaS)** Accessing a remote database management system hosted in a cloud environment.

- **Failure as a Service (FaaS)** Provisioning cloud-based infrastructure to simulate system failures.

- **Gaming as a Service (GaaS)** Services that offer cloud-based video games.

- **Hardware as a Service (HaaS)** This is the same as IaaS.

- **Information as a Service** Accessing any type of information that resides in a cloud.

- **Integration as a Service (INaaS)** Cloud services that enable the integration of enterprise assets.

- **Management as a Service (MaaS)** Cloud services that enable the consumer to manage other cloud services.

- **Mobility as a Service** Services that enable mobile users to access remote data and applications hosted in a cloud environment.

- **Monitoring as a Service** Cloud services that enable IT personnel to keep watch over networks, websites, and other IT assets.

- **Network as a Service (NaaS)** The provisioning of a virtual network infrastructure located in a cloud environment that the consumer can use as though it was part of the local network.

- **Recovery as a Service (RaaS)** Services that enable the recovery of systems or data from cloud-based backups.

- **Security as a Service (SECaaS)** Cloud-based services that enable IT workers to implement and monitor security features.

- **Storage as a Service (STaaS)** The provisioning of virtual storage located in a cloud environment that the consumer can use as though it was a physical, local resource.

- **Telephony as a Service** Cloud services that enable voice phone calls over the Internet (that is, Voice Over Internet Protocol (VOIP)).

- **Testing as a Service (TaaS)** The provisioning of cloud platform services to test applications.

- **Video as a Service (VaaS)** The hosting of video content in a cloud environment.

- **Voice as a Service** This is the same as Telephony as a Service.

REFERENCES

1 **Nico Popp**, *From Windows to the Cloud: "Nothing is created, nothing is destroyed, everything transforms."* VeriSign Infrablog, http://blogs.verisign.com/infrablog/2011/07/from_windows_to_the_cloud_noth.php (July 11, 2011).

2 **Patrick Baillie**, *Don't run your own data center if you're a public IaaS*, GigaOM, http://gigaom.com/cloud/baillie-public-iaas/ (January 8, 2012).

3 See http://aws.amazon.com/ec2/.

4 See http://aws.amazon.com/ebs/.

5 See http://aws.amazon.com/s3/.

6 See https://www.synaptic.att.com/clouduser/compute_overview.htm.

7 See https://www.synaptic.att.com/clouduser/services_storage.htm.

8 See http://www.gogrid.com/cloud-hosting/cloud-servers.php

9 See http://code.google.com/apis/storage/.

10 See http://www.hpcloud.com/. Note that HP Cloud Compute is currently in beta testing as I write this.

11 See http://www.hpcloud.com/. HP Cloud Storage is also in beta as of this writing.

12 See http://www.joyent.com/products/.

13 See http://www.windowsazure.com/en-us/home/tour/compute/.

14 See http://www.rackspace.com/cloud/cloud_hosting_products/servers/.

15 See http://www.rackspace.com/cloud/cloud_hosting_products/files/.

16 See http://cloud.savvis.com/.

17 See http://vcloudexpress.terremark.com/.

18 See http://www.verizonbusiness.com/Medium/products/itinfrastructure/computing/caas_tab.xml.

19 See http://cloudtaxonomy.opencrowd.com/taxonomy/infrastructure-as-a-service/.

20 This framework is based on original research by Richard Watson of the Gartner Group.

21 See http://aws.amazon.com/elasticbeanstalk/.

22 See http://appfog.com/.

23 See http://www.engineyard.com/.

24 See http://code.google.com/appengine/.

25 See http://www.windowsazure.com/en-us/.

26 See http://www.orangescape.com/.

27 See http://www.force.com/.

28 See http://heroku.com/.

29 See http://www.cloudfoundry.com/.

30 See http://www.wolfframeworks.com/.

31 See http://cloudtaxonomy.opencrowd.com/taxonomy/
platform-as-a-service/.

32 **Nicholas Carr**, *IT Doesn't Matter*, Rough Type, http://www.roughtype.com/
archives/2007/01/it_doesnt_matte_3.php (January 8, 2007).

33 **Steve Hughes**, Has the NIST as-a-service definition come to a crossroads?,
Colt, http://www.colt.net/se/en/blogs/has-the-nist-as-a-service-definition-
come-to-a-crossroads-en.htm (October 14, 2011).

34 **Mark Suster**, *How the cloud changed venture capitalism*, Reuters, http://
blogs.reuters.com/small-business/2011/07/18/how-the-cloud-changed-
venture-capitalism/ (July 18, 2011).

35 See http://basecamphq.com/.

36 See http://campfirenow.com/.

37 See http://highrisehq.com/.

38 See http://www.ariasystems.com/products/recurring-billing.php.

39 See https://www.dropbox.com/.

40 See https://www.egnyte.com/.

41 See http://www.staffrosteringonline.com/.

42 See http://docs.google.com/.

43 See http://quickbooksonline.intuit.com/.

44 See http://www.knowledgetree.com/.

45 See http://www.clickability.com/products/web_content_management.html.

46 See http://www.microsoft.com/en-ca/office365/online-software.aspx.

47 See http://www.microsoft.com/en-ca/office365/plans/small-business/office-web-apps.aspx.

48 See http://www.netsuite.com/portal/products/netsuite/financials/main.shtml.

49 See http://crmondemand.oracle.com/.

50 See http://www.qvidian.com/.

51 See http://www.salesforce.com/crm/sales-force-automation/.

52 See http://www.taleo.com/.

53 See http://mosaic.tatacommunications.com/.

54 See http://cloudtaxonomy.opencrowd.com/taxonomy/software-as-a-service/.

4 Cloud Deployment Models

So far I have talked about what the cloud is, how the cloud works, and what the cloud does. All along, with a few exceptions, I have assumed that the cloud's location—that is, the physical space that holds the cloud infrastructure—is somewhere *out there*. There has been no great need to get any more specific than that, since cloud consumers for the most part only care about getting services that are scalable, elastic, rapidly provisioned, on-demand, and metered, wherever they happen to be, and with a minimum of fuss from the provider. The cloud consumer is location-agnostic.

However, from a business perspective, location does matter. That is why the *NIST Definition of Cloud Computing* (see "Chapter 1: Introducing Cloud Computing") has a section devoted to service deployment that includes four models: public cloud, private cloud, community cloud, and hybrid cloud. These models differ on where the cloud infrastructure is housed, and that has tremendous implications on the business case for moving to the cloud.

But a deployment model is not just about the location of the cloud environment. It also deals with other aspects of cloud operation, including the following:

Who owns the cloud?

Who manages the cloud?

How is the cloud accessed?

Who has access to the cloud?

You cannot make an intelligent decision about how to implement cloud services within your organization without knowing the answers to these questions with respect to each of the deployment models. This chapter helps you do just that by offering a more detailed look at these deployment scenarios.

Public Cloud

A *public cloud* makes its services and resources available to anyone who has Internet access. I mentioned in "Chapter 3: Cloud Service Models" that when most people think of cloud computing, they think of the myriad SaaS applications available. More specifically, they think of the SaaS apps that are available on the *web*: Gmail, iCloud, Office Web Apps, Salesforce.com, and so on. In other words, to most people, the public SaaS cloud *is* cloud computing. However, there are plenty of other types of public clouds, including public IaaS clouds (such as Amazon EC2 and Rackspace Cloud Servers) and public PaaS clouds (such as Google App Engine and Microsoft Azure).

From a deployment perspective, public cloud has the following characteristics:

- The infrastructure is owned by the public cloud provider.

- The infrastructure is managed by the public cloud provider.

- The infrastructure is located within the public cloud provider's data center.

- Access to the public cloud is via the Internet.

- Anyone can access the public cloud.

One of the key characteristics of the public cloud is multi-tenancy, where multiple clients share the same instances of a particular resource. For example, in a typical public IaaS cloud, a single physical server is shared by multiple clients by setting up a separate virtual machine for each client. The important element here is that in trying to maximize the use of its computing assets, the public cloud provider is confronted by two antagonistic elements. On the one hand, they would like to have their assets used as much as possible to maximize utilization, which implies having different companies (each being one tenant) using the same assets at the same time. But on the other hand, each client wants to ensure that it is fully isolated from the others. So multi-tenancy is all about being able to isolate multiple tenants using the same IT assets.

Public cloud costs vary widely. Many public cloud services are free, particularly public SaaS applications such as Google Docs and iCloud. There are also some free PaaS services, such as RUN@Cloud[1] and the basic version of Google App Engine[2] (see Figure 4-1), and others that offer free trials, such as Force.com.[3] As I write this, I do not know of any major IaaS vendors that offer free services.

Google App Engine - Pricing and Features
The following pricing and features are an advance preview and not immediately available.

The following is advance notice for changes to our features, pricing as well as addition of SLA and support.

To get started with Google App Engine set up an account today. Pricing seen on code.google.com is still in effect until further notice.

	Free	Paid	Premier
Platform fee	Free	$9/app/month	$500/account/month
Dynamic scaling	✓	✓	✓
Java Runtime	✓	✓	✓
Python Runtime	✓	✓	✓
Go Runtime	✓	✓	✓
Usage based pricing		✓	✓
Infinitely scalable		✓	✓
SLA		✓	✓
Operational support			✓
Tools			
Google Plugin for Eclipse	✓	✓	✓
Code upload/download	✓	✓	✓

Figure 4-1 Some public PaaS providers, such as Google App Engine, offer free services.

Public IaaS pricing generally charges by the minute for servers, by the gigabyte per month for storage, and by the gigabyte for network bandwidth. Public PaaS pricing is usually a set charge per hour per virtual machine platform, with extra charges incurred for databases, storage, bandwidth, load balancing, and so on. However, some providers (such as Google App Engine; see Figure 4-1) charge a set monthly fee per application.

Public SaaS pricing is a real mixed bag. Some vendors use a classic cloud pay-per-use model, where they charge a per-hour or per-minute fee for using an application. However, it is more common to charge a monthly fee or to use a *freemium* strategy, where a scaled-down version of the application is free, but a premium version costs money. Also common is a tiered-price strategy, where you pay a small amount per month for a basic version of the application, and the price goes up depending on the number of bells and whistles you add. Salesforce.com's Sales Cloud[4] service is an example (see Figure 4-2).

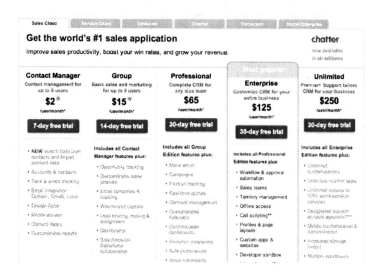

Figure 4-2 Some public SaaS providers, such as Salesforce.com, use a tiered-price model.

The common feature in all these public cloud pricing plans is that no contracts are involved. In fact, most public cloud payments are made using a credit card. However, we are also seeing many SaaS providers asking customers to sign multi-month or even multi-year deals up front, much like the old software licensing deals from pre-cloud days. This is about as far away as you can get from the metered, pay-per-use model of true cloud computing, but developers of large, complex applications aimed at enterprise users say they need the stability and income stream provided by longer-term deals. Larry Dignan, editorial director at ZDNet, summed up this state of affairs:

> It's an open secret in the IT industry that SaaS companies often are pushing multi-year deals that more resemble the licensing arrangements by on-premise vendors. On the surface, SaaS providers get predictable revenue streams and customers also get costs they can easily forecast. This predictability matters for large enterprises and the SaaS vendors increasingly catering to them...Is this really SaaS pricing as initially conceived?...Some analysts like Ray Wang are concerned about these developments. Wang argues that IT buyers should be worried. Wang argues that the key tenets of SaaS—pay as you go, seamless updates, all-in costs—are being eroded for long-term contracts, termination for cause and pricier support programs.[5]

For a more complete look at public cloud costs and other considerations related to choose a public cloud vendor, see "Chapter 10: Selecting a Public Cloud Provider." I also discuss some of the disadvantages associated with using public clouds in "Chapter 5: The Pros and Cons of Cloud Computing."

Private Cloud

As you saw in the previous section, the public cloud is a multi-tenant model where a pool of virtualized resources is available to anyone. By contrast, a *private cloud* is a single-tenant model where the resource pool is only available to members of the organization that has provisioned the cloud.

You might think that private cloud ought to be the simplest of the deployment models, since the word *private* seems to indicate that the infrastructure is owned and operated by the organization, and everything runs within the organization's data center. That can certainly happen, but there are actually *four* different types of private cloud deployment:

On-site private cloud

Hosted private cloud

On-site hosted private cloud

Virtual private cloud

The ownership, management, location, and access path varies for each of these models, as I describe in the next few sections. Therefore, it is more accurate to define private cloud as a cloud environment where the infrastructure is dedicated to a single organization, no matter who owns or manages that infrastructure.

On-Site Private Cloud

An *on-site private cloud* is a private cloud infrastructure owned and operated by an organization, and located on the organization's premises (see Figure 4-3). This is the type of cloud that most people are referring to when they use the phrase *private cloud*. You should implement this type of private cloud when you need complete control over the cloud infrastructure and data.

> "Enterprises looking to leverage the economies, efficiencies and scale of cloud providers are adopting cloud models in-house, such as OpenStack, for both compute and storage environments. These private clouds offer scale, agility and price/performance typically unmatched by traditional infrastructure solutions and can reside inside a company's firewall."[6]
>
> —Nicos Vekiarides

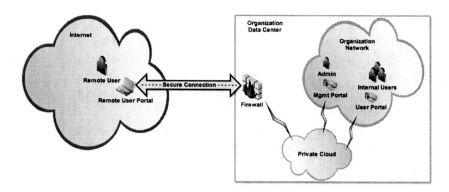

Figure 4-3 An on-site private cloud is owned and operated by the organization and resides within the corporate firewall.

For deployment, an on-site private cloud has the following characteristics:

- The private cloud infrastructure is owned by the organization.

- The private cloud infrastructure is managed by the organization.

- The private cloud infrastructure is located within the organization's data center.

- Access to the private cloud is via the organization's intranet.

- Only authorized employees or partners can access the private cloud.

For a general look at how to set up a private cloud, see "Chapter 8: Implementing a Private Cloud." I also go through some of the disadvantages associated with using private clouds in "Chapter 5: The Pros and Cons of Cloud Computing."

Hosted Private Cloud

A *hosted private cloud*—also called a *managed private cloud*—is a single-tenant, private cloud infrastructure created and maintained by a third-party cloud provider and located within the provider's data center. This type of private cloud is ideal for small- to medium-sized businesses that do not want the hassle and expense of running a data center and managing a private cloud infrastructure, but that require a secure, isolated cloud environment.

The connection between the organization's internal network and the provider's data center is handled by a virtual private network (VPN), as shown in Figure 4-4, which guarantees that only authorized users can access the hosted private cloud.

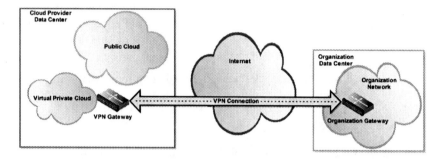

Figure 4-4 A hosted private cloud uses a VPN connection to the cloud provider to ensure data security.

The deployment of a hosted private cloud has the following characteristics:

- The private cloud infrastructure is owned by the cloud provider.

- The private cloud infrastructure is managed by the cloud provider.

- The private cloud infrastructure is located within the cloud provider's data center.

- Access to the private cloud is via the Internet.

- Only authorized employees or partners can access the private cloud.

On-Site Hosted Private Cloud

An *on-site hosted private cloud* is a private cloud infrastructure owned by the organization and residing within the organization's data center, but managed by a third-party cloud provider. This type of deployment model gives the organization complete control over choosing the cloud hardware, but leaves the complexities of managing the cloud to third-party experts. And since the cloud data sits behind the corporate firewall (see Figure 4-5), security is maximized. This type of cloud deployment is well suited to businesses with sensitive data to protect, but who do not want to devote manpower and resources to the cloud operation.

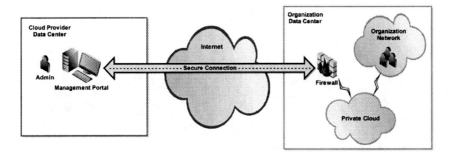

Figure 4-5 An on-site hosted private cloud resides within the corporate firewall, but is managed by a third-party provider.

On-site hosted private cloud deployment has the following characteristics:

- The on-site hosted private cloud infrastructure is owned by the organization.

- The on-site hosted private cloud infrastructure is managed by the cloud provider.

- The on-site hosted private cloud infrastructure is located within the organization's data center.

- Access to the on-site hosted private cloud is via the organization's intranet.

- Only authorized employees or partners can access the on-site hosted private cloud.

Virtual Private Cloud

A *virtual private cloud* (VPC)—it is also called a *private multi-tenant cloud*—is a single-tenant, private cloud infrastructure hosted in a multi-tenant, public cloud environment. As with a hosted private cloud, the connection between the organization's internal network and the provider's public cloud is handled by a VPN (see Figure 4-6) to ensure security.

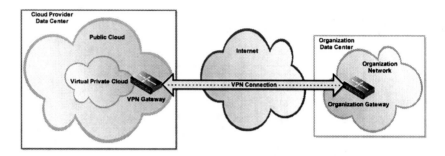

Figure 4-6 A virtual private cloud uses a VPN connection to the public cloud.

The goal here is to marry some of the best traits of private and public clouds. That is, the organization gets the elasticity, scalability, and utility benefits of public cloud services, but also the enhanced security and SLA-based quality and performance guarantees of a private cloud. The most popular VPC service is Amazon VPC.[7]

For deployment, virtual private cloud has the following characteristics:

- The virtual private cloud infrastructure is owned by the cloud provider.

- The virtual private cloud infrastructure is managed by the cloud provider.

- The virtual private cloud infrastructure is located within the cloud provider's data center.

- Access to the virtual private cloud is via the Internet.

- Only authorized employees or partners can access the virtual private cloud.

Community Cloud

Many organizations operate within sectors or industries that have extensive IT-related regulatory requirements that must be satisfied. These requirements usually include rules related to security, privacy, risk management, data location, and auditing. If such organizations

> **⚠ Note**
>
> It is important to remember that most organizations choose to implement a virtual private cloud, because it bypasses many of the negatives of an in-house private cloud (particularly costs) and provides almost all of the benefits, particularly since the single-tenant architecture if more secure and the private cloud deployment makes it easier to meet compliance rules and regulartions.

are looking to implement cloud computing, they will immediately run into problems with both public and private clouds:

- Public clouds almost always implement one-size-fits-all SLAs that do not meet these regulations.

- Private clouds can be built to satisfy industry regulations, but such clouds are necessarily more complex and more management-intensive.

In more and more cases, the solution to these problems is to bypass public and private cloud deployments in favor of a *community cloud* (also known as a *vertical cloud*), a cloud environment shared by several organizations and designed to support a specific community that has common concerns. These concerns often take the form of a common set of regulatory requirements, but they can also be a shared goal or mission, similar interests, or a shared community of customers or suppliers.

Community clouds offer a number of advantages. For example, the cloud environment can be built specifically to satisfy industry regulatory requirements, particularly with regard to data location, security, and auditing. Community clouds are usually managed by a third party (more on this below), thus relieving an individual organization of the burden of compliance. The shared cloud environment makes it easier and more efficient for organizations to collaborate on projects and common causes. And a community cloud allows businesses from the same industry to share IT services they have in common—such as a reservation system in the airline industry—which frees each company to focus on services that differentiate them from their competitors.

Here are some recent examples of community clouds:

- Penguin Computing and Indiana University teamed up to offer a cloud service called Rockhopper[9] to the U.S. science and research community. Rockhopper enables researchers to purchase high-performance computing time in a secure environment. The infrastructure is owned and managed by Penguin and resides in the IU data center.

> "Once cloud systems have proven their resilience look out for community clouds to appear and underpin a radical change in managing IT services, allowing companies to share a base layer of IT service and then continue to compete on competitive differentiation in other areas."[8]
> —Craig Boundy

- Apps.gov[10] is a U.S. government community cloud that offers computing services to federal agencies. These services including virtual machines, virtual storage, web hosting, and business, productivity, and social media apps.

- IQ Business Group created a community cloud for Australia's pension fund sector and configured the cloud to meet the industry's stringent regulatory requirements as well as offer common services such as claims processing and reporting.[11]

There are two type of community cloud deployment: hosted community cloud and on-site community cloud.

Hosted Community Cloud

In this deployment, the community cloud infrastructure resides in the data center of a third-party cloud provider. The community members work with the cloud provider to set up an environment that is beneficial to the community goals and needs. As shown in Figure 4-7, community members access the cloud over the Internet via secure links.

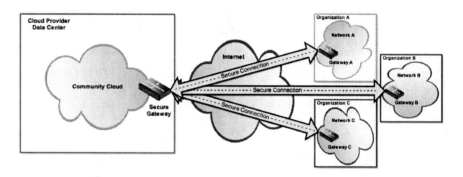

Figure 4-7 A hosted community cloud resides in a third-party data center that member organizations can access via secure connections.

A hosted community cloud deployment has the following characteristics:

- The community cloud infrastructure is owned by the cloud provider.

- The community cloud infrastructure is managed by the cloud provider.

- The community cloud infrastructure is located within the cloud provider's data center.

- Access to the community cloud is via the Internet.

- Only authorized community employees or partners can access the community cloud.

On-Site Community Cloud

In this deployment, the community cloud infrastructure resides in the data centers of one or more of the community members. When two or more organizations deploy the community cloud, each organization typically implements a different part of the cloud. For example, one organization might offer IaaS services, while another might offer SaaS applications. In Figure 4-8, for example, community organizations A and B implement the community cloud locally. Authorized members of organizations X and Y can access both the A and B community cloud deployments via secure links. Note, too, that authorized users in organizations A and B can also access each other's cloud deployments.

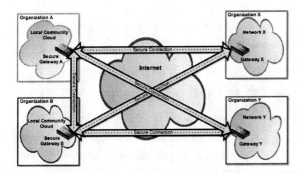

Figure 4-8 An on-site community cloud resides in one or more member organization data centers that other member organizations can access via secure connections.

On-site community cloud deployments have the following characteristics:

- The community cloud infrastructure is owned by the community.

- The community cloud infrastructure is managed by the community.

- The community cloud infrastructure is located within the data centers of one or more community members.

- Access to the community cloud is via the Internet, although users with a local community cloud use their organization's intranet to access that cloud.

- Only authorized community employees or partners can access the community cloud.

Hybrid Cloud

Of the three cloud deployment models that you have seen so far—public, private, and community—it is sometimes the case that a single model is just right for a business. For example, startups or small businesses that cannot afford a data center can still get all the server power, development tools, or software they need through public cloud services. Similarly, a company that must cope with stringent rules and regulations regarding security, privacy, geography, and compliance for all of its data would almost certainly go with a strict private cloud deployment.

However, these *one-size-fits-me* cases are probably the exception rather than the rule. Consider:

- An organization that has a private cloud might need extra computing power from time to time, in which case cloudbursting out to a public IaaS provider might be the most economical and agile way to handle peak loads.

- A business that uses public cloud services might need a private cloud to protect sensitive data.

- An organization that uses a private cloud might save money and improve collaboration by moving some services to a community cloud.

"It is becoming apparent that companies will not adopt a single cloud deployment model, but rather will use a combination of various public cloud services (including Software as a Service, Infrastructure as a Service, and Platform as a Service), private cloud services as well as their traditional computing environment....The ability to manage this hybrid environment will be the difference between success and failure."[12]

—Judith Hurwitz

For these and similar scenarios, an organization can adopt a *hybrid cloud*, which is a cloud environment that uses two or more of the three main cloud deployments—public, private, and community. Ideally, the hybrid cloud will also include mechanisms that enable the organization to move data and share services between each cloud component.

Figure 4-9 shows an example hybrid cloud that includes external public and community cloud components, as well as an internal private cloud component.

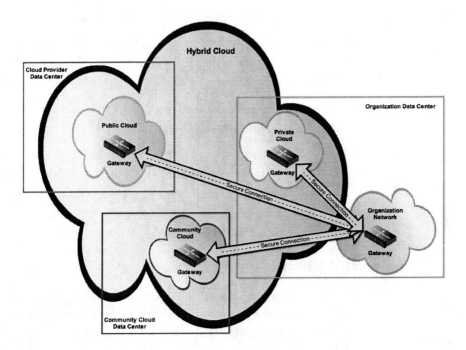

Figure 4-9 A hybrid cloud uses connections to two or more cloud deployment models.

Hybrid cloud deployments are complicated by the fact that there are actually more than three possible components. For example, the private cloud component can be on-site, hosted, on-site hosted, or virtual, while the community cloud component can be hosted or on-site. How you mix and match these deployments determines features such as ownership and location, so a general list of characteristics is not possible with a hybrid deployment.

For example, the hybrid cloud shown in Figure 4-9 uses public, on-site private, and hosted community clouds, so this deployment has the following characteristics:

- Ownership is split between the organization (private cloud), community (community cloud), and cloud provider (public cloud).

- Management is shared between the organization (private cloud), community (community cloud), and cloud provider (public cloud).

- The cloud infrastructure location is split between the organization's data center (private cloud), the community data center, (community cloud), and cloud provider data center (public cloud).

- Access to the internal (private) cloud is via the organization's intranet, while access to the external (public and community) clouds is via the Internet.

- Only authorized employees or partners of the organization can access the hybrid cloud.

- For a more detailed examination of the hybrid cloud deployment model, see "Chapter 9: Enhancing Agility with a Hybrid Cloud," which discusses the case for moving to a hybrid cloud, as well as several hybrid cloud issues you should be aware of.

Deployment Summary

You have seen many different deployment models in this chapter, with a large number of permutations and combinations with respect to the five characteristics that I outlined at the beginning (ownership, management, location, access path, and user authorization). To help you keep everything straight in your mind, Table 4-1 summarizes the eight deployment models and their characteristics.

Table 4-1 The characteristics of the cloud deployment models.

Model	Owner	Manager	Location	Access	Users
Public	Third-party	Third-party	Off-site	Internet	Unauthorized
On-Site Private	Business	Business	On-site	Intranet	Authorized (business)
Hosted Private	Business or third-party	Third-party	Off-site	Internet	Authorized (business)
On-Site Hosted Private	Business	Third-party	On-site	Intranet	Authorized (business)
Virtual Private	Third-party	Third-party	Off-site	Internet	Authorized (business)
On-Site Community	Community	Community	On-site (community member)	Internet (intranet for host)	Authorized (community)
Hosted Community	Third-party	Third-party	Off-site	Internet	Authorized (community)
Hybrid	Business and third-party	Business and third-party	On-site and off-site	Intranet and Internet	Authorized (business)

REFERENCES

1 See http://www.cloudbees.com/run.cb.

2 See http://www.google.com/enterprise/cloud/appengine/.

3 See http://www.salesforce.com/platform/.

4 See http://www.salesforce.com/crm/sales-force-automation/.

5 **Larry Dignan,** *SaaS pricing evolves: Should we be worried?*, ZDNet, http://www.zdnet.com/blog/btl/saas-pricing-evolves-should-we-be-worried/35757 (June 14, 2010).

6 **Nicos Vekiarides,** *Ten Hot Trends in Cloud Data for 2012*, Sys-Con Media, http://www.sys-con.com/node/2109293 (January 3, 2012).

7 See http://aws.amazon.com/vpc/.

8 **Craig Boundy,** *Share and share alike: Developing the community cloud*, Logica, http://blog.logica.com/blog/2011/05/27/share-and-sare-alike-developing-the-community-cloud/ (May 27, 2011).

9 See http://pti.iu.edu/ci/systems/rockhopper.

10 See https://www.apps.gov/.

11 See http://www.theregister.co.uk/2011/11/09/iq_bg_community_cloud_launched/.

12 **Judith Hurwitz,** *5 Big Cloud Trends For 2012*, InformationWeek, http://www.informationweek.com/news/cloud-computing/infrastructure/232200551 (December 28, 2011)

5 The Pros and Cons of Cloud Computing

I t is one thing to know what cloud computing is all about, including its definition, characteristics, architectures, and its service and deployment models. These fundamental facts form the backbone of any serious understanding of the cloud computing phenomenon. However, it is quite a different thing to be able to *evaluate* cloud computing to determine not only how your business might best implement cloud computing, but whether the cloud is the right place for your business at all.

So now it is time to turn our attention to some cloud computing evaluation tools. The next chapter takes you through the business case for accepting (or rejecting) the cloud, based on an examination of the relative costs of cloud and non-cloud IT infrastructures. In this chapter, you get a classic pros-versus-cons look at cloud computing. First, I offer up a long list of the substantial advantages of moving to the cloud. For balance, I then present an even longer list of cloud disadvantages, broken down between private and public clouds (since they are so different).

Does the fact that the total number of disadvantages is greater than the number of advantages mean that you should reject cloud computing right off the bat? No, not even close. You will see that most of these disadvantages demand caution, not outright rejection, and in any case you need to evaluate each disadvantage (and, yes, each advantage) within the context of your business goals, requirements, and restraints.

Why Consider the Cloud at All?

"The train is leaving the station. It's not a fad. It's not a bubble. It's not a buzzword. The technology industry is going through a major transformation. Computing is going to be universally distributed as a service, and it's anybody's game to win."[1]
—Mark Veverka

I mentioned in "Chapter 1: Introducing Cloud Computing," that one of my goals in this book was to convince you that cloud computing is not simply the latest in a long line of technology fads. I certainly hope that at least the first four chapters of this book have shown you that cloud computing rests on the solid underpinnings of mature technology and a robust set of models for delivering IT services.

Yes, cloud computing is not some passing fancy, but is that enough of a reason to consider moving some or even your entire IT department to the cloud? Of course not. If there is a single, overarching reason to consider the cloud, it is that we are at a kind of computing crossroads where there is a genuine need for a new way of doing and delivering IT. That need comes from three main factors that are bedeviling IT departments today:

- IT is too slow and cumbersome to respond to the needs of the business in a fast-paced, ever-changing world.

- IT spends most of its time and budget maintaining existing systems rather than innovating to create new services.

- IT is not prepared to handle a new generation of digitally-aware workers who have the skills and the mindset to work around IT bottlenecks and embrace new technologies.

If this sounds like *your* IT department, let's take a look at how cloud computing can help turn things around.

Increasing Agility

"The World is Flat," declared *New York Times* columnist Thomas Friedman in his 2005 bestselling book, meaning that the combination of globalization and ubiquitous Internet access have given an unprecedented number of people access to markets and to information. This represents a tremendous opportunity, because a flat world is teeming with new markets, new customers, new lines of business, and new technologies. However, it also represents a significant danger, because a flat world is rife with competitive threats, macroeconomic shifts, political upheavals, and currency fluctuations. And all of these opportunities and dangers are coming into view at an ever-faster rate, because in the same way that you can drive many times faster on the Bonneville Salt Flats than through the Rocky Mountains, a flat world is an accelerated world.

This means that today's enterprises can only take advantage of a flat world's opportunities and respond to a flat world's dangers by being fast enough to recognize them before they go whooshing by, and also by being nimble enough to produce the products, services, or systems that meet the new need or thwart the new danger.

In this world, the old *eventually on*, *siloed* way of doing things no longer delivers what business needs, when it needs it. In this world, a company must be fast and nimble—in short, *agile*—to respond quickly and effectively to both opportunities and dangers, and the cloud is an excellent way to achieve such agility. By providing on-demand, elastic, easily-provisioned, and easily-accessed services, the cloud enables a business to create new resources or expand existing resources in a fraction of the time.

Innovating Instead of Maintaining

One of the crucial functions of IT is what is known in the trade as keeping the lights on. This means performing the routine maintenance that keeps servers patched, clients updated, data backed up, and security beefed up. No modern enterprise could run for very long without these mundane IT tasks being performed every day.

The problem is that, thanks to technology silos and IT sprawl (see "Chapter 1: Introducing Cloud Computing"), a typical company's engineers, developers, and administrators have to deal with an increasing number of expensive, rigid, inefficient, and complex systems, so they end up spending at least 70% of their time and budget on operations and maintenance. That leaves just 30% to spend on innovation—creating new systems, new ways of sharing data, and new ways of differentiating the company from its competitors.

> "While the IT savings is compelling, the strongest benefit of cloud computing is how it enhances business agility – especially how the cloud can help launch entirely new businesses with little to no up-front capital."[2]
> — Jacqueline Vanacek

> "So this is the dark side of the IT story: Increasingly layered, complex, hard-coded, and sprawling, IT over time has grown inflexible, brittle and costly. Today, as a result, the typical company spends more than 40 percent of its IT budget on infrastructure maintenance and around 30 percent on application maintenance. That adds up to 70 – 80 percent of IT spending simply to maintaining the status-quo. Think of this as a complexity tax."[3]
> — VMware

So although you might want your company to be more agile in a dynamic, competitive world, you simply won't be able to achieve that agility if IT has to spend most of its time and money treading water. By helping to eliminate silos, reduce IT capital expenditures, and offer a fast and nimble way to handle IT resources, cloud computing can reverse the typical maintenance/innovation ratio, so IT spends more time innovating and less time keeping the lights on.

Supporting a New Generation of Workers

One of the little-known and largely unseen forces at work in business today is a massive generational shift that is happening at an alarming pace and will only accelerate over the next decade or so. To understand this shift, you need to realize not only that the leading edge of the Baby Boom generation is now well into its retirement years, but that the oldest of the next generation—Generation X: people born between 1965 and 1977—are closer to fifty than they are to forty. This means that, before too long, the modern workforce will consist mostly (and soon entirely) of people born in 1978 or later. This next generation is sometimes called Generation Y (since it comes right after Generation X), but a better named is Generation D, because it is the first generation that has grown up with and is completely at home with digital devices and digital culture.

These so-called *digital natives* come to the job already familiar with hardware such as computers and smartphones, and technologies such as text messaging and chat. More than that, however, their comfort with all things digital means that they think nothing of diving into new technologies and systems, metaphorically turning the dials and twiddling the knobs to gain hands-on experience and to see what the system is capable of. This generation does not read the manual and will not be bound by the old IT strictures of using only approved devices, services, and software. Instead, they will *consumerize* IT by bringing their own devices, ordering their own services, and installing their own programs.

This is an inevitable trend, but it does not have to been an inevitable headache for the IT department. By moving to the easily-provisioned

> "It was only a few years ago that the majority of our patrons were encountering computers and computer-based resources for the first time in our libraries. Their lack of familiarity with both the hardware and the software created an instant demand for assistance at the reference desk. Increasingly, computer savvy clientele no longer need as much support to use the hardware. We are no longer talking about Generation X or Y, but Generation D, the digital generation."[4]
> —Peggy A. Seiden

and device-agnostic cloud, IT can better anticipate and accommodate the needs of Generation D, securely support any device they bring, and offer services and resources that tap into the potential of this digitally-savvy workforce.

The Advantages of Cloud Computing

Transforming IT to support and encourage agility, innovation, and being Generation D-friendly would be a huge win for any business and might be enough to tilt the argument in favor of adopting the cloud without considering the *Cons* side of the ledger. Of course you, as a prudent steward of your business, want to see both sides of the argument. So, before getting to the inevitable disadvantages of cloud computing, let's take some time to run through a few more of the advantages.

Lower Capital Costs

The question of whether cloud computing necessarily lowers IT costs is more complicated than you might think, since there are scenarios that are not all that far-fetched where the cloud can actually be *more* expensive. You learn about these scenarios in particular, and the economics of adopting cloud computing in general, in "Chapter 6: The Economics of Cloud Computing." For now, I will only say that the case for lower capital costs in a cloud environment can be summarized with a simple question:

If you only need a ride, why buy a car?

For example, if you just want to get from point A to point B, then the easiest way to get there is probably to hire a taxi. If you need to make several stops over the course of a few hours or an afternoon, then it makes more sense to join a car sharing service where you can reserve a vehicle of whatever type you require and pay an hourly rate for as long as you need it. If you need a car for a longer trip or for a weekend, then your most efficient and economical course is probably a car rental agency.

Whatever the scenario, in each case you avoid the high costs associated with owning a vehicle, including loan or lease payments, insurance, gas, maintenance, and repair. Of course, if you need a car full-time, then cabs, car sharing services, and rental agencies are going to be prohibitively expensive, and you'd be much better off owning or leasing a car.

Here is the cloud computing equivalent (at least from an IaaS perspective):

If you only need CPU time, why buy a server?

For example, if you just want to test an application, the easiest way to do it these days is to rent a server from an IaaS provider for a few cents an hour. If you need to allow for demands beyond what your current IT infrastructure can handle, it makes sense to provision as many virtual servers as you need to handle the load, and then de-provision when the peak passes. If you need to develop, test, and deploy a major application, then your most efficient and economical source is probably a PaaS platform.

As with the car analogies, in each of these cases you avoid the high costs associated with owning systems, including hardware costs, software licenses, staff salaries, and data center infrastructure expenses.

Metered

A corollary to lower capital costs is that cloud computing changes from a capital expense to an operating expense because in most cases cloud computing services are *metered*. That is, in the same way that a metered utility such as electricity means that you only pay for the power you use, a metered cloud resource means that you only pay for the resource while you use it. This *pay-as-you-go* model means paying for a server by the minute, paying for storage by the gigabyte per month, paying for a hosted application by the bandwidth it consumes, and so on.

◢ Note

I am mostly talking here about provisioning public cloud services, but you can also make the same argument for private cloud. That is, by virtualizing your resources, each physical server can run multiple instances of virtual machines, virtual storage, and so on, which is significantly cheaper than purchasing new hardware.

Lower Barriers to Entry

It was not all that long ago that if you were thinking of starting a new business or a new line of business within an existing company, particularly one that was computing-related or heavily IT-dependent, you needed a huge up-front investment just to afford all the servers, storage, networking devices, and other infrastructure. How many good or even great ideas never saw the light of day because of a lack of capital?

Cloud computing changed all that by removing the barrier of high up-front computing costs. Why spend hundreds of thousands or even millions of dollars do get the IT portion of a business off the ground when you can rent cloud-based servers or platforms for pennies an hour?

Scalability

From an IT perspective, *scalability* refers to the ability to expand a computing resource to match the current workload. In a non-cloud environment, scaling computing resources almost always means adding more hardware. Depending on the type of demand, this means more servers, more processors, more memory, more storage, more routers, and so on. But hardware resources always operate under real-world constraints. Data centers can only hold so much equipment, for example, and IT budgets are all-too finite these days. When you run out of room, run out of money, or bump up against a similar hardware-related ceiling, your IT resources no longer scale.

These real-world hardware constraints vanish in a puff of smoke when you move to the cloud. That's because the cloud versions of hardware resources such as servers, storage, and networking are all virtualized and automated. This means that you can effectively add new resources at will, and there is no practical barrier to the number of resources you can add. In the cloud, your IT resources scale, and this means that you can quickly and efficiently build out your virtual IT infrastructure to meet whatever demand comes your way.

> "The cloud...allows customers to start as large OR as small as they want in a deployment, with no cost penalty. Certainly there are some economies of scale, but when compared to the deployment of onsite software, the economics of personnel, computers, licenses, storage, etc were generally so high that unless you started with, or committed to a large deployment, it was cost prohibitive to "give it a try." Cloud services enable customers to start at any scale, *and deliver value to the buyer before asking for a large commitment.*"[5]
> —Jim Melvin

Elasticity

In the previous section, I mentioned that, in non-cloud environments, scaling IT means adding more hardware, and unless IT has adopted virtualized resources, more hardware means more time. You have to get the purchase approved and ordered, wait for the hardware to arrive, set up and configure the hardware, test it, and then finally deploy it.

In IT, *elasticity* is the ability to expand or contract a computing resource on-the-fly, based on current needs. If it takes your IT department weeks or even months to get a new server or similar hardware into operation, then your IT department is *not* elastic.

Cloud computing adds elasticity to IT by enabling resources to be provisioned quickly (usually within a few minutes or hours), from anywhere (for example, a local network portal or a web-based portal), using any device (desktop, thin client, notebook, tablet, or even a smartphone). This enables the business to meet spikes in demand quickly and cost-effectively. Just as important, cloud elasticity also means that the business can quickly and easily de-provision resources when they are no longer needed.

Self-Service

A *bottleneck* is, of course, a stage in a process where progress is delayed or impeded. In our high-speed, flat world, the old style of doing IT acts as a bottleneck for creating value in a business:

- In an in-house IT department, users must jump through a long series of hoops to get new hardware, services, or software. From the initial request through the various processes for planning, approval, procurement, setup, configuration, and deployment, the user must interact and negotiate with IT every step of the way.

- In a third-party IT vendor (such as a hardware or software vendor), users must deal with sales and support to purchase, customize, and configure new resources.

All this interaction slows down the process, wastes time, and takes employees away from their core responsibilities. In other words, it creates bottlenecks that impede business.

The cloud does away with all that by giving users self-service portals to access service catalogs that enable them to peruse, configure, and provision their own IT resources, all without any interaction with a cloud provider (either internally or externally). In many cases, users can provision new resources with just a few mouse clicks.

Faster Time-to-Value

Time-to-value is a measure of how long it takes a resource to begin providing a direct benefit to a business. In this hyper-accelerated culture and hyper-competitive business environment, just creating value is not enough. What good is a new company-wide software application if employee morale is at an all-time low because users have had to put up with the existing, antiquated, held-together-by-spit-and-string system for a year? What good is a new server cluster if your customers have abandoned your website in droves because it has been so slow and unreliable for the past six months?

In the cloud, combine on-demand self-service, broad network access from any location and any device, and rapid elasticity, and new resources can be provisioned, configured, tested, and then deployed in days or weeks, instead of months or years.

Reliability

When discussing the reliability of a computing system, particularly one accessed over a network, the most common measure is *availability*, which is the percentage of time that users are able to access the system. IT personnel often express availability in *nines*, where 90% availability is *one nine*, 99% availability is *two nines*, 99.9% is *three nines*, and so on.

"The move toward self-service is only going to accelerate...analysts say, as IT departments face increasing demand, from the newest hire to the most senior executive, for faster, better access to corporate services and data."[6]
—Tracy Mayor

Note

You can also make the argument that not only does cloud computing create value for your business faster, but it also creates more value than does a comparable in-house resource. For example, many SaaS applications are mashups that tie in to huge databases, such as Google Maps data or government census data. Unless you have the in-house expertise to create similar applications, these in-cloud equivalents will be more useful and therefore more valuable to your business.

Note

An availability of three nines (99.9%) sounds amazingly high, but over the course of a year it translates into approximately 8 hours and 45 minutes of total downtime. For comparison, note that four nines (99.99%) results in about 52 minutes of yearly downtime, while five nines (99.999%; the *Holy Grail* of network availability) means just over five minutes of downtime in a year.

 Note

Public cloud systems are getting more reliable every day, but they still do not offer the same level of availability as a well-architected private data center. So, although I include reliability as a point in favor of public clouds, they are not yet robust enough for your most important applications. See my discussion of "Mission-Critical Applications" later in this chapter.

All network-based resources have *some* downtime, planned or otherwise. For example, a network server will have occasional planned downtime to install updates, perform scheduled maintenance, repair a component, or reboot to complete a software install. And, unfortunately but inevitably, network resources also have unplanned downtime caused by malfunctions, bugs, or other unforeseen glitches.

IT departments and their networks are usually quite reliable, but most analysts agree that public cloud-based resources are coming close to the same levels of reliability. That is because high availability is a function of having lots of redundant hardware (for backups, backups of backups, and so on) as well as a network architecture that enables *failovers* (bringing another system online to take over from a failed system). Most large cloud providers have massive hardware investments, so redundant machines aren't a problem. Also, since large cloud providers can afford to hire the cream of the engineering crop to deploy and maintain their systems, they have sophisticated network architectures that offer extremely robust IaaS, PaaS, and SaaS offerings.

Energy Savings

One perhaps surprising benefit to moving to the cloud is that it is remarkably more energy efficient than doing the equivalent work in your own (non-cloud) data center. For example, Salesforce.com recently hired WSP Environment & Energy to compare the energy use and carbon footprint of the cloud with that of the in-house data center. Perhaps the most remarkable finding was that a cloud SaaS transaction was 95% more carbon efficient than the equivalent transaction performed in the data center.[7]

Why should that be? Mostly it is because large cloud providers have much higher server utilization rates. For example, a typical data center server might be in use 5 or 10% of the time, while most cloud servers are in use 30 to 40% of the time. Also, it is more energy efficient to have a single physical server running a dozen virtual servers than it is to have thirteen physical servers gulping electricity.

So if you are considering converting some or all of your current data center into a private cloud, you should see distinctly reduced energy costs.

The Disadvantages of Private Cloud Computing

The cloud computing advantages that you learned about in the previous section are for the most part location-agnostic. That is, it doesn't matter whether you use a public or private (or hybrid) cloud environment, you still get scalability, elasticity, self-service, faster time-to-value, higher availability, and energy savings.

However, when it comes to the disadvantages associated with the cloud, we need to separate private and public cloud environments because the negatives are very much location-specific. In this section, I take you through some disadvantages of private cloud deployments, and you learn about public cloud disadvantages a bit later in this chapter.

New Infrastructure Costs

Running a cloud requires hardware:

- The physical servers that will host the virtual machines

- Hard drives to store virtual machine images and data

- Routers, cables, and other networking equipment to tie the cloud together

- Physical plant hardware such as power, lights, and cooling

Running a cloud requires software:

- A cloud operating system

- A hypervisor to create and manage virtual machines

- A development platform for building cloud applications

- A database management system for storing and managing data

> "A large percentage of global GDP is reliant on [Information Communications Technology] – this is a critical issue as we strive to decouple economic growth from emissions growth. The carbon emissions reducing potential of cloud computing is a thrilling breakthrough, allowing companies to maximize performance, drive down costs, reduce inefficiency and minimize energy use – and therefore carbon emissions – all at the same time."[8]
> —Paul Dickinson

 Note

I am talking here about on-site private clouds. Most of these disadvantages disappear in hosted private cloud and virtual private cloud deployments (see "Chapter 3: Cloud Service Models").

Running a cloud requires people:

- Engineers to install, configure, and maintain the physical servers

- A system administrator to manage the network and the virtual machines

- Developers to build the cloud interface and applications

All of these cloud components cost money, of course, so perhaps the main disadvantage of private cloud deployments is the cost associated with setting up, configuring, and maintaining the cloud. Yes, you might be able to convert some or all of your existing infrastructure into a private cloud, but you might still need to add memory and storage to your servers. In any case, hardware obsolesces, so you will eventually have to replace your physical machines.

Server Underutilization

When you plan your private cloud, one of the key considerations is capacity planning. That is, how many nodes (virtual machines) do you need to run your cloud services, be they hardware, platform, or software services. If you think the demand for these services will be more or less steady, then capacity planning becomes a relatively simple exercise of determining the number of nodes that will serve that demand, then dividing by the number of nodes per physical machine to calculate the number of servers you need to purchase. For example, if you believe 100 nodes will do the job, and you can run 10 nodes per physical machine, then you need 10 servers in your data center.

Life, of course, is never that straightforward. A much more likely scenario is that you can handle normal loads with 100 nodes, but you will occasionally experience peak demands that might require an extra 40 or 50 nodes to keep your cloud services running and responsive. In this scenario, you have no choice but to purchase an extra five servers so that you can scale your cloud up to handle demand peaks. What this means, however, is that during non-peak times—which will be most of the time—all those servers will be underutilized. So not only do you incur extra capital costs to purchase those peak-demand servers, but all your servers will now run less efficiently.

> "Typically, in situations where there is a need for a huge IT infrastructure to deal with voluminous data, for example 'on-and-off workloads' during the holiday rush for the websites of retail companies, [public] cloud infrastructure is very useful. These instances may happen once or twice in a year and the cloud is the perfect alternative to heavy IT investments that will remain underutilized all year around."[9]
> —Sanjay Sharma

Cloud Expertise

Any decent-sized cloud deployment is going to be complex, perhaps even dauntingly so. By their very nature, clouds are complicated systems that require special expertise to plan, build, deploy, secure, and maintain. Public and third-party cloud providers have this expertise in spades, since that is their business, and they would not stay viable for very long without that expertise (and without training their employees in the latest cloud technologies).

Achieving similar levels of expertise in your own IT department, while not impossible, is certainly challenging. It requires a huge investment in training existing employees to get them up to speed on cloud technologies, as well as hiring new personnel with solid cloud backgrounds. And remember, too, that if you want to allow access to your private cloud from outside the network (say, by a virtual private network connection), then that seriously raises the security stakes, which in turn means developing or hiring the security expertise needed to keep your cloud safe from unauthorized access.

> "If you are looking to cloud computing to simplify your IT environment, I'm afraid I have bad news for you." [10]
> —James Urquhart

The Disadvantages of Public Cloud Computing

By its very nature, the public cloud is always going to bring to the table many more disadvantages than the private cloud. That is, because the public cloud is, by definition, located *outside* the enterprise, you necessarily lose some control over the design, implementation, and management of various aspects of the cloud: hardware, software, platforms, databases, networks, security, and so on. This does not mean you should write off the public cloud, far from it. We are entering an era where having a public cloud component—whether it involves cloud bursting for extra infrastructure when needed, testing new applications, or giving employees access to useful software —is a necessary part of any company's IT strategy. Businesses who don't take advantage of the resources available in public clouds will be at a major competitive disadvantage.

> "From a practical standpoint, the most important lesson to be learned from earlier infrastructural technologies may be this: When a resource becomes essential to competition but inconsequential to strategy, the risks it creates become more important than the advantages it provides."[11]
> —Nicholas Carr

So all the more reason to understand the potential pitfalls associated with public cloud deployments, so you and your IT people can make decisions on which public cloud resources make sense and how best to minimize the risks.

Security

When cloud pundits and IT types talk about the downside of public cloud, they almost always start with (and sometimes also end with) security. This is a vital issue and an obvious starting point, since public cloud infrastructure and services are under the control of a third party, so security threats are more frequent and measures designed to block those threats are harder to analyze. In many ways, the security issue completely determines whether some companies implement public cloud services at all, which is why I devote an entire chapter to security (see "Chapter 13: Cloud Security Issues"). For now, let's take a quick look at the major security concerns with public cloud:

- **Insider threats** Cloud provider employees and affiliated vendors can have direct access to customer data and proprietary assets such as customer application code. Nefarious use of this data can include fraud, theft, industrial espionage, and deletion or sabotage of data.

- **Insider errors** Not all provider employee dangers are deliberate. Via error, insufficient training, or misunderstood instructions, employees can expose sensitive data. For example, in 2009 a Wyoming bank employee accidentally sent the tax IDs and Social Security numbers of more than 1,300 businesses and individuals, as well as their names, addresses, and loan data to the wrong Gmail account.[12]

- **Outsourcing** A public cloud provider might outsource some of their services to another cloud provider. For example, a SaaS vendor might get its PaaS or IaaS infrastructure from a third party. In such cases, although you might have security agreements with your own provider, similar agreements between your provider and the third party are opaque.

- **Authentication** By definition, public cloud services are accessed externally, usually via a web-based portal (for simplicity, I am ignoring programmatic access via the provider's APIs). This access requires authentication—a user name and password —to ensure that only authorized users can enter the cloud and to specify which activities the user can perform in the cloud. All login systems are vulnerable to various cracking techniques, including shoulder surfing (reading a password as it is typed), social engineering (for example, posing as a member of the IT department and asking a user for login data), and packet sniffing (monitoring network traffic to steal passwords sent unencrypted).

- **Multi-tenancy** Public cloud services are multi-tenant, and there are rare but not impossible circumstances where code on one virtual machine can access data on another.[13]

- **External attacks** Like all Internet destinations, public cloud providers are vulnerable to external exploits, such as denial of service attacks and malware.

Data Location

Most big-time cloud providers maintain multiple data centers. This is a good strategy because it enables the cloud provider to shift loads from one data center to another to increase performance and decrease latency (how long it takes network signals to travel between the cloud and the customer). Unfortunately, some of these data centers might reside in a different state or even a different country. That is bad news if your business must follow strict rules, regulations, or laws that require you to know exactly where your data is stored at all times. For example, you might have compliance regulations that prevent customer data from being stored out-of-state or out-of-country.

You can sometimes work around this by asking your cloud provider to keep your information in a specific data center that meets your compliance needs. Otherwise, the public cloud is not for you and you need to bring your data in-house.

 Note

Location concerns are not always based on jurisdictional boundaries. For example, in the U.S., the regulations of the National Archives and Records Administration stipulate that any building holding federal records must be situated at least five feet above and 100 feet away from any 100-year flood plain.

Data Loss

You probably know from your own personal computing experience that non-backed-up data is vulnerable to permanent loss. A physical disk failure or lightning strike can render a hard drive unusable, and therefore its data unreadable.

The same is true for data stored in a public cloud which, after all, is built from basically the same hardware (at least from a reliability standpoint) that you use yourself. Physical machines can fail, virtual machines can lose their integrity, and so your data can vanish without a trace. Unfortunately, for many cloud providers backups are not a standard feature, and must either be provisioned at extra cost or performed by a third-party cloud provider.

Data Portability

If you provision public SaaS or PaaS services, at some point you will use those services to create data. For example, a public SaaS customer relationship management application will have customer contact data, meeting notes, to-do lists, and more. This is crucial data for the enterprise, and it will be accessible as long as you maintain your relationship with the provider, the provider keeps offering the service, and the provider stays in business. But what happens if you no longer need the service, or the provider announces that it is cancelling the service or terminating operations?

You, of course, want to extract your data. However, many public cloud providers do not offer a method for exporting data to a standard format, performing bulk extraction of the data, or porting the data between the public cloud and your in-house data center.

Availability

Earlier I mentioned that network gurus often use measures such as three nines (99.9%) or four nines (99.99%) when referring to network availability. It is also common to refine these measures with "quarter nines" (0.25%) or "half nines" (0.5%). So, for example, one common availability metric defined in cloud service level agreements is three and a half nines, or 99.95%.

Three and a half nines is considered high availability for a cloud service, but it still means that the cloud is unavailable for about four hours and 23 minutes every year, or just a bit over five minutes a week. Where do these minutes and hours come from? Here are the most common causes of cloud downtime:

- **Server reboots** Just like a physical server, a virtual server requires maintenance, particularly for the installation of operating system updates and security patches. Unfortunately, many of these updates require rebooting the server, so your virtual servers will occasionally have to go offline for a minute or two while the patch is installed. In most cases, the IaaS provider will give you advance notice about a reboot, so you can prepare. However, there will times when an emergency reboot is required—for example, to plug a security hole that has a known virus or other exploit—so your prep time might be minimal or non-existent.

- **Unplanned short-term outages** A software bug, a bad hard drive sector, a recalcitrant memory module, or a broken network interface can all cause outages, usually up to a few hours. Also, lightning strikes and electrical failures can take down parts of a data center.

- **Unplanned long-term outages** As I mentioned earlier, cloud computing is a complex bit of business, so it is inevitable that this complexity will rear its head in ugly ways from time to time, causing prolonged outages. The most famous example of this was the Amazon Web Services outage that lasted several days in the spring of 2011 (see Figure 5-1), and was caused by an apparently innocuous *network change*.[15]

> "If you run infrastructure, regardless of whether it's in your own data center, in hosting, or in cloud IaaS, you should have a plan for 'what happens if I need to mass-reboot my servers?' because it is something that *will* happen. And add 'what if I have to do that immediately?' to the list, because that is also something that *will* happen, because mass exploits and worms certainly have not gone away."[14]
>
> —Lydia Leong

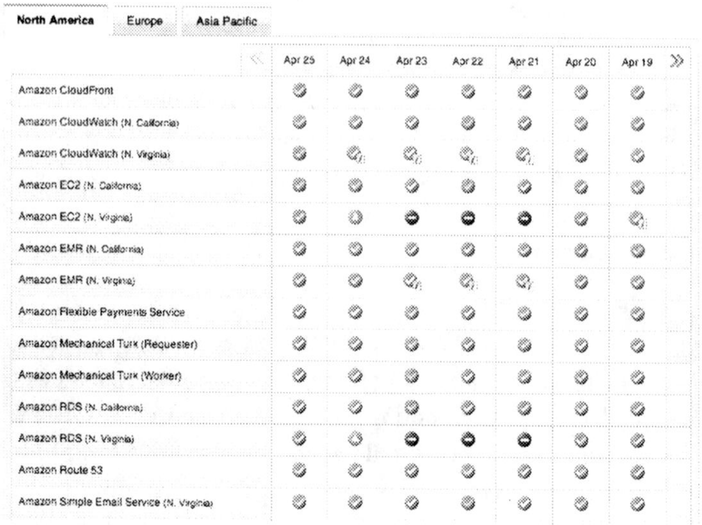

	North America	Europe	Asia Pacific

	Apr 25	Apr 24	Apr 23	Apr 22	Apr 21	Apr 20	Apr 19
Amazon CloudFront	✅	✅	✅	✅	✅	✅	✅
Amazon CloudWatch (N. California)	✅	✅	✅	✅	✅	✅	✅
Amazon CloudWatch (N. Virginia)	✅	⚠️	⚠️	⚠️	⚠️	✅	✅
Amazon EC2 (N. California)	✅	✅	✅	✅	✅	✅	✅
Amazon EC2 (N. Virginia)	✅	✅	⛔	⛔	⛔	✅	⚠️
Amazon EMR (N. California)	✅	✅	✅	✅	✅	✅	✅
Amazon EMR (N. Virginia)	✅	✅	⚠️	⚠️	⚠️	✅	✅
Amazon Flexible Payments Service	✅	✅	✅	✅	✅	✅	✅
Amazon Mechanical Turk (Requester)	✅	✅	✅	✅	✅	✅	✅
Amazon Mechanical Turk (Worker)	✅	✅	✅	✅	✅	✅	✅
Amazon RDS (N. California)	✅	✅	✅	✅	✅	✅	✅
Amazon RDS (N. Virginia)	✅	✅	⛔	⛔	⛔	✅	✅
Amazon Route 53	✅	✅	✅	✅	✅	✅	✅
Amazon Simple Email Service (N. Virginia)	✅	✅	✅	✅	✅	✅	✅

Figure 5-1 For a few days in the spring of 2011, some Amazon Web Services offerings were off the grid due to a network glitch.

Unknown Costs

When you examine the offerings available from a public cloud provider, either on their website or in their service catalog, you will see a price for each offering. For example, Figure 5-2 shows a portion of the Amazon EC2 Pricing page.[16]

Region: US East (Virginia) ▾	Linux/UNIX Usage	Windows Usage
Standard On-Demand Instances		
Small (Default)	$0.085 per hour	$0.12 per hour
Large	$0.34 per hour	$0.48 per hour
Extra Large	$0.68 per hour	$0.96 per hour
Micro On-Demand Instances		
Micro	$0.02 per hour	$0.03 per hour
Hi-Memory On-Demand Instances		
Extra Large	$0.50 per hour	$0.62 per hour
Double Extra Large	$1.00 per hour	$1.24 per hour
Quadruple Extra Large	$2.00 per hour	$2.48 per hour
Hi-CPU On-Demand Instances		
Medium	$0.17 per hour	$0.29 per hour
Extra Large	$0.68 per hour	$1.16 per hour
Cluster Compute Instances		
Quadruple Extra Large	$1.30 per hour	$1.61 per hour
Eight Extra Large	$2.40 per hour	$2.97 per hour
Cluster GPU Instances		
Quadruple Extra Large	$2.10 per hour	$2.60 per hour

Figure 5-2 Public cloud vendors provide a price list for their services, such as the one shown here for Amazon's EC2 IaaS offerings.

Does this mean that, for example, if you rent a Small Windows server from Amazon, you will only pay 12 cents per hour for that server? Almost certainly not. In Amazon's case, if you scroll down the pricing page, you see also see the following charges:

- Per-gigabyte charges for bandwidth.

- Per-gigabyte charges for transferring data between zones (for example, if one zone goes down—see Figure 5-1!—or experiences high volume)

- Per-gigabyte charges for storage

- IP address charges

- Monitoring charges

- Load balancing charges

Some of these are optional (or have default levels that are free), but the point is that the amount you pay for that server is going to be more than twelve cents an hour, probably a lot more.

"Unfortunately comparing public cloud services is often like comparing budget airlines. The only consistent fact is that what you end up paying does not bare [sic] any resemblance with the advertised price. And this is due to the additional costs for inbound/outbound traffic, for writing to storage, for an IP address etc."[17]
—Christian Verstraete

At least Amazon does a good job of specifying exactly what it charges for each level of service and each feature. Many public cloud providers hide or, at least, make it difficult to find, these extra charges, so it becomes very hard to know exactly how much the service will cost you.

Vendor Lock-in

Vendor lock-in occurs when a customer becomes dependent on a vendor for the delivery of a particular product or service, and is unable to switch to a different vendor because the cost of doing so (in terms of effort, money, or data and system incompatibilities) is too high. Many companies choose a public cloud service and later find that the switching costs of moving to another cloud provider are too expensive, so vendor lock-in is a major public cloud disadvantage. Public cloud lock-in comes in two main flavors:

- **Horizontal lock in** This type of lock-in prevents a company from replacing an existing service with a comparable service from another cloud provider. The usual difficulties here revolve around either the difficulty of moving SaaS application data to the new provider, or migrating code to a new PaaS development platform.

- **Vertical lock-in** This type of lock-in means that a company is stuck with whatever infrastructure and platforms are offered by the cloud service provider. For example, provisioning a PaaS system might necessitate using a particular operating system and database.

Performance

An application running on a public cloud infrastructure, through a pipe that supports transmission speeds of up to a few megabits per second, is always going to feel slower and more sluggish than a comparable app running over an internal network that supports transmission speeds of up to a gigabit per second.

Not only is the public cloud pipe smaller, but it is also longer. Most obviously, the total distance between the customer and the cloud provider's data center is going to be vastly longer than the distance to the customer's own data center. Beyond that, public cloud data often has to bounce around between different areas within the same data center and between data centers in different regions or even different countries. At best, these extra hops slow down cloud performance even more, but, at worse, they can cause application delays and even timeouts.

Cloud Sprawl

In "Chapter 1: Introducing Cloud Computing," I introduced you to *IT sprawl*, an infrastructure problem where a large number of silo technologies require IT to support legacy hardware and software systems on increasingly complex networks. Moving to the cloud helps reduce IT sprawl by getting rid of technology silos, trimming IT capital expenditures, and offering your company an agile way to handle IT resources for the benefit of the business.

As you have seen, part of this newfound agility is the on-demand, self-service nature of cloud computing. This is particularly true in the public cloud, where employees can quickly and easily source a huge catalog of infrastructure, platforms, and software from a wide variety of vendors. The *quickly and easily* part means that many public cloud services can be provisioned with just a few mouse clicks and the proffering of a corporate credit card.

This makes business more agile, indeed, but the ease with which public cloud services can be provisioned can lead to these services infiltrating every corner of the business. This is known as *cloud sprawl* and it is nearly as bad as IT sprawl because it raises costs and prevents IT from implementing a coherent cloud strategy.

Shadow Cloud

In "Chapter 1: Introducing Cloud Computing," you also learned about *shadow IT*, the use of technologies, devices, services, and applications outside of the IT infrastructure and without IT's approval or knowledge. The main cause of shadow IT is the amount of time and effort that it takes to get anything done through the IT department, so managers and employees take IT into their own hands.

This can happen in the cloud, as well. If the IT department is brokering services through its own private cloud and through public cloud providers, the old IT mindset might still prevail, which means it can take an inordinate amount of time to get new services approved and deployed. The ease with which employees can provision services on their own (leading to cloud sprawl) also means that they will be just as willing to provision their own public cloud services if IT is too slow. This is called shadow cloud (or stealth cloud) and it is a huge problem for businesses, particularly those with compliance rules regarding issues such as data privacy and security. What data are employees storing in these stealth cloud services? Where is it being stored? How is it being protected?

Transparency

When you provision a public cloud service, particularly a SaaS offering, you probably think you are dealing with a single company. For example, if you are using Foursquare, Hootsuite, Kickstarter, Reddit, or Quora, your data resides on those companies' servers, right? Not really. Every one of those companies relies on Amazon's EC2 IaaS services for their infrastructure, so your data *actually* resides in an Amazon data center.

That is not so surprising, since I mentioned earlier in this chapter that it often makes a lot of sense for SaaS startups to rent infrastructure instead of investing in their own data centers. The problem, however, is that these companies—and, in fact, the vast majority of public SaaS (and PaaS) providers— do not disclose who they partner with for their infrastructure. This means that you usually have no way of telling which company is actually storing your data, so you have no way of judging how well they are securing that data. You also have no way of establishing the physical location of your data, which can be a big problem if the infrastructure provider has data centers in multiple countries and your compliance rules come with restrictions on the geographic location of your data.

When *Not* to Consider the Public Cloud

I began this chapter by offering you several reasons why you should definitely consider implementing some sort of cloud environment in your company: increasing business agility, transforming IT into an innovator rather than a maintainer, and supporting the rapidly increasing Generation D workforce.

Let's close this chapter by looking at the opposite case. That is, are there any scenarios where you should *not* consider implementing cloud services, particularly those of a public cloud provider?

Compliance Requirements

Depending on the nature of your business, the data you collect, and the partners, agencies, and vendors you deal with, you might have a list (perhaps a *long* list) of responsibilities to operate your business in accordance with laws, regulations, standards, and corporate guidelines. This all falls under the rubric of *compliance*, and it can be a complex, many-headed beast consisting of federal laws, state laws, local government regulations, industry standards and best practices, and more.

You should not consider any public cloud environments or services that would contradict your company's compliance regulations. In particular, the public cloud is no place for the following:

- Data that must remain private, such as data tied to individuals, financial information, health records, and academic transcripts.

- Data that must remain secure, such as corporate secrets, intellectual property, and research results.

- Data that must be stored in a specific geographic location, such as a state or country, or with specific geographic requirements, such as away from a known flood plain.

Mission-Critical Applications

A mission-critical application is, by definition, an application that your business simply cannot do without. In your own data center, you can ensure that such an application achieves *five nines* (99.999%) availability by implementing a number of insurance and safety features, including dedicated high-performance hardware, storage redundancy, load balancing, data backups, sophisticated monitoring, failover systems, and recovery plans.

Compare five nines reliability and its five or so minutes of total annual downtime to the typical public cloud's three and a half nines (99.95%) availability and its more than four *hours* of yearly downtime. This alone is reason enough not to consider public cloud for mission-critical apps and services. Add in the fact that most public cloud providers only implement one-size-fits-all services that do not offer more than commodity hardware and rudimentary application management and monitoring features, and you see that the public cloud is not the place for your mission-critical jobs.

> ### ◢ Note
>
> I should probably be more specific here and say that the public cloud is *currently* not the place for mission-critical applications. Many public cloud providers and third-party vendors are hard at work putting together systems that are designed to make the public cloud fast, reliable, and secure enough for mission-critical tasks. This work involves revising cloud architecture to ensure that mission-critical apps do not go offline during standard server reboots, beefing up SLAs to require more uptime, supporting existing applications without modification, and optimizing cloud performance.

Physical Access to Server

Public cloud servers are virtualized, so they are just software, not hardware. However, in some cases you might require hardware instead of software because you need physical access to the server:

- For maximum security, access to the server might require a hardware encryption key, such as a specially configured USB flash drive.

- A particular application on the server might require a hardware dongle to be physically connected to the machine.

- The server might require special equipment, such as an internal circuit board (such as a fax card) or an external USB device.

In these and similar scenarios where access to a physical server is required, the public cloud is not for you.

REFERENCES

1 **Mark Veverka**, *Verizon Leaps for the Clouds*, Barron's, http://online.barrons. com/article/SB50001424052970203876704576102170890208378.html (January 29, 2011).

2 **Jacqueline Vanacek**, *The Social Impact of Cloud*, Forbes, http://www.forbes. com/sites/sap/2012/01/10/the-social-impact-of-cloud-2/ (January 10, 2012).

3 *VMWare vSphere, the First Cloud Operating System, Provides an Evolutionary, Non-disruptive Path to Cloud Computing*, VMWare, http://www.vmware.com/ files/pdf/cloud/VMW_09Q2_WP_Cloud_OS_P8_R1.pdf (June 1, 2009).

4 **Peggy A. Seiden**, *Where Have All the Patrons Gone?*, Reference & User Services Quarterly, March 22, 2000.

5 **Jim Melvin**, *CEO Notes: Another Benefit of Cloud Computing...Elastic means SMALL too!*, AppNeta, http://blog.appneta.com/2011/10/07/ceo-notes-another-benefit-of-cloud-computing-elastic-means-small-too/ (October 7, 2011).

6 **Tracy Mayor**, *Self-service IT: Are users up for the task?*, InfoWorld, http:// www.infoworld.com/d/the-industry-standard/self-service-it-are-users-the-task-183553 (January 9, 2012).

7 **Josh Whitney**, et al., *Salesforce.com and the environment*, http://www. salesforce.com/assets/pdf/misc/WP_WSP_Salesforce_Environment.pdf

8 **Paul Dickinson**, *Cloud Computing — The IT Solution for the 21st Century*, Carbon Disclosure Project, https://www.cdproject.net/Documents/Cloud-Computing-The-IT-Solution-for-the-21st-Century.pdf (July 19, 2011).

9 **Sanjay Sharma**, *Cloud Computing for SMBs: A Level Playing Field*, Cloud Computing Journal, http://cloudcomputing.sys-con.com/node/1907291 (July 14, 2011).

10 **James Urquhart**, *Cloud is complex—deal with it*, GigaOM, http://gigaom. com/cloud/cloud-is-complex-deal-with-it/ (January 8, 2012).

11 **Nicholas Carr**, *IT doesn't matter, part 7*, Rough Type, http://www.roughtype. com/archives/2007/01/it_doesnt_matte_6.php (January 11, 2007).

12 **Kim Zetter**, *Bank Sends Sensitive E-mail to Wrong Gmail Address, Sues Google*, Wired, http://www.wired.com/threatlevel/2009/09/bank-sues-google/ (September 21, 2009).

13 **Thomas Ristenpart**, et al., *Hey, You, Get Off of My Cloud: Exploring Information Leakage in Third-Party Compute Clouds*, University of California, San Diego, http://cseweb.ucsd.edu/~hovav/dist/cloudsec.pdf (November 9, 2009).

14 **Lydia Leong**, *Cloud IaaS is not magical, and the Amazon reboot-a-thon*, CloudPundit, http://cloudpundit.com/2011/12/07/cloud-iaas-is-not-magical-and-the-amazon-reboot-a-thon/ (December 7, 2011).

15 See *Summary of the Amazon EC2 and Amazon RDS Service Disruption in the US East Region*, Amazon Web Services, http://aws.amazon.com/message/65648/ (April 29, 2011).

16 See http://aws.amazon.com/ec2/pricing/.

17 **Christian Verstraete**, *Private Cloud, how do we define that?*, HP Supply Chain Management Blog, http://h30507.www3.hp.com/t5/Supply-Chain-Management-Blog/Private-Cloud-how-do-we-define-that/ba-p/83621 (November 29, 2010).

18 *'Cloud sprawl' is a growing concern for European companies: survey*, Computer Business Review, http://appdev.cbronline.com/news/more-than-half-of-european-employees-use-public-cloud-apps-and-services-without-prior-permission-from-it-department-survey-020611 (June 2, 201).

19 **Christian Teeft**, *Defining, differentiating and debunking common assumptions when making cloud computing decisions*, Smart Business, http://www.sbnonline.com/2012/01/defining-differentiating-and-debunking-common-assumptions-when-making-cloud-computing-decisions/?full=1 (January 1, 2012).

6 The Economics of Cloud Computing

When it comes to deciding how to use cloud computing in your business—or even *whether* to use cloud computing at all—you have seen so far that there are many factors to consider. These include security, reliability, performance, compliance, as well as the current needs and future goals of your company. In some cases, these considerations will be deal-makers or deal-breakers, and you will know right away that the cloud is either perfect for your business, or something you need to avoid at all costs.

However, it is more likely that you will view cloud computing as a mixture of pros and cons, advantages and disadvantages, opportunities and challenges, and that all of these considerations will come out more or less even.

What do you do then? How can you decide whether cloud computing is right for your company in the absence of a compelling or persuasive argument one way or the other? In that case, it is time to crunch the numbers. It is time to take a cold, hard look at the business case for (or against) cloud computing.

Understanding Cloudonomics

Doing cost/benefit analyses is often a fairly straightforward bit of business. You add up a few things on each side of the ledger, calculate the difference, and you are done! I wish I could tell you that an economic analysis of cloud computing is just that easy but, alas, it is not. For example, cloud computing's different delivery models and their varied implementations and mechanisms confuse the issue quite a bit, so that, say, comparing public cloud's pay-per-use model with a private cloud's physical-servers-in-a-data-center model is anything but simple. So, let's begin this chapter with a look at a few of the twists and turns that cloud computing brings to the economics table.

> "The significant benefits of agility and cost savings delivered by cloud computing are too compelling to ignore. Forward-thinking enterprises are answering the questions of cloud computing not with an 'if' but with a 'when.' The challenge is to understand, based on a risk/reward evaluation, what cloud services are appropriate for adoption, when they are appropriate, and the best practices, technologies and vendors that should be employed."[1]
> —Gartner

Understanding Pay-Per-Use

I have used the term *pay-per-use* many times throughout this book, and I have generally used the phrase to mean a cloud computing business model in which services are paid for only when they are used. In the real world of cloud computing, however, the *use* part of this phrase varies dramatically depending on the cloud provider and the service being offered:

- **Pay-per-time-used** In the purest sense of the term, the *use* part refers to the time a resource is provisioned. That is, like a long-distance phone call, the meter starts running as soon as you provision the resource (initiate the call) and does not stop until you de-provision the resource (end the call). In this pure pay-per-use model, resources are charged at a set fee per time unit (usually per hour), and that fee is charged whether you use the resource constantly, only part of the time, or not at all.

- **Pay-per-unit-consumed** Another type of cloud payment model that often falls under the rubric of pay-per-use is the consumption-based model where the provider measures the amount of resources you use and charges a set fee per unit of consumption. This could be gigabytes for storage or bandwidth, cores for CPUs, and so on. This is the *utility* pricing model, since it is analogous to how utilities charge for consumables such as electricity and natural gas.

- **Pay-per-instance-provisioned** In this payment model, the provider charges a set fee when you provision a resource. The most common example is an operating system license fee which the provider charges when you provision a virtual machine or platform. A real-world equivalent would be a taxi ride where the cab charges you an initial fee (the starting charge on the meter).

- **Pay-per-user** This is a common SaaS pricing model where you pay a set charge per person per month for each user who needs access to the software. This is akin to the Netflix pricing model, where you pay (or, really, your household pays) a flat fee per month that enables you to access any available movie.

It is important to realize that in many instances your cloud costs will be a mixture of two or more of these pay-per-use models. For example, if you provision infrastructure from an IaaS provider, you will pay for the time you use the virtual machine (pay-per-time-used). You will also almost certainly have to pay extra for more CPU cores, memory, and storage (pay-per-unit-consumed). If the VM includes an operating system, then you will also pay a license fee (pay-per-instance-provisioned). If you use the VM to set up a development platform, the software might require a fee for each developer (pay-per-user).

Pay-Per-Use Versus In-House

Perhaps the most contentious cloudonomics debate is the argument over the relative costs of public cloud versus private cloud, or pay-per-use (in its pure sense of pay-per-time-used) versus investing in dedicated, in-house servers. The debate is a complex one, with spreadsheet jockeys tossing formulas around like digital grenades. However, for our purposes we can simplify the debate by assuming the following:

- Both the pay-per-use and in-house models have a unit cost, which is usually expressed per unit of time (for example, x cents per hour).

- The unit cost of pay-per-use resources can be expressed relative to the unit cost of in-house resources. This is called the *utility premium*. If it equals 1, it means the unit costs are the same; if it is less than 1, it means pay-per-use is less expensive; if it is greater than 1, it means that pay-per-use is more expensive. For example, if the in-house unit cost is 10 cents and the utility premium is 1.5, then the pay-per-use unit cost is 15 cents.

- The demand for resources can be expressed numerically as the average demand over some fixed time period. During that same time, there will also be a value for the peak demand.

- An in-house model must be built to handle peak demand, so the cost of this model per unit of time is the unit cost of the in-house resources, multiplied by the peak demand value.

- A pay-per-use model is used for both demand peaks and demand troughs, so its usage is based on the average demand. Therefore, the cost of this model per unit of time is the unit cost of the dedicated resources, multiplied by the utility premium, multiplied by the average demand value.

So, which is cheaper, pay-per-use or in-house? The short answer is: it depends. In particular, it depends on two main factors: the utility premium and the size of the peak demand. The utility premium is important because it determines the relative unit cost of pay-per-use versus in-house. The size of the peak demand is important because it determines how much infrastructure you need in-house to meet that demand. The interplay between these two factors is complex, but we can break it down into the following three scenarios:

- **Pay-per-use unit costs are lower than in-house unit costs** This is the scenario where the utility premium is less than 1. Not only do you pay less for resources, but you also only per for what you use, so, in this scenario, pay-per-use will always be cheaper than the in-house model.

- **In-house unit costs are lower than pay-per-use unit costs, and demand is flat** This is the scenario where the utility premium is greater than 1. Since demand is flat, the in-house model needs no extra infrastructure, so both the in-house and pay-per-use costs are calculated using average demand. Since in-house unit costs are cheaper, in this scenario, in-house will always be cheaper than pay-per-use.

- **In-house unit costs are lower than pay-per-use unit costs, and demand is variable** Again, in this scenario, the utility premium is greater than 1. However, since demand is variable, the in-house model needs extra infrastructure to handle the peak usage. The two factors—the utility premium and the extra peak demand costs—are pulling this scenario in opposite directions. To get a handle on this, note that the utility premium is a ratio (of the pay-per-use unit cost to the in-house unit cost), so the equivalent in the second factor would be the ratio of peak demand to average demand (because in-house is priced based on the peak and pay-per-use is priced on the average). When you do the math,[2] you end up with three possibilities:

  - **The utility premium is greater than the peak-to-average ratio** In this case, the cost of pay-per-use outweighs the cost of the extra peak infrastructure, so the in-house model is cheaper.

  - **The utility premium is the same as the peak-to-average ratio** In this case, the two ratios exactly offset each other, so the cost is the same for both.

  - **The utility premium is less than the peak-to-average ratio** In this case, the cost of the extra peak infrastructure outweighs the pay-per-use premium, so we end up with the surprising result that, despite higher pay-per-use unit costs, the pay-per-use model is cheaper than in-house.

What about hybrid clouds? So far we have just looked at pure public and pure private models, but what about the common scenario of handling average demand in-house and sourcing cloud bursting peak demand out to a pay-per-use cloud? Under what conditions is a hybrid cloud cheaper than either a pure private cloud or a pure public cloud?

Let's look at the hybrid versus private scenario first. In this case, the hybrid total cost is the sum of the following:

- **In-house costs** The amount of non-peak resources used, multiplied by the unit cost, multiplied by the amount of time those resources are used.

- **Pay-per-use costs** The amount of peak resources used, multiplied by the unit cost, multiplied by the utility premium (which is greater than 1), multiplied by the amount of time those resources are used.

✏ Note

Why must the utility premium be greater than 1? Because, all other costs being equal, in any scenario where the utility premium is less than 1, a pure pay-per-use model will always be cheaper.

The key ratio here is the total time the peak resources are used to the total time all resources are used. In this scenario, this ratio works in opposition not with the utility premium, but with the *inverse* of the utility premium, which means in-house unit costs divided by pay-per-use unit costs. It turns out that if the peak time to total time ratio is less than the inverse of the utility premium, then the hybrid model will always be cheaper than a pure private model.

This makes sense because in a hybrid model the data center can only handle non-peak loads (so its infrastructure costs are less than with an in-house model), but it must burst to the more expensive public cloud during peak periods. So, there must be some maximum value below which the extra public cloud expenses do not offset the infrastructure savings.

The opposite case is comparing a hybrid cloud to a public cloud. In this case, we ignore peak demand (since it will be handled in the public cloud in both cases), so the case reduces to seeing whether hybrid or public is cheaper for handling the non-peak demand. The total cost of the non-peak usage is calculated as follows:

- **In-house** The amount of non-peak resources used, multiplied by the unit cost, multiplied by the total time.

- **Pay-per-use** The amount of non-peak resources used, multiplied by the unit cost, multiplied by the utility premium (which, again, is greater than 1), multiplied by the amount of time those resources are used.

The main difference is that in-house resources are always available, even if no one is using them, so in a sense they are constantly being paid for. By contrast, in the public cloud you only pay for resources when you use them. The key ratio here is the total time resources are used over the total time available, and this is in opposition not to the utility premium, but to the inverse of the utility premium. The math shows that if the ratio of time used over total time available is greater than the inverse of the utility premium, then a hybrid model will always be cheaper than a pure public model.

This makes sense because the longer a resource is used, the more the in-house infrastructure is utilized, and the more the in-house and pay-per-use costs converge. If a resource is used 100% of the time, then the cost difference is simply the utility premium, so there must be some minimum amount of time above which the lower in-house unit costs more than offset the public cloud's pay-only-when-you-use-it savings.

The Economic Value of On-Demand

I have mentioned several times in this book that one of the key advantages of cloud computing is its on-demand nature that enables a business to provision resources quickly when they are needed, and then de-provision those resources just as quickly when they are no longer required. This rapid elasticity is not just a better way to run a business, it is a better way to *do* business:

- **Minimize forecasting errors** When you do not have resources available on demand, you must forecast future demand based on historical data, current trends, expected future events, and so on. As you no doubt know from hard-won experience, this process is anything but foolproof and more often than not a forecast will either woefully underestimate or wildly overestimate future demand, particularly peaks and extreme events. Underestimation results in not having the capacity to handle demand, while overestimation results in spending too much for infrastructure to handle non-existent demand. With on-demand provisioning, however, you can quickly bring resources online when peaks or extreme events appear, and you never overspend because, thanks to pay-per-use, you do not pay for what you do not use.

> "The ability to rapidly provision capacity means that any unexpected demand can be serviced, and the revenue associated with it captured. The ability to rapidly de-provision capacity means that companies don't need to pay good money for non-productive assets. Forecasting is often wrong, especially for black swans, so the ability to react instantaneously means higher revenues, and lower costs."[3]
> —Joe Weinman

- **Maximize agility** Being able to provision resources quickly and easily is a key component of the agile business. When your company needs to respond to customer needs, sales opportunities, new technologies, or external factors, being able to provision the necessary resources quickly means a faster, more targeted response. This helps the bottom line by enabling your business to turn sales opportunities into actual sales, and to minimize any expenses that would otherwise be incurred through a slow or inefficient response to a problem.

- **Minimize opportunity costs** If your business either does not have sufficient infrastructure to meet peak demands, or you have not yet devised a cloud strategy that enables you to provision extra resources when required, then you run the risk of creating opportunity costs. That is, if your customers cannot access your website or purchase your product, they will go elsewhere and you will lose that person's business.

- **Maximize revenue** This is a direct corollary to the previous point. That is, if you have sufficient capacity (either in-house or via a public cloud) to handle all demands, the people who want to buy your product will be able to do so, and you will maximize revenue form those customers.

Cloud Computing and ROI

Another way to look at the economics of cloud computing is by examining the rate of return a pure public cloud implementation generates versus a pure in-house data center. The return on investment (ROI) is a measure of how much a company earns for each dollar of investment it makes. Generally speaking, a public cloud investment requires no initial cash outlay, but sizable annual expenses, while an in-house data center requires a large initial investment and relatively small annual expenses. Which scenario generates the superior ROI?

Let's simplify things by looking at an example that makes the following assumptions:

- The in-house data center requires an initial $5 million dollar investment, and the company earns a $1 million profit each year.

- The public cloud requires no initial investment, but it does cost $750,000 each year, resulting in a yearly profit of $250,000.

Table 6-1 lays out the cash flows over eight years for Startup A, which implements an in-house data center, and Startup B, which uses a public cloud.

Table 6-1 Comparing cash flows, total profit, and rate of return for an in-house data center and a public cloud implementation.

| Date | Startup A (In-House) | | Startup B (Public Cloud) | |
	Cash Flows	Type	Cash Flows	Type
1-Jan-2012	$(5,000,000)	Initial investment	$(750,000)	First year expenses
1-Jan-2013	$1,000,000	Profit	$250,000	Profit
1-Jan-2014	$1,000,000	Profit	$250,000	Profit
1-Jan-2015	$1,000,000	Profit	$250,000	Profit
1-Jan-2016	$1,000,000	Profit	$250,000	Profit
1-Jan-2017	$1,000,000	Profit	$250,000	Profit
1-Jan-2018	$1,000,000	Profit	$250,000	Profit
1-Jan-2019	$1,000,000	Profit	$250,000	Profit
TOTAL	$2,000,000		$1,000,000	
Annualized IRR	9.2%		27.1%	

On the surface, Startup A looks like the better bet since it generated $2 million dollars in net profit, versus just $1 million for Startup B. But the annualized internal rate of return (IRR) tells a different story: 27.1% for Startup B versus just 9.2% for Startup A. In other words, Startup B's investment earned nearly three times more per dollar than Startup A's.

This is not to imply that public cloud will always generate a higher rate of return that an in-house data center. Table 6-1 represents an extremely simplistic scenario, and in the real world costs are much more complex and are highly dependent on the needs and goals of individual companies and the industries in which they operate. To get a more nuanced view, the next section gives you a closer look at cloud computing costs.

Understanding Cloud Costs

As you saw earlier when I discussed pay-per-use costs versus in-house costs, determining the *cheapest* cloud implementation is not even remotely straightforward. In fact, cloud pundits and pros have been arguing the relative cost benefits of public versus private clouds for years. Some say that public cloud is always cheaper, and put forth sophisticated arguments to prove their point, while others counter with equal force that private clouds are always cheaper.

The goods news is that it does not matter which side is right. First, you now know full well that cost is only a piece of the larger cloud pie, and how large a piece depends on how much you value other cloud metrics, such as agility, elasticity, scalability, and increased innovation. Second, even if the cost argument is vital to your organization, the bottom line will be determined almost entirely by your company's unique situation. For that to happen, you need to not only take an honest and thorough look at both your current expenses and your potential expenses in whatever cloud model you use, but you also need to prioritize those costs so they are in line with your company's needs and goals.

> "[Public] cloud services don't actually save many businesses very much money, and in some cases they boost costs because they require companies to add new staff with the relevant cloud expertise."[4]
> —Jon Stokes

> "I will, however, grant that public cloud computing offerings are almost certainly cheaper resources than private."[5]
> —Lori MacVittie

Fixed Costs Versus Variable Costs

I have talked a lot about transforming your business so that it can quickly and nimbly respond to changing conditions in the market, the global economy, the political landscape, technology, and so on. However, it is just as important that your company's cash flow and expenses are as nimble and responsive to changing conditions.

For example, a data center has certain costs attached to running it, including electricity, cooling, physical plant expenses, and maintenance. The key point is that over the lifecycle of the hardware, these costs will remain relatively constant, even if external conditions change. In a down market, for example, if your revenues fall, you might trim your staff or ask employees to freeze their wages short-term, but you will still have to pay those fixed data center costs.

You might be thinking that at least in an up market, when revenues are on the rise, those fixed data center costs will look awfully good. That is true, but only to the extent that your existing data center has the capacity to meet peak demand. If it does not, then you lose sales and incur the opportunity costs of customers taking their business elsewhere.

In other words, from a pure expense standpoint, a data center and its fixed costs have no relation to sales: those costs do not go down when revenues drop, and they do not rise to meet new demand.

Public cloud costs are the opposite, because instead of fixed costs you have variable costs. That is, you have no up-front investment, and the pay-per-use model (particularly pay-per-time-used and pay-per-unit-consumed) means that your costs are directly related to your computing needs. In a down market, with falling revenues, you can scale back your public infrastructure (for example) to compensate. In an up market, you can quickly provision new infrastructure to ensure that you do not lose sales when demand peaks.

> "Disconnect price from cost; reconnect price to value."[6]
> —Daryl Plummer

Capital Costs

Depending on the type of cloud you intend to implement, one of the most important cost factors is capital expenses, particularly when you are looking to compare cloud costs with the costs associated with a non-cloud data center. The latter includes the capital costs associated with the data center itself and its equipment, as well as the computing infrastructure costs (servers, networking, and so on), which must be built up to handle peak demand. Let's see how these stack up against the cloud deployment models:

- **Public** This type of cloud has no capital expenses.

- **Private** This cloud type does come with some capital costs, including costs associated with the data center that holds the private cloud, and the servers and other infrastructure that create the private cloud. Note, however, that since the cloud includes virtualized resources, it can provision to peak demand using far fewer physical servers than with a non-cloud data center.

> **Note**
>
> For a proper comparison of capital costs between a cloud implementation and a non-cloud data center, you might be tempted to reduce the in-house costs by the amount of existing equipment your company already owns. However, you need to know where that equipment resides in its operational lifecycle. If it has been in operation for several years and is, therefore, nearing the end of its tenure, then you need to factor replacement equipment into your calculations.

■ **Hybrid** Since this type of cloud includes a private cloud component, it does come with a list of capital costs that are similar to those of the private cloud. However, since the private portion of the hybrid cloud environment is only provisioned to handle average demand (with peak demand loads *cloudbursted* out to the public cloud component), capital costs overall will be less than for a pure private cloud implementation.

Operating Costs

Capital costs tend to be large, one-time expenses and are treated in a special way by the accounting department (for example, using depreciation). Operating costs, on the other hand, are ongoing expenses involved in the day-to-day running of the business. These costs are myriad, but from a cloud computing perspective you need to look at the following:

IT staff salaries

Data center staff salaries

Data center management

Electricity, cooling, lights

Fire and theft protection

Taxes

Insurance

These are all costs that a public cloud provider takes on, so you eliminate these costs to the extent that you implement public cloud in your IT strategy.

> "From an accounting point of view, however, it is important to consider that moving to the Cloud will almost certainly result in reduced capital expenses (fixed Capex costs) and increased operating expenses (variable Opex costs)... The move, from Capex to Opex will be an attractive prospect to many corporations and business units, allowing them to pay for only the IT services they consume."[7]
> —Ralph Presciutti

System Costs

By system costs I mean those costs required to implement a complete computing system for your company, from servers to operating system licenses. (Yes, there will necessarily be some overlap with both capital costs and operating costs.) When comparing the costs of a public, private, or hybrid cloud implementation with an in-house, non-cloud data center, you need to take all the relevant system costs into consideration. Here is a list of the most important items to include:

- Servers

- Storage, including storage for applications, data, backups, and disk images

- Networking equipment, including routers, switches, cables, and load balancers

- Networking access costs, particularly bandwidth

- Security equipment, including physical firewalls and VPN endpoints

- Client hardware, including desktops, notebooks, tablets, and smartphones

- Software licenses, including those for operating systems and applications

- Software development, including platforms, databases, and development of new applications

- Technical support, including employee support and customer support

The costs involved will be highly dependent on the type of system. A purely public cloud system will have mostly virtualized, pay-per-use resources, while the data center spectrum as it increases from hybrid cloud to private cloud to non-cloud will have increasing numbers of non-virtualized, capital-cost resources.

> "For organizations over $1 billion [in revenue], private clouds are more cost effective in general, and provide significantly higher availability and security functionality."[8]
> —David Floyer

Physical Plant Costs

Physical plant costs are the expenses required to *keep the lights on* in the data center, including (of course) lighting, power, cooling, maintenance, and personnel:

- **Public** This type of cloud has no physical plant costs.

- **Private** This cloud type requires a data center, so it does come with physical plant costs. However, since a typical private cloud environment uses fewer physical servers than a non-cloud environment, the data center is usually smaller and, therefore, cheaper.

- **Hybrid** This type of cloud has a private cloud component, so it does have physical plant costs. However, the data center will be smaller than one used for a straight private cloud (since the hybrid cloud does not need to handle peak demand loads), so the plant costs will be corresponding smaller.

Staffing Costs

On the one hand, it follows that moving to a cloud environment will necessarily reduce staffing costs. For example, a pure public cloud implementation barely needs an IT department at all. Similarly, private and hybrid environments implement virtualized resources deployed automatically via self-service portals, so they no longer require a large staff to handle resource configuration, deployment, and provisioning.

On the other hand, you have learned that one of the goals of moving to the cloud is to transform IT so that it spends less time on operations and maintenance and more time on innovation and helping the business differentiate itself in the marketplace. Most of us would want fewer IT staff *keeping the lights on*, but it might make sense to have *more* IT staff innovating and making the business more efficient and focused.

Migration Costs

It is important to understand that there is no such thing as a free ride to the cloud. The journey from here to there has migration costs that you need to factor into your calculations. Here are some examples:

- **Costs associated with migrating data to the cloud** For example, you might have to clean up the data, export the data to a format suitable for migration, or analyze the data to ensure that the cloud portion complies with any data regulations and laws your company must follow.

- **Costs associated with migrating applications to the cloud** Converting an in-house app into a cloud-friendly app almost always involves reprogramming, optimizing, and updating code, as well as building new functionality, such as portals.

- **Retraining costs** Employees used to performing tasks in-house will need to be retrained to use any new cloud-based platforms and software. This is particularly true of IT staff, who may need extensive retraining for new cloud technologies and systems.

Fortunately, these are almost always one-time-only costs, not recurring expenses.

REFERENCES

1   *Cloud Computing: The Why, When and How of Adoption*, Gartner, http://www.gartner.com/technology/summits/na/applications/track-2-cloud-computing.jsp (November 15, 2010)

2   If you literally want to do the math, see Joe Weinman, *Mathematical Proof of the Inevitability of Cloud Computing*, http://joeweinman.com/Resources/Joe_Weinman_Inevitability_Of_Cloud.pdf (November 30, 2009).

3   **Joe Weinman**, *The 10 Laws of Cloudonomics*, GigaOM, http://gigaom.com/2008/09/07/the-10-laws-of-cloudonomics/ (September 7, 2008).

4   **Jon Stokes**, *What Moore's Law Means for the Future of the Cloud*, Wired Cloudline, http://www.wired.com/cloudline/2011/12/moores-law-cloud/ (December 9, 2011).

5   **Lori MacVittie**, *It's Called Cloud Computing not Cheap Computing*, F5, http://devcentral.f5.com/weblogs/macvittie/archive/2010/12/06/itrsquos-called-cloud-computing-not-cheap-computing.aspx (December 6, 2010).

6   **Daryl Plummer**, *The Real Truth About Cloud, SaaS, & What To Do With Your Money*, Gartner, http://www.gartner.com/it/content/1525600/1525617/february_15_real_truth_about_cloud_saas_dplummer.pdf (February 15, 2011).

7   **Ralph Prescuitti**, *From Capex to Opex: How the Cloud Affects Cash Flow and Accounting*, Tatum LLC, http://blog.tatumllc.com/?p=586 (December 13, 2011).

8   **David Floyer**, *Private Cloud is more Cost Effective than Public Cloud for Organizations over $1B*, Wikibon, http://wikibon.org/wiki/v/Private_Cloud_is_more_Cost_Effective_than_Public_Cloud_for_Organizations_over_$1B (December 13, 2010).

7   Devising a Cloud Strategy

One of the central themes of this book is that if businesses want to be agile enough to compete in an increasingly globalized, competitive, fast-paced world, one of the best ways to do that is to transform the IT department to include some kind of cloud environment, be it private, public, or hybrid. It is true that there may be a tiny subset of businesses that would derive little or no benefit from cloud computing, but the cloud offers tangible benefits to the vast majority of enterprises, including yours.

If you find yourself fired up about cloud computing and its potential to transform your business, you might be tempted to just get on with it already. After all, the business landscape is shifting under your feet as you read this, and the pace of change is only going to get faster. You are convinced the cloud is the place to be, so why delay the journey?

To put it another way, you have got the starting gun in your hand, why not just pull the trigger to start the race? Because at this point you do not know where the gun is pointing, and *ready-fire-aim* is a dangerous way to do business. To help remedy that, this chapter is all about the *aiming*, as I take you through various ways of developing a strategy for moving some or all of your IT operations into the cloud.

General Considerations for a Cloud Computing Strategy

With all the greatest-thing-since-sliced-bread hype surrounding cloud computing these days, you can be forgiven for thinking that doing the cloud thing sounds effortless. With "cloud consultants" lurking around every corner promising a smooth transition to the cloud, you can be forgiven for thinking that moving to the cloud sounds practically automatic. In short, you can be forgiven for thinking that implementing cloud in your business does not require a strategy.

Of course, once you get beyond the hype and smooth talk, you see that cloud computing is as complex and involved as any other significant piece of technology. This means that a successful move to the cloud is pretty much impossible without a detailed strategy that looks at every aspect not only of cloud computing, but also your business and its needs and goals. To help you get started, this section presents a few general ideas that should be a major part of your cloud computing strategy.

Identify Your Competitive Distinctiveness

Ever since the first computers came rumbling to life in the middle of the twentieth century, computing technology has offered a competitive advantage for early adopters. The first mainframes, the first networks, and the first data centers, to name but a few innovations from the past decades, gave companies a leg up on their rivals by making them more efficient and more productive. Unfortunately, computing technology tends to disseminate relatively quickly, so whatever competitive advantage a technology created for a company was soon gone, as rival firms caught up. This simple fact goes to the heart of writer Nicholas Carr's argument in his seminal essay, *IT Doesn't Matter:*

> What makes a resource truly strategic – what gives it the capacity to be the basis for a sustained competitive advantage – is not ubiquity but scarcity. You only gain an edge over rivals by having or doing something that they can't have or do. By now, the core functions of IT – data storage, data

processing, and data transport – have become available and affordable to all. Their very power and presence have begun to transform them from potentially strategic resources into commodity factors of production. They are becoming costs of doing business that must be paid by all but provide distinction to none.[1]

Of course, none of this means that you should not have an IT department! As Carr says, routine IT tasks are costs that "must be paid by all," because these tasks are crucial to the functioning of any modern enterprise. The key is to recognize that there are actually two main classes of IT function: routine tasks such as email and backups, and those *secret sauce* tasks that serve to differentiate your company from your competitors.

In his book, *Dealing with Darwin*, the consultant and author Geoffrey Moore refers to these classes as *context* and *core*, respectively, and sees the dichotomy between them as crucial for replacing inertia with innovation:

> *Core* is defined as any aspect of a company's operations that creates differentiation leading to customer preference during a purchase decision. It is innovation in service to competitive advantage. *Context*, by contrast, represents everything else, all other work performed by the enterprise. The work is extremely important and can be highly valued, but it does *not* differentiate you from your competition. It does, however, play host to the forces of inertia. The formula for tackling innovation and inertia in tandem is simple: Extract resources from context to repurpose for core.[2]

This idea of repurposing IT investments from context functions to core functions should be at the heart of your cloud computing strategy. First, it is crucial that you identify those aspects of your business that distinguish your company from your competitors. Once you have done that, you then determine what IT resources your need to maintain and nurture those aspects. For most companies, their competitive differentiators are where they need to be most agile and flexible, so these are best implemented in a cloud environment.

Transforming IT into a Strategic Service Broker

One of the main advantages to adopting cloud computing is that it enables IT to spend less time *keeping the lights on* and more time innovating, particularly on resources that differentiate your company from its rivals. But does that mean that *all* this innovation must be created in-house by the IT department? Not necessarily. In today's cloud world, innovation can just as easily come from public cloud services. If a public SaaS product gives your company a leg up on its competitors, then that is every bit as innovative as any resource created in-house and deployed in a private cloud.

How do you decide which route to take? That should be part of your cloud strategy. Specifically, you need a plan for sourcing services, either internally via the IT department, or externally via the public cloud.

This plan (and, again, by extension your cloud computing strategy) begins by identifying not only the services your company requires, but also their relative importance to the business. This means getting personnel from IT and business together to work out a governance model that identifies and prioritizes these services.

Next, you need to decide whether there are extenuating issues that might require keeping certain services in-house. For example, a particular service might have privacy, security, or compliance rules that require it to be provided internally. For each service that must be provided in-house, you next need to decide whether an existing application can be adapted to work within the private cloud, or whether IT needs to create a new service from scratch.

If a service can be sourced from a public cloud provider, then both IT and business need to evaluate potential providers and their services to ensure you choose one that not only satisfies the needs of the business side, but also meets IT requirements for security and integration with other resources.

With all the legwork done, the final step is to either to adapt or create the service internally, or source the service from the public cloud.

In the end, IT ends up with a service catalog that includes internal services adapted from legacy applications, internal services created from scratch, and external services sourced from the public cloud. To effectively manage all of these resources, IT must transform itself into a *strategic service broker* that sources services internally or externally, makes those services available to the business using a flexible, automated, on-demand hybrid cloud model, and periodically reviews these services to ensure they are providing the right resources to enable the business to innovate and improve its competitiveness.

> "Post-modern businesses will even re-imagine the roles that IT departments will play. Three out of 10 IT organizations will become cloud brokers for their business, and that is one way they will survive."[3]
> —Daryl Plummer

Data Integration

The importance of data does not go away when you move to the cloud, particularly if you plan on implementing a hybrid cloud that includes private and public components. In fact, it becomes even more important because you will end up with some data remaining in-house (because of security, privacy, or compliance rules) and some migrating to the public cloud, so now you have to decide how to integrate your internal and external data.

As part of your cloud strategy, you need a data integration strategy that determines how the private and public data is linked. First and foremost, you need to examine all your data and determine which types are allowed to reside in the public cloud and which must remain in-house. (See "Chapter 11: Migrating to the Cloud," for more information on this data classification problem.)

> "As businesses continue to deploy cloud-based systems, many are ignoring the fact that there needs to be some mechanism to synchronize data to and from your cloud and the core enterprise systems."[4]
> —David Linthicum

Once you have done that, you can then determine the integration strategy you prefer. There are three main possibilities (again, see "Chapter 11: Migrating to the Cloud" for the details):

- Keep all public data in-house and allow remote access.

- Maintain internal and external copies of the public data and synchronize.

- Migrate data from the private cloud to the public cloud as needed.

Implementing a Cloud Computing Strategy: The *Eight Hows*

In the rest of this chapter, I take you through a couple of examples of cloud computing strategies. Whether you follow these approaches in some form when devising your own strategy, or create your own approach, it is important to keep a few key concepts in mind. I call these the *eight hows* of implementing a cloud computing strategy, and they consist of the following questions:

- **How does cloud make our company better?** This is the fundamental question for *any* IT endeavor (or, really, any *business* endeavor). Determining where cloud computing will improve your business—or, to put it slightly differently, determining where your business needs the advantages of cloud computing—will go a long to helping craft your strategy.

- **How much does it cost initially?** Obviously, you need a budget for any new business project. However, in the context of cloud computing, this question is really a private versus public decision. A private cloud will almost certainly have significant up-front costs for servers and other data center infrastructure, while the public cloud almost always has very small initial costs.

- **How much does it cost to maintain?** Ongoing costs are a crucial part of the budgeting process. For a cloud project, public services will usually have higher monthly costs than private services.

- **How do we use it?** Cloud computing is all about giving users a scalable, elastic, on-demand, automated way to provision resources. Your cloud strategy must include some thought as to how users will access the service catalog, provision services, and then de-provision them when they are no longer needed.

- **How do we manage it?** Your cloud strategy must include a management layer, where both IT and business are able to oversee cloud services. Cloud management includes monitoring performance and availability, configuring services, ensuring compliance and governance rules are being followed, managing resource lifecycles, and monitoring costs, particularly for public cloud services.

- **How do we secure it?** Any aspect of your cloud strategy that will reside outside the corporate firewall (even temporarily) needs to have a robust security component. This will include examining the security sections of SLAs and negotiating with cloud providers to allow third-party security audits.

- **How do we back it up?** All aspects of your cloud implementation—whether private or public—require foolproof backup strategies that minimize (or, ideally, eliminate) the risk of data loss through backups, data redundancy, synchronized copies, and so on.

- **How do we recover if it fails?** Your cloud computing strategy should *assume* that some aspect of your private or public environment will eventually fail, and so, therefore, it should include a strategy for recovering from that failure. For the private cloud, this includes system image backups and failover protocols, while for the public cloud it means examining the availability and failover provisions of the SLA and, perhaps, negotiating a more robust recovery strategy.

The U.S. Government's Decision Framework for Cloud Migration

Under the stewardship of its former CIO, Vivek Kundra, the U.S. Federal Government realized a couple of years ago that it needed to move government IT services into the cloud to reduce costs, make government more efficient, and better serve the public. As part of that initiative, the government created a document called *Federal Cloud Computing Strategy,*[5] which laid out in detail not only the benefits of cloud computing to government IT operations, but also a detailed decision framework for migrating those operations to the cloud.

Although this framework is aimed at the Federal Government, the overall strategy is easily and usefully applied to businesses, as you see in this section. The decision framework is divided into three basic steps: select, provision, and manage.

> "The broad scope and size of the cloud transformation will require a meaningful shift in how government organizations think of IT. Organizations that previously thought of IT as an investment in locally owned and operated applications, servers, and networks will now need to think of IT in terms of services, commoditized computing resources, agile capacity provisioning tools, and their enabling effect for American citizens. This new way of thinking will have a broad impact across the entire IT service lifecycle – from capability inception through delivery and operations."[6]
> —Vivek Kundra

STEP 1 Select Services to Move to the Cloud

One of the most important concepts to understand about planning a cloud migration is that you do not have to move everything to the cloud all at once. In fact, from a migration point of view, there are three main types of IT resources:

- Resources that would benefit from an immediate cloud deployment

- Resources that are good cloud candidates, but not right away

- Resources that should not be moved to the cloud

How do you decide which resources fall under which category? The government's decision framework offers a resource migration roadmap that focuses on two key dimensions: readiness and value.

Assessing Readiness

Readiness refers to whether or not a resource is currently a suitable candidate for cloud migration, from the point of view of both the resource itself and the cloud provider. The decision framework breaks down readiness into seven main categories:

- **Security needs** A higher readiness score is given to cloud providers or environments that can meet or exceed a resource's security requirements, including legal or regulatory compliance, privacy protection, data access safeguards, data integrity procedures, and the management and governance tools to assess and monitor these requirements.

- **Resource needs** A higher readiness score is given to cloud providers or environments that can meet the needs of a resource. These needs vary from service to service, but could include minimum levels for performance and reliability, data portability (say, between the cloud and your local network), service interoperability (say, between a public cloud and your private cloud), scalability, and support.

- **Market characteristics** For a cloud provider market that is suitable for hosting a particular service, a higher readiness score is given to a market that is mature, has lots of competition, enables the service to be easily moved from one provider to another, enables the service to be distributed between multiple providers, and supports recognized technical standards to avoid vendor lock-in.

- **Network readiness** A higher readiness score is given to cloud providers that offer a network infrastructure capable of handling the demand required by a service, as well as the redundancy required to ensure the service remains available.

- **Application and data readiness** A higher readiness score is given to applications and that can be directly migrated to the cloud, particularly those applications that are *well-defined,* in the sense that they are fully documented, have clearly articulated algorithms and business rules, and interoperate simply and clearly with other applications, databases, and so on. A higher readiness score also applies to legacy applications where the cloud provider can offer an equivalent SaaS application.

- **Organization readiness** A higher readiness score is given to departments and lines of business that are prepared to migrate their resources to the cloud. Such preparation includes managers who are not only capable and reliable, but who fully embrace and understand the cloud idea, as well as employees who have the required technical skills.

- **Resource lifecycle** A higher readiness score is given to resources that are nearing the end of their lifecycle. This includes services that are ready to be updated, those that are nearing the end of their contracts, and those that currently run on or depend on old or inefficient technology.

 Note

It is important to note that the lowest readiness score is given to applications that simply cannot be migrated to the cloud. You will find that in many cases it is not technically feasible to move an application to the cloud, so you must include in your cloud strategy some other way to encapsulate these legacy applications.

You need to prioritize these categories based on your company's unique characteristics and goals, as well as the requirements of each resource.

Assessing Value

Value refers the advantages that cloud computing brings to business, and, in particular, how those advantages would help your existing resources. Although you saw in "Chapter 5: The Pros and Cons of Cloud Computing," that cloud computing brings many advantages, the decision framework refers to just the following three categories:

- **Efficiency** A higher value score is given to resources that can most take advantage of the higher efficiencies inherent in cloud computing. This would include services that are expensive to maintain and/or are underutilized (and so have very high per-user costs).

- **Agility** A higher value score is given to resources that are most suited to the greater agility that comes with a cloud environment. Prime candidates would be resources that currently take a long time to provision, deploy, or upgrade, as well as new resources, particularly those deemed urgent for the business.

- **Innovation** A higher value score is given to resources that are most in need of improvement, and so can take advantage of the greater scope for innovation that comes with a cloud implementation. Examples are services that are clearly inferior to similar services on the market, that require a relatively high level of support, that receive above average user complaints or below average user ratings, or that show declining usage trends.

As with the readiness scores, you need to prioritize these categories based on your company's characteristics and goals and the needs of each resource.

Selecting Services

The overall idea is to examine each of your services and IT resources and assign a relative weight for both readiness and value based on the above characteristics and criteria. You can then use these two dimensions to graph the resources, with value on the vertical axis and readiness on the horizontal axis. As you can see in Figure 7.1, resources that fall near the top right of the chart (high readiness, high value) should be the first services that migrate to the cloud. The next wave would be those services that score high on only one dimension, or that score in the middle on both dimensions (*Medium-term movers* in Figure 7.1). Finally, those services that score extremely low on one dimension or somewhat low on both dimensions (*Long-term movers* in Figure 7-1) would be the last to migrate, or might not migrate at all.

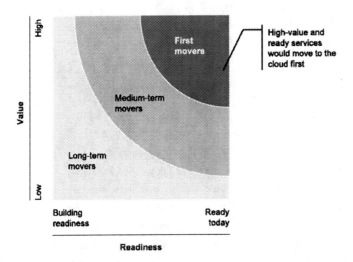

Figure 7-1 Using readiness and value scores to select the order in which resources migrate to the cloud.[7]

STEP **2** Provision Cloud Services

Once you have used readiness and value scores to determine your best cloud candidates, your next step is to provision the necessary cloud services. In the decision framework, this involves four key components: aggregating services across departments, ensuring service integration, researching cloud providers, and shutting down or repurposing legacy resources.

Pooling Commodity Services

Commodity IT refers to services that are required by or are used by a large percentage of the users or departments in a business. For example, email is a commodity IT service because it is used by nearly everyone. Similarly, customer relationship management could be considered commodity IT if it is required by sales and other staff in multiple departments.

Before migrating services to the public cloud, you should identify those commodity IT services in your business. This enables you to aggregate the demand across the entire company, which gives you more leverage, since you can pool the purchasing power across multiple departments, and less overhead, since you only have to manage one provider relationship and one service.

Ensuring the Integration of Cloud Services

Most of the cloud services you provision should not (and probably could not) stand alone. (An exception here might be a one-off development platform for testing a new application.) Applications, databases, and other cloud services are going to have to interoperate with not only those services that remain in-house, but also other services that you have migrated to the cloud. Before embarking on this migration, you need to understand the extent to which each service integrates with other IT resources, as well as the technical hurdles that must be overcome to ensure the same level of integration once the service moves to the cloud.

Researching Cloud Providers

Note

I go into SLAs in more detail in "Chapter 10: Selecting a Public Cloud Provider."

When it comes time to choose a cloud provider, you need to do your research to ensure the provider meets your needs both short-term and long-term. For example, as I described in "Chapter 5: The Pros and Cons of Cloud Computing," it is important to avoid vendor lock-in so that you have the most flexibility when it comes to changing providers or porting your data to another environment. You should also take lots of time to examine each provider's SLA to ensure it meets your minimum requirements for availability, quality of service, and security.

Shutting Down or Repurposing Resources

Once you have made the move to the cloud, even if only in part, you should not leave your existing resources in their previous state. Instead, you need to extract value from those resources. For example, if you have legacy servers and applications, you should shut them down to reduce costs and maintenance time. If you have a data center you no longer need, either sell the real estate or repurpose the building to house higher-value tasks and resources. Employees should be retrained and redeployed to work with the higher-value cloud services.

STEP **3** Manage Cloud Services

The old way of doing IT is to see computing resources as a collection of assets to manage: servers to configure, operating systems to update, development projects to code, and applications to support. The new way—that is to say, the *cloud* way—sees computing resources as a set of *services* to manage. In the decision framework, managing services is crucial, and making the switch from assets requires the following.

Shifting the Focus from Assets to Services

It is likely that everyone in your company—not just IT personnel, but executives, managers, and end users—is used to dealing with IT resources as assets. That makes sense in the IT department, where employees routinely install, configure, and deploy hardware and software products. However, it also applies to users, who are used to treating IT resources as objects with certain characteristics that can be configured and customized.

In a cloud environment, however, you are dealing with services rather than products. This means that the point of the resource is not what it is, but what it can do, what problems it solves, and what advantages it brings to the business. It means that you are no longer interested in internally-focused product metrics such as how many servers you have, but rather in externally-focused service metrics such as the percentage of time a service is available.

Monitoring Services Actively

Cloud computing should not be seen as a *set-it-and-forget-it* environment. To extract the maximum value out of the cloud and to avoid cloud pitfalls, you need to monitor your cloud investment. For example, the SLA is, above all, a contract between your company and the cloud provider that stipulates minimum levels for service metrics such as availability and quality. The only way to make sure the provider is living up to its end of the contract is to monitor these and any other metrics that are spelled out in the SLA. In a pay-per-use environment, it also crucial to monitor the *use* part to ensure that your expenses remain in line with your expectations (and budget). You should also assign IT personnel to monitor emerging security threats related to your services, so that they can take steps to thwart those threats.

Reevaluating Services Periodically

Note

The U.S. Federal Government is not the only public sector organization to draft and make public a cloud computing strategy. The Australian Government also recently released a document called *Cloud Computing Strategic Direction Paper,*[8] which offers an excellent cloud computing backgrounder and a useful strategy overview for migrating to a cloud environment.

Although hopefully you made optimum decisions in terms of which services to send to the cloud and how best to provision those services, it does not follow that those decisions will always be optimal. As circumstances, technologies, and company needs change, you need to reevaluate your choices to ensure that the value goals of enhanced efficiency, agility, and innovation are met. You also need to keep evaluating your remaining non-cloud resources to determine when the time is right to migrate them to the cloud. Finally, you should also periodically reevaluate your existing cloud providers and research new vendors to ensure you are getting the most out of your cloud computing investments.

HP's Journey to the Instant-On Enterprise

In a world of rampant globalization, accelerated change, and near-instant information delivery, today's companies must be agile entities that can quickly and effectively respond to new shifts, opportunities, and trends. Today's companies must be innovation engines that drive growth, creativity, and service quality. Today's companies must by highly optimized and highly efficient to keep operating costs to a minimum, while simultaneously raising productivity. Finally, today's companies must be expert managers of risk, whether it comes from security dangers, competitive threats, or compliance pitfalls.

In short, today's companies need to become *instant-on* enterprises that use technology—particularly cloud services—to achieve all of these goals. This is HP's vision of the corporate future, and they have a roadmap to get there called Journey to the Instant-On Enterprise. The purpose of this strategy is to transform IT so that it can deliver on the following five success factors:

- **Flexibility** IT delivers applications and services that are designed for high availability (so users can access them when they need them) and easy adaptation (so they can respond to new opportunities).

- **Automation** IT delivers services that can be provisioned and de-provisioned rapidly and automatically in response to current demands and changing needs.

- **Security** IT delivers services that minimize risk and maximize reliability.

- **Insight** IT delivers services that provide business decision-makers with the tools and information they need.

- **Speed** IT delivers services that give the business what it needs, when it needs it.

Fundamental Tasks

Before getting to the specifics of the journey to the instant-on enterprise, let's step back a bit and understand in general terms what the overall journey requires. There are five fundamental tasks that your IT department must undergo to transition from its current state to supporting an instant-on business:

- **Modernize** Every effort towards making the instant-on enterprise a reality stems from the core idea of modernizing IT. This means replacing products with services and embracing the latest technologies. It means setting up IT resources to quickly and easily respond to change, so that today's cutting-edge services do not become tomorrow's legacy applications.

- **Transform** IT must rid itself of slow, rigid, and expensive technology silos and replace them with rapid, agile, and efficient services.

- **Secure** In the instant-on enterprise, data, code, proprietary knowledge, and intellectual property must be protected, but in a way that does not discourage innovation. The right people—whether they are employees, partners, clients, or consumers—need the right level of access to the right assets at the right time.

- **Optimize** The instant-on business recognizes that we live in a world that is becoming flooded with data, but also that lying somewhere within that data are the facts, connections, and knowledge that the business needs to make the right decisions. IT must, therefore, provide technologies and services that enable employees to capture, organize, search, analyze, retrieve, and protect the data that powers the business.

- **Deliver** In the instant-on enterprise, IT must create or make available the services required by the business, and deliver those services quickly, efficiently, and cost-effectively.

With all of these fundamental tasks in mind, you are now ready to examine the journey that takes you to the instant-on enterprise. Figure 7-2 provides you with a roadmap for that journey. In each phase, I will give you an overview of what the phase entails, and then I will break down the requirements of each phase into five categories: applications, infrastructure, security, information, and delivery model.

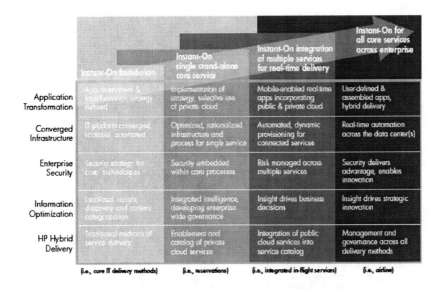

Figure 7-2 The roadmap for the Journey to the Instant-On Enterprise.

PHASE 1 Instant-On Foundation

As its name implies, this phase is used to create a foundation to support the upcoming phases. This foundational work includes the initial steps required to transform the company's core IT resources so that they can deliver services rapidly and on-demand. This phase requires the following:

- **Applications** All applications that deliver or support core business services must be assessed. This assessment includes identifying applications that can be moved to the cloud, prioritizing those applications in terms of readiness and value to the business, understanding how each application needs to be transformed to become cloud-ready, and creating a plan for the migration.

- **Infrastructure** IT infrastructure must begin the transformation to a converged infrastructure. That is, IT must begin virtualizing its resources, particularly servers, networking, and storage so that they can be later offered as a resource pool that can be allocated dynamically.

- **Security** You must set up a security strategy that not only identifies the risks involved in a cloud delivery model, but also identifies ways to thwart those risks, particularly methods that tie directly into the new converged infrastructure.

- **Information** You need an information management strategy that not only brings all core business data under centralized control, but also categorizes and organizes that data. The goal is to enable users to easily and profitably search for information and extract insights from that information.

- **Delivery model** At this stage, IT still delivers its resources in the traditional, in-house model, although there may be limited tests or trial runs of cloud-based services.

PHASE 2 Instant-On Single Stand-Alone Core Service

In this phase on the road to instant-on, you implement at least one stand-alone core business service within a private cloud environment. In other words, it means that you have transformed enough key IT resources that you can get a private cloud up and running and migrate at least one core enterprise service to that cloud. This phase requires the following:

- **Applications** You have the necessary software configured and deployed to implement a private cloud. Also, the application assessment from Phase 1 is complete and is now well on its way to being implemented. Some applications have been transformed, and at least one stand-alone core service has been migrated to the private cloud.

- **Infrastructure** Once a critical mass of virtualization is reached, IT creates a pool of all the virtualized resources, so that they can be allocated dynamically and efficiently and provisioned automatically. In particular, the infrastructure has been set up to provide the capacity, workflow, and management features required by the stand-alone core service that is moving to the cloud.

- **Security** The infrastructure has been augmented with the necessary security features—both hardware and software—required by the stand-alone core cloud service.

- **Information** The information management strategy from Phase 1 has been implemented company-wide. In particular, information-related tools, interfaces, and support have been put in place for the stand-alone core cloud service.

- **Delivery model** The traditional, in-house IT model has been expanded to include a private cloud environment. This cloud includes a service catalog and has been optimized and configured to deliver the stand-alone core service.

PHASE 3 Instant-On Integration of Multiple Services for Real-Time Delivery

With this phase of the instant-on journey, your company implements multiple cloud services. These include multiple in-house applications migrated to the private cloud, as well as multiple services made available through one or more third-party public cloud providers. This hybrid cloud enables the company to dynamically combine multiple services into higher-level applications, and to interoperate between cloud environments as needed. This phase requires the following:

- **Applications** Your company's core applications have been transformed as needed and migrated to the cloud, making them true on-demand services. Services from third-party public cloud providers have also been included, and those services are fully integrated into the service catalog.

- **Infrastructure** The converged infrastructure is fully functional, allowing users to automatically and dynamically provision and de-provision resources as demand and needs require.

- **Security** The security framework has been expanded to include both in-house private services and third-party public services. The security strategy has been enhanced to include risks inherent in public cloud environments and to offer guidance on the security clauses that must be added to public cloud provider SLAs.

- **Information** The information management strategy has been extended to include the capture and categorization of data from the public cloud implementation. Together with the data from the in-house private cloud, the company now has the capability to leverage both types of data to offer insight and intelligence to company decision-makers.

- **Delivery model** The in-house private cloud service catalog is now integrated with one or more public cloud environments. Users can quickly and easily provision services from both environments.

PHASE 4 Instant-On for All Core Services Across the Enterprise

In this final phase of the instant-on journey, your company completes the migration of all core resources that can be moved to the cloud, and replaces any applications that are not cloud candidates with new in-house or public cloud services. Any service that the company offers internally to its employees or externally to its customers and clients can now be rapidly and elastically provisioned. The fundamental interoperability of these services enables the company to build new services on the fly to meet changing demands or circumstances. This phase requires the following:

- **Applications** Service interoperability allows users to innovate by creating new applications based on existing services through the use of mashups and similar techniques.

- **Infrastructure** The converged infrastructure now supports the automatic provisioning of services in real-time across the entire IT resource spectrum, including both in-house private cloud services and third-party public cloud services.

- **Security** For each service, the security layer has been integrated so seamlessly that the security mechanisms and features no longer slow down or stifle business processes. Instead, this higher-level, organic security gives the company a competitive advantage and does not get in the way of innovation.

- **Information** The information management capabilities are fully service-centered, allowing the company to derive profound insights from service delivery, which in turn enables intelligent goal setting, strategy planning, and innovation.

- **Delivery model** The company implements a full hybrid cloud environment, with IT acting as a strategic service broker to source resources as needed by the company, its employees, and its customers.

REFERENCES

1   **Nicholas Carr,** *IT Doesn't Matter*, Rough Type, http://www.roughtype.com/archives/2007/01/it_doesnt_matte.php (January 3, 2007).

2   **Geoffrey A. Moore,** *Dealing with Darwin* (New York: Penguin, 2008), xvi.

3   **Daryl Plummer,** Gartner Says Now More Than Ever Is the Time to Re-Imagine the Role of IT, http://www.gartner.com/it/page.jsp?id=1824816 (October 17, 2011).

4   **David Linthicum,** *The data-integration buzzkill for cloud computing*, InfoWorld, http://www.infoworld.com/d/cloud-computing/data-integration-buzzkill-cloud-computing-587 (March 25, 2010).

5   **Vivek Kundra,** *Federal Cloud Computing Strategy*, http://www.cio.gov/documents/federal-cloud-computing-strategy.pdf (February 8, 2011).

6   **Kundra,** 11.

7   **Kundra,** 12.

8   See http://www.finance.gov.au/e-government/strategy-and-governance/docs/final_cloud_computing_strategy_version_1.pdf.

8 Implementing a Private Cloud

When most people talk about cloud computing these days, they are almost always talking about public cloud. That is not surprising since public cloud offers many significant benefits, including on-demand servers and storage without massive capital costs, a safe and robust platform for testing applications away from the local network, and third-party applications that can be deployed company-wide in minutes.

However, public cloud also comes with its share of drawbacks, most notably questions about its reliability and security. Many IT managers also look askance at public cloud because of its overall lack of transparency. You put your servers, platforms, and applications *out there* in the hands of a third party, and suddenly large chunks of your infrastructure are no longer under your control. Yes, the public cloud excels at rapid, elastic deployment, but it also increases complexity because it is so much more difficult to manage. Public cloud computing is, in short, a *more-chaos-faster* environment.

Perhaps that is why many businesses are realizing that they can derive the benefits of cloud computing and avoid the negatives of public cloud by implementing their own private clouds. That is, by essentially implementing a public cloud within its local network, a company gets rapid, elastic, scalable, on-demand services, *and* it gains control over aspects such as security, availability, governance, and management.

So, what am I talking about when I talk about private cloud? Recall from Chapter 1 that the *NIST Definition of Cloud Computing* defines a private cloud as one where "the cloud infrastructure is operated solely for an organization. It may be managed by the organization or a third party and may exist on premise or off premise." As you then saw in Chapter 4, this led to not one but *four* different types of private cloud: on-site private cloud, hosted private cloud, on-site hosted private cloud, and virtual private cloud. However, it is still accurate to define private cloud as a cloud environment where the infrastructure is dedicated to a single organization, no matter who owns or manages that infrastructure.

An on- or off-site hosted private cloud or a virtual private cloud is a relatively easy way to get your company's feet wet in cloud computing. However, if you want maximum control over the cloud and what you put in it, then an on-site private cloud is the way to go. This chapter offers you an overview of what is required to implement an on-site private cloud.

Private Clouds: The Prerequisites

Most data centers that have been around for a while are essentially custom-designed, with a hodgepodge of components from multiple vendors, different sets of tools running on different servers, disparate collections of processes and rules, isolated technology silos, and complex integration procedures for getting everything to somehow work together.

These jerry-rigged data centers are not only inefficient, but are difficult to manage and maintain, expensive to operate, and prone to errors. Why? For several reasons:

- Isolated applications and their infrastructures cannot be easily scaled, so business agility suffers.

- It is difficult to find all the weak points in a diverse collection of software and hardware, so the data center becomes more vulnerable to attack.

- Hosting a wide variety of applications and infrastructure makes it difficult and costly to maintain and manage those resources and to train personnel to operate and support those resources.

- Applications built on custom, proprietary infrastructure make it very difficult to share data with other parts of the business, leading to a loss of flexibility and the need for slow, expensive integrations.

You can overcome these problems and make your data center cloud-ready by implementing four key redesigns: standardization, virtualization, automation, and self-provisioning.

Standardization

The core problem of the cobbled-together data center is the dizzying array of technologies that make up such an operation. You cannot create a private cloud out of an inefficient data center, and the number one cause of computing inefficiency is a lack of standards. So the first step towards solving that problem is *standardization*, which means rationalizing the data center to use consistent technologies, processes, rules, and management structures across the enterprise.

The first move is usually the *consolidation* of IT resources, which involves bringing isolated resources into a common framework. This means gathering all technology silos and disparate networks into a single enterprise-wide network, and combining all isolated instances of storage—called *storage islands*—into a single *storage area network* (SAN), as shown in Figure 8-1.

"In 2010 an IBM survey of more than 1,500 CEOs worldwide revealed a troubling gap: Close to 80% of them believed their environment would grow much more complex in the coming years, but fewer than half thought their companies were well equipped to deal with this shift. ...Their technology environments actually impede their ability to sense change and respond quickly."[1]
—Andrew McAfee

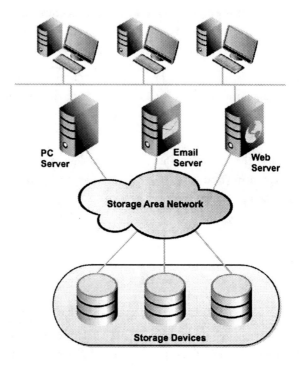

Figure 8-1 A storage area network

From there, standardization means working with IT, business, and vendors to come up with uniform IT resources, including the following:

- IT hardware resources, including networks, server architectures, and storage technologies

- IT software resources, including operating systems and development environments

- Data center infrastructure, including power, cooling, server racks, and cabling

- IT processes, including assessment, procurement, configuration, and deployment

- Business rules

- Management and monitoring tools

By implementing a standardized approach to IT, you end up with infrastructure that is scalable, portable, and interchangeable, and IT personnel are better able to learn systems, prevent errors, and anticipate problems.

Virtualization

As you learned in Chapter 1, *virtualization* is the process of creating a simulation of a resource using software. As you see later in this chapter, you can virtualize a wide variety of IT resources, including servers, networking, storage, and applications. This leads to a more efficient data center because a single physical resource can be used for multiple applications.

For example, consider the virtual machine (VM), which is a software simulation of a fully operational computer that can have its own operating system, storage, and applications. A single physical server can host perhaps ten or twelve VMs. This increases your overall infrastructure efficiency because a standalone server might be utilized five to 10% of the time, whereas a machine running multiple VMs might reach 40% utilization or better, a four- to eightfold improvement.

Virtualization also augments your standardization efforts, because now all your VMs and other virtualized resources run in a standard environment, and the process for provisioning virtual resources is the same for all.

Finally, virtualization also improves IT efficiency by greatly reducing the time it takes to provision resources. With virtualization, applications are uncoupled from hardware, which means that IT can create *virtual machine images* that are essentially large files that contain all the information required by the VM, including its operating system, configuration files, and hard disk space.

> "Within many data centers around the world, the most visible consequence of these priorities has been the rapid expansion in the use of server virtualization technology. By the end of the year, more than half of all applications deployed will be running as virtual machines on a virtualized server."[2]
> —Richard L. Villars

⚡ Note

Although I have listed virtualization here as a prerequisite for private cloud, recall from Chapter 1 that a cloud does not necessarily have to provision virtual resources. However, in the real world, virtual resources *are* required in order to realize the rapid elasticity that is one of the main characteristics of cloud computing.

Automation

In the old, inefficient way of doing IT, working with non-standard, physical resources meant (in most cases, literally) getting hands-on with those resources to set up, configure, deploy, and maintain them. As you have seen, this is costly, time-consuming, and inefficient.

So from an IT perspective, one of the main benefits to having standardized, virtualized resources is that such resources are now programmable, meaning that they can be controlled and configured via software instead of via human intervention. This is called *automation,* and it is the next step towards transforming the data center into an efficient, cloud-capable environment.

For example, with automation, IT can set up virtual machine images (which, remember, are just files) and a front-end program for perusing the available images, which can then be provisioned by non-IT users with a minimum of fuss.

Automation also enables IT to deploy monitoring programs that can probe, test, and measure virtual resources to look for things like slowing response times, application faults, and whether new resources are needed. In this last case, automation also enables either monitoring programs or virtual applications themselves to provision new resources as needed during periods of high demand, and to de-provision those resources when demand ebbs.

Self-Provisioning

Once IT resources are standardized, virtualized, and automated, then there is no longer any need for IT personnel to waste their valuable time working directly with end users to assess, configure, and deploy resources. Instead, those end users can now *self-provision* their own resources, which means they can select those IT resources they need, when they need them. This not only frees up IT to spend more time concentrating on innovating for the business, but it also improves overall business productivity because the business side is able to deploy new applications and environments in a fraction of the time.

> "The innovation that is going to happen down there [in IT]... is really about automation and management. It will be a constant theme for our releases going forward... taking resources and really stitching those into a giant computer that can be increasingly automatically managed."[3]
> —Paul Maritz

The Components of a Private Cloud

A data center reorganized and transformed around the principles of standardization, virtualization, automation, and self-provisioning is well on its way to becoming a private cloud. However, while these *big picture* technologies are certainly necessary for any private cloud implementation, they do not represent the whole story. In this section, I delve into virtualization a little more deeply, and I also introduce you to a few more components of a typical private cloud.

Virtualization

Even companies that have no intention of implementing a private cloud are virtualizing their IT resources. They are heading down the virtualization path not just because it improves server utilization rates, enhances standardization, and speeds provisioning, as I described earlier in this chapter. Virtualizing resources also brings the following benefits to the business:

- With fewer physical hardware resources required, you can reduce the size of the data center, which means either relocating to a smaller (and cheaper) building, or repurposing some of the current data center floor space to higher-value projects.

- Lower overall energy costs not only because of fewer physical devices consuming energy, but also because of fewer data center infrastructure resources (such as cooling devices).

- If you can repurpose most or all of your existing hardware to host virtual resources, then you reduce operational costs, and future capital costs are reduced as well, since you will need to purchase fewer replacement devices.

Again, virtualization is not a strict necessity for implementing a private cloud, but I would not recommend going the cloud route without it, because it offers tremendous advantages in elasticity, speed, and on-demand self-provisioning. To ensure you have got a good handle on virtualization, the next few sections take a closer look at the five main types: server, storage, network, desktop, and application.

Server Virtualization

The server is by far the most common type of virtualized hardware. In this case, a single physical server uses software—such as vSphere (from VMware), Hyper-V (Microsoft), and Xen (Citrix)—to create virtual machines. Each of these VMs has its own operating system (see Figure 8-2), and the OS acts just as though it was running on a physical system complete with a virtualized hard drive and network interface, and sometimes also virtualized devices such as an optical drive or printer. Depending on the virtualization software used and the physical resources of the host computer (number of CPUs, amount of installed memory, total hard disk storage, and so on), a single physical server can run as many as ten or twelve virtual machines.

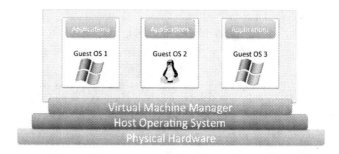

Figure 8-2 With a virtual machine manager installed, a single physical server can host several different virtual machines, each with its own operating system.

Although there are virtualization machine managers that enable some interaction between the host computer and a VM (for example, shared folders or a shared clipboard that enables cut, copy, and paste operations between the two systems), private cloud VMs are completely isolated from each other and from the physical server. This isolation offers several key advantages:

- A single physical server can host multiple operating system platforms, including various flavors of Windows and Linux.

- Since each VM is unaware of the others, security is enhanced because there are no common elements (such as a clipboard memory area) that can be used to launch exploits against another VM.

- If one VM fails, the other VMs are not affected.

Each VM is actually just a file—called a virtual machine image or a disk image—that can be easily moved into place, so creating a new VM or recovering a failed VM is as easy as copying its image file to a new machine. And since the entire state of a VM can be saved to an image file, you can easily and quickly make system backups, a crucial aspect of disaster recovery.

> "The driving force for virtualization is consolidation, but disaster recovery is the second phase."[4]
> —Tom Bittman

Storage Virtualization

Storage virtualization takes multiple physical storage devices—hard drives, RAID arrays, SANs, and so on—and adds an abstraction layer that brings all these disparate devices into a single resource pool from which virtual disks can then be provisioned. Users and applications no longer need to care where data is stored or what type of device is being used, since virtualized storage appears as a single, homogeneous device. Storage virtualization decouples physical storage devices from their traditional connection to a physical system (such as a server) and instead enables a collection of physical storage mechanisms to be shared across multiple systems.

Storage virtualization offers the following advantages:

- **Rapid storage provisioning** Virtual disks can be created, configured, and assigned to a host machine in minutes.

- **Higher device utilization rates** When a storage device is attached to a single computer, its utilization rate is often quite low, as the system often spends time without needing to read from or write to the device. In a virtualized storage environment, however, physical storage devices are shared across multiple servers and applications, so they spend less time in an idle state.

- **Easy migration of data** Since virtual storage is not allocated to a physical system, it can be easily moved from one system to another without disrupting its data or applications.

- **Improved uptime** In a virtual storage environment, servers and applications are not tied to physical storage, so when a particular storage device needs maintenance, repair, or replacement, technicians can do so without affecting servers, applications, or users.

- **Increased performance** Rather than using a single storage device that can be readily overburdened by a sudden surge in demand, virtualized storage distributes each task over multiple storage devices, so no single device is overwhelmed and overall performance improves.

- **Thin provisioning** This means that a server or other resource is allocated only the amount of storage space it needs at the time of creation, not all the storage space it requests. For example, a Windows VM might request 100GB of storage, but at the time of creation it requires only 30GB. Thin provisioning ensures that the VM gets 30GB of storage at first (although to the VM it appears as though it has 100GB), and then extra storage is added to the VM as needed.

- **Central storage management** The storage virtualization software provides a single management interface that offers services for monitoring and allocating storage, and for performing standard storage management tasks such as mirroring data and replicating data.

> "Storage virtualization has played a major role in advancing how we use our storage infrastructure and reap the benefits from our investments."[5]
> —Bill Hill

Network Virtualization

Network virtualization takes multiple physical networking resources—switches, network adapters, firewalls, load balancers, network storage, cables, and so on—and adds an abstraction layer that brings all these elements into a single resource pool from which virtual switches and virtual network ports—that is, virtual networks—can then be provisioned.

The most common type of virtual network is the *virtual LAN*, or VLAN, which is a collection of nodes that can communicate with each other via network protocols no matter where they happen to be located. In other words, a VLAN appears to users and applications as a local area network, but the hosts can be physically separated and do not even have to be connected to the same switch.

Here are the main advantages of network virtualization:

- **Improved performance** If two VMs on the same physical server need to exchange data over the network, virtualization ensures that the traffic between them is exchanged using the server's memory, rather than the physical network itself.

- **Efficient resource usage** When you need separate networks for particular applications, network virtualization enables you to create those networks without having to invest in extra hardware.

- **Enhanced security** When you have applications that must remain segregated—for example, human resources and accounts payable—network virtualization enables you to isolate these data streams while still using the same physical network infrastructure.

Desktop Virtualization

Desktop virtualization refers to a virtual machine running a desktop operating system and installed in a cloud environment so that the user can access the desktop from multiple locations using multiple types of thick or thin client devices. In other words, the user's desktop is no longer a static object that resides in a physical PC. Instead, the desktop is a virtual machine image file residing in the private cloud. This means that any client device that can be used to access the private cloud—a desktop PC, notebook PC, tablet, even a smartphone—can be used to access the desktop.

In a world where the rampant consumerization of IT means that end users are increasingly choosing which devices they prefer to use to access IT resources, moving these users to virtual desktops gives IT at least some control over securing those desktops and preventing them from causing havoc should they fall into unauthorized hands.

"Combined with server and storage virtualization, network virtualization facilitates a fluid and responsive data center, where you can move resources from one network to another without having to reconfigure hardware."[6]
—Logan G. Harbaugh

"If virtual desktops are more secure than physical ones, then a major cost justification for the move materializes. A virtual user interface that can move from device to device resolves some of the conflicts preventing the transition to bring-your-own-computer to work."[7]
—Charles Babcock

Application Virtualization

Application virtualization is the encapsulation of an application so that it thinks it is directly interfacing with a particular operating system, no matter which operating system is in reality being used to host the encapsulated instance. A virtualized application is really just an image file that can be loaded onto a VM and used instantly. The virtual application is already configured, so it does not require a lengthy installation procedure. A virtualization layer between the application and the VM's operating system controls the application's access to the OS. For example, the virtualization layer intercepts requests to modify operating system files (such as the Windows Registry). The layer makes the application think (and act as though) the request was successful, but no actual changes are made to the OS. This ensures that each virtual application does not interfere with or cause problems for other virtual applications running on the same VM. Also, since the requested changes are stored in a separate location (such as a file), it means the virtualized application can be easily migrated to a new VM with its system modifications intact.

Hypervisor

A *hypervisor* is a virtualization software layer that distributes the physical server's resources among multiple virtual machines. This program—it is also known as a *virtual machine manager*—also ensures that multiple VMs running on a single physical server remain isolated, thus guaranteeing that no two VMs can interfere with each other. You might think that adding an extra layer between the physical hardware and the operating system would cause a drastic (or, at least, noticeable) drop in performance compared to systems that have direct access to the hardware. Fortunately, that is not the case because modern hardware (particularly the CPUs) are designed with virtualization in mind and so can run multiple VMs with very little overhead.

Converged Infrastructure

In your journey to a private cloud, you begin by virtualizing a few IT resources, particularly servers. From there, you slowly virtualize more resources, not just servers but also networking, storage, and so on. Once a critical mass of virtualization is reached, you then implement *infrastructure convergence*, which creates a pool of all your virtualized resources so that they can be allocated dynamically and efficiently (see Figure 8-3).

"Faced with a future in which they will need to deploy and effectively use hundreds, thousands, and even tens of thousands of server (and/or desktop) application instances in a virtual environment, companies should consider deploying optimally (e.g., densest, greenest, simplest) configured converged infrastructure systems (server, storage, network) that are managed as unified IT assets."[8]

—Richard L. Villars

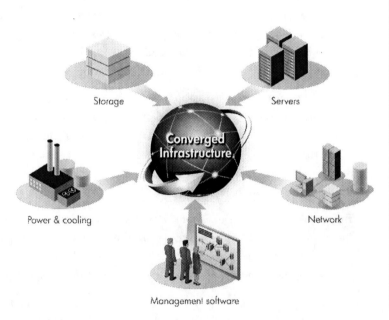

Figure 8-3 A converged infrastructure creates a pool of virtualized resources.

Private Cloud Software

Once you have your standardized, virtualized resources gathered together in a converged infrastructure, how do you get from there to a private cloud? What is missing is a software layer that enables you to deploy, configure, and manage your private cloud, and to allow end users to access the cloud.

This is one area of the private cloud that is actually more difficult than the old system of provisioning only physical infrastructure. In that system, resource allocation, costs, and security were (at least theoretically) straightforward because you know who was going to use the hardware and why they were using it. This made it relatively easy to determine the required specifications, configure and secure the hardware, and then determine the final cost for everything.

In a private cloud, however, all hardware resources are virtualized and shared by everyone. How much do they cost (that is, how much do you charge back to the department requesting them)? How do you secure them? How do you allow business users to self-provision those resources? In a self-provisioning environment, how do you automate the selection of resource specifications?

The answer to all these questions is that you need a private cloud *operating system* that ties everything together. This can be a single platform that offers a full range of private cloud tools, or a suite of applications designed to work together. Here are some examples:

- **OpenStack**[10] This is an open source cloud platform project founded by IaaS provider Rackspace and NASA and now supported by a large community of technology companies, including HP, Intel, Cisco, AT&T, and Dell.

- **Eucalyptus**[11] This is one of the most popular private cloud software platforms and is currently installed in more than 25,000 cloud environments. Eucalyptus is compatible with Amazon Web Services, enabling your private cloud to burst out to Amazon when it needs extra resources, so you can easily transform your private cloud into a hybrid cloud.

> "Your infrastructure has been fully virtualized when you have server virtualization, storage virtualization and network virtualization. The crossover point from a virtual infrastructure to private cloud comes when you have the management tools that treat all three types of resources—servers, storage and networks—as a single pool that can be allocated on demand."[9]
> —Bill Claybrook

- **Cloud.com**[12] Now owned by Citrix, this is an open source cloud platform that supports multiple hypervisors, including VMware vSphere and Xen.

- **VMware**[13] This company takes the suite approach, and its private cloud offerings include vSphere (a virtual machine hypervisor), vCenter Server (for managing vSphere environments), vCloud Director (for provisioning IaaS, migrating resources, and overall management), vShield (for security), and vCenter Chargeback (for charging back costs to business units).

- **Microsoft**[14] This company offers private cloud tools based on its Hyper-V, Windows Server, and System Center technologies.

- **HP**[15] This company offers HP CloudSystem, which includes HP CloudSystem Matrix for private cloud IaaS services and HP CloudSystem Enterprise for hybrid XaaS services.

Is a Private Cloud Really a Cloud?

The cloud computing version of the "How many angels can fit on the head of a pin?" argument is the "Is a private cloud really a cloud?" debate. Those who would answer in the negative assert that private clouds lack many of the features and advantages of public clouds, including the lack of up-front capital expenses, metered pay-per-use costs, near-limitless scalability, and the elasticity to reduce resources when demand is low.

Are these arguments enough to make the private cloud a non-cloud? I do not think so, particularly when you remember that a private cloud still provides many other features and advantages of a cloud environment, including standardized, virtualized, and automated resources, on-demand self-provisioning, resource pooling, services instead of assets, faster time-to-value, reduced energy costs, as well as the bonus advantages of greater reliability, easier compliance, and enhanced security.

"These services share computing capabilities within a single company. If IT organizations go beyond the virtualization of infrastructure and use flexible self-service provisioning tools, the relationship between IT and business can be described as a private cloud."[16]
—Stefan Reid

Private Clouds: The Issues

A private cloud offers many advantages to a business, and the private cloud market is getting mature enough that the prospect of converting some or all of your data center to a private cloud environment is not the scary proposition that it was just a couple of years ago. However, none of this means that the decision to implement a private cloud is a no-brainer. You need to compare the advantages of a private cloud with the all-too-real issues that surround such an implementation. To that end, I use the rest of this chapter to take you through a few of those issues.

Corporate Culture

One of the key aspects of implementing a private cloud is that many of the traditional burdens once shouldered by IT are now borne by the business side. Determining resource needs, provisioning servers and other virtual resources to meet those needs, and then managing those virtual resources are all tasks that fall to business units in a private cloud environment.

This is usually listed on the *advantage* side of the ledger because self-service means that business no longer has to run the IT gauntlet to get things done. Business units get what they need when they need it, resulting in faster time-to-value, while IT gets to focus on innovation.

However, there is a rather bold assumption that underlies all this: that business units have the interest, time, and expertise—in short, the corporate culture—to take on these IT functions. You have probably seen *old school* managers, business units, or even entire companies that you just know would have a hard time adjusting to a self-service world.

> "Just because one of your subordinates is telling you that an internal cloud is the right way to go, as a senior executive your job is to assess the likelihood of the success of your initiatives and make decisions based on that assessment. If you're not confident your organization can pull a complex infrastructure project like an internal cloud off, don't go forward just to make your staff feel good."[17]
> —Bernard Golden

If this applies to *your* company, then implementing a private cloud is almost certainly not going to work. However, if you are just talking about a department or two, you might be able to work through the problem with extensive end-user training, educating managers on the long-term benefits of using a cloud, or hiring someone (perhaps from Generation D!) to deploy and manage cloud services for that department.

Scaling and Elasticity

Earlier, I talked about the arguments in favor of the idea that a private cloud is not a cloud at all. I could also have mentioned that the arguments mostly fall apart when you recall the NIST definition of cloud computing:

> Cloud computing is a model for enabling convenient, on-demand network access to a shared pool of configurable computing resources (e.g., networks, servers, storage, applications, and services) that can be rapidly provisioned and released with minimal management effort or service provider interaction.[19]

With one exception, there is nothing here that says a private cloud is not a cloud. The exception is the "resources...that can be rapidly provisioned and released" portion of the definition:

- In a private cloud, you *can* rapidly provision resources, but only to the capacity of the data center. If you have ten servers each capable of hosting a dozen VMs, then you can provision up to 120 virtual servers. If demand goes beyond that, in a pure private cloud you have to add physical servers to meet that demand.

- In a private cloud, you *can* rapidly de-provision resources. However, even if you reduce your virtual resources to zero, you still have physical resources in your data center that you must maintain and pay for.

> "Deploying a full-featured private cloud in an environment where business units do not have the scale, interest, or ability to take advantage of its self-service capabilities would be a massive waste of time and money. Not everyone has business units with the IT expertise necessary to deploy and manage their servers, even with a portal."[18]
> —Matt Prigge

So, yes, a private cloud is not as scalable and elastic and a public cloud. This is why most pundits and cloud gurus today recommend implementing a hybrid cloud that uses in-house capacity to meet normal demand, and then bursts out to a public IaaS provider to handle demand spikes. I talk about hybrid clouds in more detail in Chapter 9.

Costs

Another perennial cloud computing debate is whether private cloud or public cloud is cheaper. It is not an easy argument to make either way. For example, a recent article on Wikibon argued that because of economies of scale and other factors, private cloud is cheaper than public cloud for enterprises that have more than a billion dollars in revenue or budget.[20] The same article also showed that for small- and medium-sized businesses, private cloud is cheaper than public cloud for important applications. Why? Because such applications tend to run constantly, so the pay-per-use charges of the public cloud soon add up.

On the other hand, you also need to examine the fixed costs associated with a private cloud (as opposed to the variable costs associated with a public cloud). As I mentioned in the previous section, a major issue with private clouds is that you pay for them even when you are not using them, so those fixed costs can really start to burn a hole in your budget.

With some new private clouds, you can get away with repurposing legacy equipment to keep up-front costs down, but that is only a temporary solution. You will eventually have to replace that old equipment, so recurring capital costs will always be a concern with a private cloud. This is particularly true if you (or your IT manager) have expensive taste in equipment because of concerns of reliability and robustness. Not every shop requires Rolls Royce-quality servers and networking hardware.

"If you had an application running constantly, where the size is the same, the load is the same, you're pretty much winding up paying more to have that constant load running on the public cloud than in a dedicated environment."[21]
—Paul Carmody

"Not everything has to be engineered to five nines of availability....Instead, cloud infrastructure should be tiered—one management portal, one API, multiple levels of service at different price points. 'Everything we do is enterprise-class' unfortunately implies 'everything we do is expensive.'"[22]

REFERENCES

1 **Andrew McAfee**, *What Every CEO Needs to Know About the Cloud*, Harvard Business Review, http://hbr.org/2011/11/what-every-ceo-needs-to-know-about-the-cloud/ar/1 (November, 2011)

2 **Richard L. Villars**, *Measuring the Business Value of Converged Infrastructure in the Data Center*, IDC, http://h17007.www1.hp.com/docs/ci/Measuring_the_Business_Value_of_CI_in_the_Data_Center.pdf (October, 2011).

3 **Paul Maritz,** quoted in Jennifer Scott, *IT as a Service: the virtualisation goal*, http://www.itpro.co.uk/627604/it-as-a-service-the-virtualisation-goal (October 12, 2010).

4 **Tom Bittman**, quoted in *Server Virtualization and Disaster Recovery*, Overland Storage, http://ipexpo.co.uk/content/download/3176/39793/file/BCA_ServerVirtualizationWP.pdf

5 **Bill Hill**, *Storage Virtualization: An Overview*, Tintri, http://blog.tintri.com/2012/01/storage-virtualization-an-overview/ (January 27, 2012).

6 **Logan G. Harbaugh**, *Tech that should be on your radar for 2012*, InfoWorld, http://akamai.infoworld.com/d/computer-hardware/tech-should-be-your-radar-2012-182698?page=0,1 (December 29, 2011).

7 **Charles Babcock**, *6 Ways Cloud Computing Will Evolve In 2012*, Informationweek, http://www.informationweek.com/news/cloud-computing/infrastructure/232301052?pgno=2 (December 27, 2011).

8 **Richard L. Villars, et al.**, *Measuring the Business Value of Converged Infrastructure in the Data Center*, IDC, http://resources.idgenterprise.com/original/AST-0056751_Measuring_the_Business_Value_of_CI_in_the_Data_Center.pdf (October, 2011).

9 **Bill Claybrook**, *Building a private cloud: Get ready for a bumpy ride*, http://www.computerworld.com/s/article/9180941/Building_a_private_cloud_Get_ready_for_a_bumpy_ride?&pageNumber=4 (August 24, 2010).

10 See http://openstack.org/.

11 See http://www.eucalyptus.com/.

12 See http://www.cloud.com/.

13 See http://www.vmware.com/cloud-computing/private-cloud/datacenter-challenges.html.

14 See http://www.microsoft.com/en-us/server-cloud/private-cloud/default.aspx.

15 See http://www8.hp.com/us/en/business-solutions/solution.html?compURI=1079455.

16 **Stefan Reid, et al.**, *The Evolution of Cloud Computing Markets*, Forrester Research, http://fm.sap.com/data/UPLOAD/files/Forrester%20-%20 The%20Evolution%20Of%20Cloud%20Computing%20Markets.pdf (July 6, 2010).

17 **Bernard Golden**, *The great cloud computing pricing debate*, InfoWorld, http://www.infoworld.com/d/cloud-computing/the-great-cloud-computing-pricing-debate-180201?page=0,3 (December 27, 2011).

18 **Matt Prigge**, *How I learned to stop worrying and love the private cloud*, http://www.infoworld.com/d/data-explosion/how-i-learned-stop-worrying-and-love-the-private-cloud-167869?page=0,3&1325018873= (July 25, 2011).

19 **Peter Nell and Tim Grance**, *The NIST Definition of Cloud Computing*, National Institute of Standards and Technology, Information Technology Laboratory, http://www.nist.gov/itl/cloud/upload/cloud-def-v15.pdf (October 7, 2009).

20 **David Floyer**, *Private Cloud is more Cost Effective than Public Cloud for Organizations over $1B*, http://wikibon.org/wiki/v/Private_Cloud_is_more_Cost_Effective_than_Public_Cloud_for_Organizations_over_$1B (December 13, 2010).

21 **Paul Carmody**, quoted in Robert L. Scheier, *Need an agile infrastructure? Do your homework*, http://www.computerworld.com/s/article/359309/The_Agile_Infrastructure?taxonomyId=154&pageNumber=2 (January 16, 2012).

22 **Lydia Leong**, *Common service provider myths about cloud infrastructure*, http://cloudpundit.com/2011/11/09/common-service-provider-myths-about-cloud-infrastructure/ (November 9, 2011).

9 Enhancing Agility with a Hybrid Cloud

One of the main themes of this book has been that, although today's businesses must always keep an eye fixed firmly on the bottom line, in our highly competitive, constantly changing, and fast-paced world, agility is at least as important. And the way to make your company more agile is to adopt cloud computing technologies, which feature the rapid elasticity, scalability, and on-demand provisioning that are the perquisites of the agile enterprise. As you saw in the previous chapter, you can get all of this and more by implementing a private cloud.

Another aspect of agility is flexibility, and you achieve that in your company by transforming your IT department from an asset provider to a service broker. By *broker* I mean that IT uses its expertise to create a catalog of services that meet minimum standards for quality, reliability, and security. Most importantly, IT sources these services not only through its own offerings created in-house, but also through IaaS, PaaS, and SaaS third-party public cloud providers, as well as one or more community clouds.

In other words, you can only achieve maximum business agility through cloud computing by implementing a hybrid cloud that offers services from private and public (and also community) cloud services (see Figure 9-1). This chapter gives you an overview of how a hybrid cloud enhances business agility.

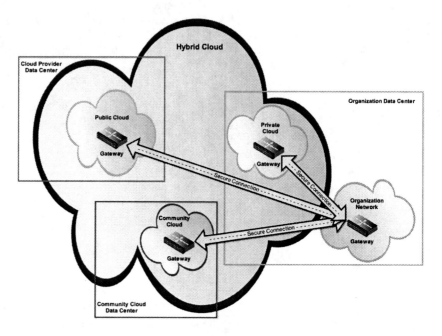

Figure 9-1 A hybrid cloud implementation combines a private cloud with either a public cloud or a community cloud (or both).

Do You Need a Public Cloud Component?

After reading the previous chapter, you might be inclined to think you can get away with just using a private cloud in your business. Certainly a private cloud is an excellent way to get started with cloud computing while minimizing risk and maximizing performance. And if your company is burdened with stringent rules and regulations regarding security, privacy, and geography for all of its data, then you have no choice but to go with a pure private cloud deployment.

If your compliance needs are not so strict, then you are free to pursue other cloud types, including public and community clouds. Why go to the trouble? Consider the silos I talked about in "Chapter 1: Introducing Cloud Computing." These technological islands-unto-themselves are the bane of IT because they are rigid, expensive, inefficient, and difficult to maintain and manage. Even if getting rid of computing silos is the only thing you do to modernize your company's IT operations, you will still see an enormous benefit.

However, if you dismantle physical computing silos in favor of a strict private cloud-only IT deployment, then in a sense you are just exchanging one silo for another. Certainly a private cloud environment with its standardized, virtualized, automated, and self-provisioned resources is orders of magnitude more efficient than an old-school, silo-infested data center, but it is not *maximally* efficient. I consider an IT department to be maximally efficient if, for every business problem, IT offers not just one, but several solutions, each with its own characteristics, costs, and configuration. This enables the business side to examine the available services and decide which one best serves its needs.

You no doubt have a talented IT crew that is more than capable of creating some variety in its service catalog, but no single IT department can meet the vast array of offerings that are out there in public clouds. The maximally efficient IT department is one that leverages *all* available assets, whether they are local services coded by your IT shop, or remote services offered by third-party cloud providers.

Beyond that, however, you can also make the case in favor of adding a public cloud component to your cloud environment by noting that there are use cases where adding public cloud services takes IT to a level that it is simply not possible to attain in a purely private implementation. The next three sections take you through three such use cases: demand spikes, disaster recovery, and business intelligence.

> "Over time, it became clear that hybrid cloud computing approaches have valid roles within enterprises as IT tries to mix and match public clouds and local IT assets to get the best bang for the buck."[1]
> —David Linthicum

Demand Spikes

No doubt there are data centers that experience a steady state of demand 24 hours a day, 365 days a year. However, such sleepy IT departments are increasingly rare these days because changeableness, far from the occasional state it once was, is now the default setting for business. As is quickness, because now, information moves at the speed of light, so you never know when a huge wave of data is going to descend upon your IT infrastructure.

Even if your business is predictably cyclical, that is no guarantee against the unexpected. That is because it is not only data that moves at the speed of light, but also (and these days, perhaps more importantly) people's *attention*. A seemingly innocuous mention on a social networking site or a popular blog can send a tsunami of users to a particular site. (In the early 2000s, when the *News for Nerds* website Slashdot.org was at the height of its popularity, a site mention could produce an overwhelming increase in that site's traffic, a phenomenon dubbed the *Slashdot effect*.[2])

Even if such demand spikes are relatively rare, you ignore them at your peril. At best, a rapid increase in demand could slow your data center to a crawl, but at its worst a sharp spike can lead to error messages, lost data, even browser crashes. Users are notoriously unforgiving for such lapses, which often lead to a tarnished reputation, disgruntled customers, and lost sales.

One way to ensure your data center is built to withstand demand spikes is to provision it with enough servers (physical and virtual) to handle peak loads. However, this is problematic on two fronts:

- Even if you have predicted the maximum demand using the most sophisticated modeling possible, you cannot predict *black swans*, which are extremely rare and unexpected events. If such an event occurs, you will be forced to either live with the disruption for its duration (not good), or provision more physical server resources, which could take days or weeks to get up and running (also not good).

- Any nonlinear demand curve necessarily means that it has not only high-demand peaks, but also low-demand troughs, and long stretches that hover around the average demand. In other words, most of the time the data center infrastructure will be running at less than peak usage, which means you will have physical resources that are considerably underutilized. This is inefficient and wasteful because those underutilized resources are costing you money even when they are not being used.

You can work around both problems by architecting your cloud environment as a hybrid cloud. That is, you maintain a private cloud infrastructure designed to handle your average demand load (or even your minimum demand load), and then contract with a public IaaS provider to shift anything outside of your data center's capacity to

> "It all comes down to performance because any slowdowns impact the revenue of a company. It used to be OK if you had, say, a six-second response time to load a page. But now it's really a second or less to load. Otherwise you're going to lose those customers to another site, because the competition is just a click away."[3]
> —Robinson Schoeller

the public cloud. This is called *cloudbursting* (see Figure 9-2) and it is the easiest and most economical solution to peak demand problems:

- Since you can provision extra servers from the public cloud provider as required, there is no need to predict peak demand (except possibly for budgeting purposes since there will be pay-per-use charges for the public cloud infrastructure), and no need to worry about black swans because any unusually large spike still gets bursted out to the public cloud.

- Provisioning in-house for average (or minimum) demand keeps capital costs low. The capital expenses you would have spent building up your data center to handle peak loads are replaced by the (much smaller) operating expenses for pay-per-use public cloud servers.

- On-demand pricing for public cloud servers is elastic, meaning that once the demand peak passes you can de-provision the servers and they no longer cost you anything.

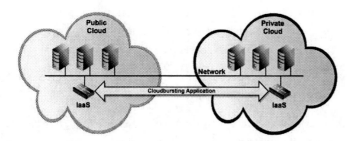

Figure 9-2 You can provision your private cloud for average demand and then cloudburst out to a public IaaS provider to handle demand spikes.

Disaster Recovery

The stark truth is that every business these days is utterly dependent on information technology, not just to perform day-to-day tasks, but to *survive*. If a data center was to suffer a major catastrophe that extended for even a short time, the viability of the business would be severely compromised. So it is all the more surprising that so many companies are willing to spend large sums of money to build, maintain, and improve IT infrastructure, but fail to put together a comprehensive and effective disaster recovery plan.

Why should this be so? Mostly because businesses live in an it-cannot-happen-to-us world, where catastrophic IT failures are either rare or they happen to *other* businesses. However, it takes but a moment's thought to see the folly in this outlook, and it disappears altogether when you list the myriad ways in which IT (and therefore a company) can go down for the count: hardware failure, software crashes, data corruption, viruses and other malware, malicious hacking, sabotage, terrorism, theft, fire, and natural disasters such as floods, tornadoes, ice storms, and hurricanes.

Even businesses that have gone as far as to recognize the potential for calamity can be still vulnerable if they fail to come up with an adequate plan for disaster recovery:

- In the event of a major data loss, you need to know where to find your latest backup.

- In the event of a fire or similar disaster that destroys company property, if backups were stored on-site, then a recovery might not be possible if those backups were also destroyed.

- Even if you have backups of company data, what about other digital property such as third-party software?

Then, even if you have planned for disaster recovery, the actual process is not going to be quick. If your hardware is destroyed, it might take weeks to provision and deploy new servers and other infrastructure. If your backups are on tape or scattered over several drives, it could take days to complete the restore process.

You can solve many of these problems by including a public cloud component as part of your disaster recovery plan. For example, you can contract with a public IaaS provider to create a virtual replica of your in-house data center. That way, if you lose your physical infrastructure, you can temporarily divert traffic to the cloud. Similarly, you can use virtual storage on a public cloud to store backups and disk images. Implementing a hybrid cloud to use the public environment for disaster recovery offers many advantages:

- In the event of a hardware failure, you can get the virtual replacements up and running within hours.

- In the event of data loss, you can begin the restore process within minutes.

- The use of disk images means you can restore full machine configurations automatically.

- You reduce the need for on-site hardware (that is, storage devices) for backups. (Notice I said *reduce*. You should still augment your public-cloud recovery strategy with a robust local recovery plan.)

Business Intelligence

You cannot make good decisions about your company unless you have good knowledge about your company. That is a fact of business life, so most enterprises today are fully engaged in organizing, identifying, querying, and analyzing business data, all of which falls under the rubric of *business intelligence* (BI). BI has traditionally involved huge datasets and the harnessing of massive amounts of processing power, so it is a quintessential in-house service. Surely there is no place for BI services in the public cloud?

You would be surprised. For example, as businesses migrate applications to the public cloud, most are keeping sensitive data behind in the company data center. However, in many cases it is much more efficient to store data along with the application to avoid the inherent network latencies involved with transferring files from the data center to the cloud environment. So, once you have customer data (or whatever) in the public cloud, it makes sense to analyze it there, too.

Public cloud-based BI also makes sense when it requires public data. For example, if your BI services are mashups that need data from, say, Google Maps or Hoovers, it is much easier to just build everything in the public cloud.

"The average length of downtime per disaster recovery event was 8 hours for non-cloud users, and 2.1 hours by cloud user standards (nearly four times faster)....Non-cloud users may depend on traditional and time-consuming tape backup methods with complex recovery paths for their disaster recovery plan."[4]

"More than 50% of the world's largest companies will have stored customer-sensitive data in the public cloud by year-end 2016, Gartner predicts.... more than 20% of organizations are already selectively storing customer-sensitive data in a hybrid cloud environment."[5]
—Ann Bednarz

> "Expect some of the greatest demand and the next wave of enterprise adoption to come from database-as-a-service (DbaaS) which would include ubiquitous access to things like business intelligence (BI) tools, whether online or off."[6]
>
> —Jocelyn DeGance Graham

For smaller datasets, business can keep sensitive data local and migrate non-sensitive data to the public cloud for analysis. One common scenario is to set up a development environment with a PaaS provider and use it to create BI services such as dashboards, querying tools, database applications, and reporting systems.

Understanding Hybrid Cloud Categories

So far in this chapter, I've been using the term *hybrid cloud* as though it was a uniform concept, but that is not the case. There are actually several different types of hybrid cloud, depending on how data and services are transferred (or not) between the private and public portions of the hybrid cloud. These categories are the static model, the replication model, and the migration model[7].

Static Model

In the *static model* of hybrid cloud, data and services generally do not transfer between the private and public environments. This is most often because the equivalent private and public services are not interoperable, usually due to incompatible standards. This is often the model used in early hybrid implementations, where the focus is on using the public portion of the cloud to lease computing resources from IaaS providers, while whatever limited PaaS and SaaS services are in play have not yet been standardized to allow the migration of code and data.

Replication Model

In the *replication model* of hybrid cloud, some data and services can be transferred between the private and public environments. These data and services are transferrable because there is some level of compatibility and standardization between the data structures and other components. One common scenario here is to use the public cloud provider's API to transfer the data, but a middleware application manipulates the incoming or outgoing data to ensure compatibility.

Note that the data and services are merely replicated on each platform, meaning there is no interaction at the service level between the private and public components.

Migration Model

In the *migration model* of hybrid cloud, the data, services, and entire virtual machines move seamlessly between the private and public cloud. Data structures and service interfaces are fully standardized to ensure complete compatibility. In this model, there is no functional difference between private virtual resources and public virtual resources, so data, code, services, and VMs can move as needed between the platforms. Note that this is more of an ideal model than anything you will see in practice today. Initiatives such as TOSCA (Topology and Orchestration Specification for Cloud Applications) are endeavoring to create the standards and requirements that would enable the easy migration of data and services, particularly between public cloud providers.

Hybrid Clouds: The Issues

You have seen that augmenting a private cloud with one or more public cloud (or community cloud) environments can increase business agility, save capital costs, increase reliability and safety, and spur innovation. However, once you have transformed your IT department into a multi-cloud environment, a few problems arise, mostly related to making all your clouds work together as seamlessly as possible. And once you start including public cloud services in your IT catalog, then all the issues related to using public cloud providers rear their heads. To give you an appreciation of the hurdles that might need to be cleared in your path to a hybrid cloud, the rest of this chapter takes you through a few of these issues.

> "TOSCA's aim is to enable broad cloud portability by providing an open standard to describe a complex application running on a complex environment. This is a critical missing link for customers that want to take full advantage of hybrid cloud architectures and the full range of available cloud services."[8]
> —Mary Johnston Turner

> "The problem comes when enterprises rely too much on vendor promises and not enough on their own architectural requirements. The vendors show up with their interpretation of what a hybrid cloud should be, enterprises understand the actual limitations too late, the budget runs out, and the plug is pulled."[9]
> —David Linthicum

Interoperability

In a cloud context, *interoperability* is the ability for multiple cloud environments to work together, including exchanging data, code, and services, particularly across multiple deployment models. So, in a hybrid cloud deployment, you are really talking about interoperability between your in-house private cloud and a public cloud.

The greater the interoperability, the more you reduce the risk of public cloud vendor lock-in, increase data portability, and avoid the creation of a public cloud silo that cannot communicate with the rest of your hybrid cloud.

When discussing interoperability with your IT department, you will need to break down the strategy into three main areas:

- **Data** The goal here is to be able to migrate databases, XML data, and even VM image files from one cloud environment to another without having to modify the data.

- **Services** In an ideal hybrid cloud, you should be able to deploy the same service locally or on the public cloud platform.

- **Management** This refers to the layer that orchestrates your various cloud environments, including the provisioning and de-provisioning of servers, storage, and other virtual resources.

To achieve this level of interoperability, either you will need to contract the services of a cloud broker that acts as a middleman between your in-house private cloud and your public cloud provider, or you will create and manage your own orchestration layer to coordinate the various cloud components.

"With the presence of numerous vendors, the need is emerging for interoperability between clouds so that a complex and developed business application on clouds is interoperable."[10]
— A V Parameswaran

Consistency

All cloud services are provisioned and configured through the use of interfaces, which could be web pages, in-house portal applications, dashboards, and so on. When you are dealing with a pure private cloud, chances are your IT team has created these interfaces internally, so there will likely be a consistent layout and consistent operational standards between the various interfaces.

However, that consistency pretty much goes out the window as soon as you move to a hybrid environment that includes public cloud services. Now you are dealing with multiple interfaces, even with tasks that are otherwise exactly the same (such as provisioning servers). This necessitates extra training for users, as well as some due diligence by IT to ensure that the new public cloud interfaces are doing what IT and business want them to do. Finally, inconsistent interfaces also means that users are more prone to errors, because someone used to a particular way of performing a task in-house might bring certain assumptions and habits to the new system, with unfortunate results.

Integration

A *hyper-hybrid cloud* combines an internal private cloud with two or more public cloud environments. A hyper-hybrid cloud makes a lot of sense for most businesses, because having multiple public cloud providers reduces the risk of vendor lock-in, increases competition, allows you to set up multiple failover strategies, and increases the overall variety of your service catalog.

However, the biggest problem with this type of cloud is the difficulty getting all these platforms to integrate with your core business services. Given your company's existing business rules, workflows, management applications, and other core services, implementing a hyper-hybrid cloud will necessitate the creation of custom integration tools that ensure the public cloud components are connected to your business needs.

Compliance

Almost all companies have some compliance concerns and, depending on factors such as the partners, agencies, and vendors you deal with and the types of data you collect and store, you might have significant compliance responsibilities to run your business in accordance with laws, regulations, industry standards and best practices, and corporate guidelines.

In a pure private cloud, you have complete control over your services,

> "This shift from 'cloud' to 'clouds' provides new opportunities, but it also brings challenges beyond just integration – security, data integrity and reliability, and business rules management for business processes that depend on enterprise IT assets composed with one or more cloud services. Welcome to the world of hyper-hybrid cloud."[11]
> —Mark E. White

systems, infrastructure, and data, so you can design a comprehensive compliance strategy. This becomes considerably more complex once you add a public cloud component to your cloud environment. When deciding what services and data can migrate to the public cloud, compliance regulations must be at the forefront. This usually means keeping in-house any data that must remain private, such as data tied to individuals, financial information, health records, and academic transcripts; data or code that must remain secure, such as corporate secrets, intellectual property, and research results; and any information that must be stored in a specific geographic location, such as a state or country.

Security

Security is not foolproof in a pure private cloud setup. For example, IT consumerization creates new attack vectors by introducing non-secure devices such as home computers, smartphones, and tablets, and there is always the threat of a malicious employee stealing or destroying data. But generally speaking, a private cloud does offer IT the best chance to lock down data and systems and thereby maximize security.

However, public cloud infrastructure and services are under the control of a third party provider, so not only are security threats more frequent, but measures designed to block those threats are harder to implement and to analyze. As I described in "Chapter 5: The Pros and Cons of Cloud Computing," public cloud security concerns fall into six main categories: insider threats, insider errors, outsourcing, authentication, multi-tenancy, and external attacks. You can address some of these concerns through service level agreements, but security will be a major public cloud concern for the foreseeable future.

REFERENCES

1 **David Linthicum**, *Why the hybrid cloud model is the best approach*, http://www.infoworld.com/d/cloud-computing/why-the-hybrid-cloud-model-the-best-approach-477 (January 17, 2011).

2 See http://www.wordspy.com/words/Slashdoteffect.asp.

3 **Robinson Schoeller** quoted in Colin Neagle, *Valentine's-related traffic spikes cause heartache for ill-prepared sites*, Network World, http://www.networkworld.com/news/2012/021312-valentines-traffic-spikes-256054.html (February 13, 2012).

4 *2011 Cloud & IT Disaster Recovery Statistics*, SmartData Collective, http://smartdatacollective.com/node/39384 (August 25, 2011).

5 **Ann Bednarz**, *Mobility, cloud, analytics to reshape IT in 2012*, http://www.computerworld.com/s/article/9223096/Mobility_cloud_analytics_to_reshape_IT_in_2012?taxonomyId=158&pageNumber=4 (January 3, 2012).

6 **Jocelyn DeGance Graham**, *Cloud Computing Trends*, Grail Research, http://grailresearch.com/pdf/ContenPodsPdf/Grail-Research-Horizons-Watch-Cloud-Trends.pdf (April 2011).

7 Based on David Linthicum, *Guidelines for implementing a hybrid cloud*, InfoWorld, http://www.infoworld.com/d/cloud-computing/guidelines-implementing-hybrid-cloud-033 (November 4, 2010).

8 **Mary Johnston Turner** quoted in Nathan Eddy, *Cisco, EMC, SAP Back Cloud Portability Standards Initiative*, eWeek, http://www.eweek.com/c/a/Cloud-Computing/Cisco-EMC-SAP-Back-Cloud-Portability-Standards-Initiative-259941/ (January 17, 2012).

9 **David Linthicum**, *The hybrid cloud is not a silver bullet*, InfoWorld, http://www.infoworld.com/d/cloud-computing/the-hybrid-cloud-not-silver-bullet-175327 (October 10, 2011).

10 **A V Parameswaran and Asheesh Chaddha**, *Cloud Interoperability and Standardization*, SETLabs Briefings, http://www.infosys.com/infosys-labs/publications/setlabs-briefings/Documents/cloud-interoperability-standardization.pdf (January 6, 2010).

11 **Mark E. White**, *Tech Trends 2012: Elevate IT for digital business*, Deloitte, http://www.deloitte.com/assets/Dcom-UnitedStates/Local%20Assets/Documents/us_cons_techtrends2012_013112.pdf (January 31, 2012).

10 Selecting a Public Cloud Provider

Whether you have decided to implement a pure public cloud environment, or whether you have opted to supplement an existing private cloud with one or more public cloud services to create a hybrid cloud, you will need to choose a provider (or providers) for those public resources.

As you learn in this chapter, one of the important things to remember when conducting a search for a cloud service provider (CSP) is that it is not the same process as procuring products such as hardware or software. You need to always bear in mind that you are looking for *services*, not products, so considerations such as security, service quality, available interfaces, terms and conditions, and payment models all come into play.

This chapter helps you in your search for a cloud service provider by running through the key requirements to look for, the important characteristics to use when evaluating CSPs, and the main contract points to examine.

What to Look for in a Cloud Provider

When you begin your search for a cloud service provider, you will of course be looking for services that align with your organization's needs and goals. Beyond those specific requirements, however, there are also a few higher-level requirements that you should to consider before signing a contract with a public cloud vendor: security, service quality, and interfaces.

Security

Security is by far the number one concern that IT managers have with moving data and services to the public cloud. On-premise resources are safe behind the company firewall, but when they migrate beyond the data center, they come under the jurisdiction of a third-party and its security practices.

So, when you evaluate public cloud providers, security should be top of mind. Most importantly, make sure the cloud provider does not offer just a single layer of security, particularly one implemented as a software-based service running on a virtual server. Any cloud provider that takes security seriously will implement a *defense-in-depth* strategy that implements multiple layers of software- *and* hardware-based security. These could include a firewall, an intrusion detection system (IDS), a virtual private networking (VPN) connection, isolated virtual machines, and separate authentication mechanisms for management tools and end-user interfaces.

A security-conscious CSP will document its security strategy, so you and your IT security personnel should examine any such documents in detail. A good example is the *Overview of Security Processes* whitepaper published by Amazon Web Services[1].

Service Quality

Service quality refers to the overall reliability and performance of a cloud environment. In-house cloud services can be engineered to provide extremely high levels of service quality that minimize both downtime and network latencies. Moving to a public cloud means the level of service quality will almost certainly drop, but in your research you should look for public environments where the quality reduction is not too drastic:

- Check the service level agreement to see the minimum percentage of availability guaranteed by the provider. Most providers nowadays offer a 99.95% uptime guarantee, so that should probably be your starting point.

- Look for CSPs that implement technologies to help improve or maintain performance. These include load balancing (distributing traffic and data among multiple servers so no one server gets overwhelmed) and auto-scaling (automatically scaling virtual infrastructure up or down to match current demands).

- Look for tools that the CSP offers to monitor the performance of your virtual resources. These monitoring tools should cover metrics such as CPU utilization, network bandwidth, disk reads and writes, and memory use.

- If you have special performance requirements, looks for CSPs that offer high-performance options specially designed to provide extreme amounts of computing power combined with very low network latencies.

Interfaces

All public cloud services offer some sort of end-user interface to use as a service front-end for logging in and using services. There should also be a separate management interface for provisioning, configuring, and controlling services. Beyond these, however, make sure the CSP offers an application programming interface (API) for controlling services programmatically. This is a crucial requirement for the IT department, because having an API enables IT to write scripts, applications, and services that quickly and automatically perform routine cloud tasks such as provisioning resources, controlling servers, and configuring services.

The downside to API access is that most APIs are proprietary. That is, each CSP creates and maintains its own set of API functions, and the names and syntax of these functions will be unique to the provider.

> "If there were an industry standard, Amazon certainly has a strong claim for it. They're the clear leader, with technology second to none. They've made huge contributions to advance cloud computing. Their API is highly proven and widely used, their cloud is highly scalable, and they have by far the biggest traction of any cloud."[2]
> —Ellen Rubin

This is a hassle for IT because it means relearning and rewriting the code if you change from one CSP to another, or if you decide to use multiple CSPs for the same type of service. Some public cloud vendors are standardizing on the Amazon Web Services API, so if you already use AWS, then adding only AWS-compatible cloud providers could become a key criterion for your company.

Researching Cloud Providers

When you are doing your public cloud provider homework, it is important to align your company's goals and needs with the services and terms offered by the cloud provider. Using your cloud strategy as a starting point (see "Chapter 7: Devising a Cloud Strategy"), you need to understand the benefits and risks, the specific requirements of each service, the restrictions you face, and how you need the public service to work together with your existing IT services. With these ideas in mind, the next few sections explore some of the issues and concerns related to researching public cloud providers.

Compliance

At this point, you should already know which types of corporate data will be remaining behind in your data center due to compliance regulations for privacy and security. However, that does not mean that your compliance issues are dealt with. You may have other types of data that are safe for the public cloud, but still come with compliance restrictions.

The most common of these is requiring that data be stored in a specific geographic location, such as a state or country, or with specific geographic requirements, such as away from a known flood plain. In this case, your CSP research should include asking the following questions:

- Where will your data be stored?

- Does the CSP offer a mechanism that enables you to specify the location of the data?

- Are there any circumstances under which the data will be moved to a different location?

- Is there a way to prevent data from being moved to a new location?

- Does the CSP use a third-party provider (for example, to provision infrastructure) and, if so, will your data be stored on the third-party provider's servers?

Costs

Most public cloud providers charge using the pay-per-use model, where you only pay for services while they are provisioned. First, remember that *provisioned* here means different things depending on the service, and, therefore, employs different cost models. For a virtual server, it usually means a per-hour charge while you use the server; for storage, it usually means a per-gigabyte charge per month; for a SaaS application, it usually means a per-user charge per month.

These are the up-front charges, but there will almost always be secondary charges that you need to consider. For example, if you provision virtual infrastructure from an IaaS provider, you will pay not only the per-hour fee for the server rental, but also fees for storage and bandwidth. The provider may also offer optional fee-based services such as high-performance clusters, extra CPUs, load balancing, and monitoring.

STAR Registration

I mentioned a few issues related to public cloud security earlier in this chapter, and I take you through some contract-related security and privacy issues later in this chapter. Clearly, security is one of the more important issues to consider when choosing a public CSP. Fortunately, evaluating cloud provider security is about to get quite a bit easier. An organization called the Cloud Security Alliance (CSA) has created a project called the CSA Security, Trust and Assurance Registry (STAR). This relatively new initiative (it was first announced in the fall of 2011) is a free and publicly available registry that details the security procedures, technologies, and certifications used by cloud providers. It is a voluntary registry, so the entries are self-assessments (see Figure 10-1), but the CSA verifies the accuracy of the assessments. This should prove invaluable in the long run for assessing and comparing the security of CSPs. As of this writing, Google, Verizon, Intel, McAfee, and Microsoft have announced plans to submit reports (and, indeed, Microsoft has already published its STAR report for Office 365[3]).

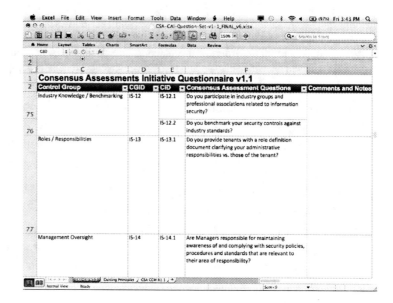

Figure 10-1 Companies get in the STAR by submitting security details and security questionnaires, such as this Excel spreadsheet.[5]

Integration

You need to investigate the cloud provider's infrastructure and services to see if they can be successfully integrated with your core business services. That is, knowing your company's business rules, workflows, management applications, and other core services, is there a way to integrate the public cloud resources across the enterprise? Is there a way to create company-wide interfaces and tools to integrate key features such as authentication, security profiles, billing, and document management?

Understanding Service Level Agreements

The key contract between your company and a public cloud service provider is the *service level agreement*, or SLA. This contract spells out the minimum level of service you can expect from the provider, particularly in terms of availability. The SLA should also detail how services are monitored, what penalties your company is entitled to should the provider not meet its uptime guarantee, and what forms of downtime are excluded from the calculations. The next few sections provide the details.

 Note

You can find an excellent overview of public cloud computing contracts in the paper *Contracts for Clouds: Comparison and Analysis of the Terms and Conditions of Cloud Computing Services,*[6] prepared for the Cloud Legal Project.

Availability Guarantees

One of the biggest concerns most IT managers have with using public clouds is availability: the percentage of time the public service is up and running. Indeed, it is a huge step to go from, say, five nines availability (99.999%, or about 5 minutes total annual downtime) to the 3.5 nines availability (99.95%, or about 4.4 hours total annual downtime) typically offered by public service providers.

Still, many businesses decide they can live with a lower downtime value if using a public cloud leads to a more agile enterprise. However, it is important to check the SLA to make sure that the availability guarantee is not too low. For example, while 99.95% uptime might be acceptable, 98% (7.3 days total annual downtime) probably is not, and you should take your business elsewhere. Also, make sure you understand how the provider calculates uptime. See, for example, the portion of the Amazon EC2 SLA shown in Figure 10-2.

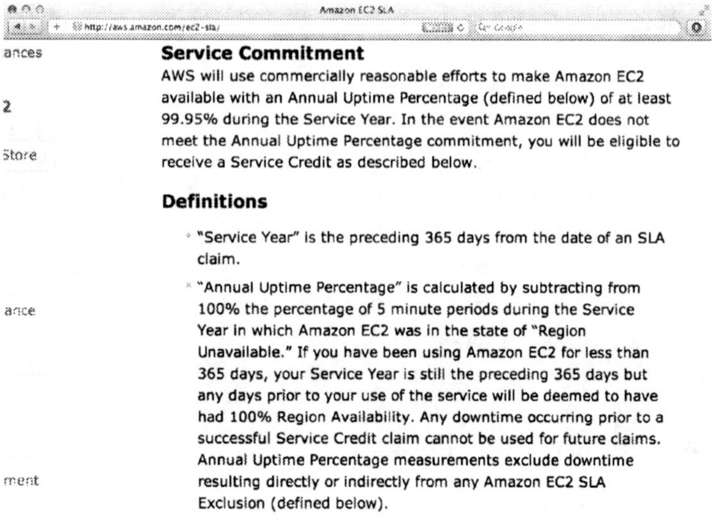

Service Commitment

AWS will use commercially reasonable efforts to make Amazon EC2 available with an Annual Uptime Percentage (defined below) of at least 99.95% during the Service Year. In the event Amazon EC2 does not meet the Annual Uptime Percentage commitment, you will be eligible to receive a Service Credit as described below.

Definitions

- "Service Year" is the preceding 365 days from the date of an SLA claim.
- "Annual Uptime Percentage" is calculated by subtracting from 100% the percentage of 5 minute periods during the Service Year in which Amazon EC2 was in the state of "Region Unavailable." If you have been using Amazon EC2 for less than 365 days, your Service Year is still the preceding 365 days but any days prior to your use of the service will be deemed to have had 100% Region Availability. Any downtime occurring prior to a successful Service Credit claim cannot be used for future claims. Annual Uptime Percentage measurements exclude downtime resulting directly or indirectly from any Amazon EC2 SLA Exclusion (defined below).

Figure 10-2 The Amazon EC2 SLA specifies an Annual Uptime Percentage and details how that value is calculated.[7]

Even more important, make sure that the SLA *has* an availability guarantee in the first place. While it is now rare for a public cloud provider to not include an uptime guarantee in their SLA, it does happen, and you should never sign a contract with a public cloud vendor that offers an SLA that makes no mention of availability guarantees.

> "While all cloud computing providers offer a contractual service level agreement, most are written to protect the vendor rather than the customer. In 2012, customers will begin demanding Service Level terms based on their governance and customer requirements."[8]
>
> **—Judith Hurwitz**

Monitoring

Ideally, the cloud service provider will offer a monitoring service that periodically checks the availability of your servers. If so, the provider should tell you how it checks availability (for example, a simple PING command), how often those checks are performed, and under what conditions it considers the server to be unavailable (for example, three consecutive PING fails). Finally, given a server failure, the provider should tell you what mechanism it uses to alert you to that failure.

Availability Penalties

Not only should the SLA specify an availability guarantee, but it should also stipulate the specific penalties the cloud provider will incur should its availability percentage fall below the contacted amount. Most cloud vendors now offer service credits as penalties. For example, Amazon EC2 offers a service credit equal to 10% of the customer's bill, should annual uptime fall below 99.95%.

Other providers offer a sliding scale of credits. For example, Rackspace Cloud Files service guarantees 99.9% availability, and offers a 10% credit if availability falls to between 99.89% and 99.5%, 25% if availability falls to between 99.49% and 99%, and so on (see Figure 10-3).

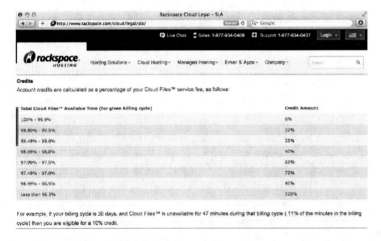

Figure 10-3 The SLA for the Rackspace Cloud Files service offers a sliding scale of availability service credit penalties.[9]

Penalty Exclusions

You should also make sure you understand under what conditions the cloud provider will *not* pay availability penalties. These are usually described as *exclusions* in the SLA, and they specify the situations under which the service commitment does not apply. For example, the Amazon EC2 SLA states that its uptime commitment does not apply to downtime "caused by factors outside of our reasonable control, including any force majeure event or Internet access or related problems beyond the demarcation point of Amazon EC2."

That is reasonable, but later in the same exclusion clause Amazon states that its service commitment does not apply to availability issues "that result from failures of individual instances not attributable to Region Unavailability." Here, *Region Unavailability* is defined as "more than one Availability Zone, in which you are running an instance, within the same Region, is 'Unavailable' to you." In other words, this refers to a broad outage that affects an entire region within an Amazon data center. It does *not* refer to individual servers going down, either via failure or for maintenance or upgrades.

Security and Privacy Practices

I argued in "Chapter 1: Introduction to Cloud Computing," that public cloud security is not as bad as many people think, because many public clouds are operated by giant enterprises that can hire the most knowledgeable and experienced cloud security personnel, and that can install the most advanced cloud security hardware and software.

So, security may not be all that big an issue after all. As long as it falls within the parameters of your company's compliance rules, you can send some resources out to the public cloud. Before doing that, however, examine the provider's agreement terms to see what provisions are made for security. In particularly, look for the following:

- **Security audits** Check to see if the cloud provider has successfully completed security audits, such as a Statement on Auditing Standards (SAS) 70 Type I or Type II audit. [10]

- **Security certifications** Check that the provider has achieved security certifications that are appropriate to your own security needs. For example, the Federal Information Security Management Act (FISMA)[11], ISO 27001,[12] and the Payment Card Industry Data Security Standard (PCI DSS) Level 1. [13]

- **Service security architecture** Examine the technologies, standards, and procedures that the provider uses to ensure the security of the services it provides. These should meet or exceed any security compliance requirements that your company must follow.

- **Physical access to the cloud data center** Access to the public cloud provider's data center should be restricted to company personnel and vendors who require access. Ideally, the data center will be staffed 24 hours a day, every day of the year, and access to the data center should require special authorization technology (such as security codes or hand scanners).

- **Security breaches** Make sure the company stipulates that it will notify you immediately if it detects a security breach.

- **Data privacy policies** The cloud provider should offer a privacy policy that details the steps it takes to ensure that no unauthorized users gain access to your data. Ideally, the company's privacy policies will adhere to the Safe Harbor privacy principles agreed to by the U.S. and the European Union.[14] The privacy policy should also tell you how data moves through the cloud, particularly with respect to the company's backup and data redundancy procedures. You also need to know whether the cloud provider offers tools that enable you to encrypt your data within the cloud. Finally, make sure the agreement explicitly states that the cloud provider will not share your data with any third party.

Major companies will offer extensive background information on their security practices. For example, Amazon Web Services offers an AWS Security and Compliance Center that details the company's security procedures and practices (see Figure 10-4). These documents should be examined closely by security experts in your IT department.

 Note

There are some exceptions that can be made for the sharing of customer data with a third-party. For example, the provider may be required to disclose data due to a subpoena or court order. Similarly, if you are contracting with a public SaaS or PaaS provider, that company might provision its infrastructure from a third-party IaaS vendor, so your data will need to be stored on the third-party's servers. In such cases, the original public cloud vendor's agreement should state the nature of this data sharing.

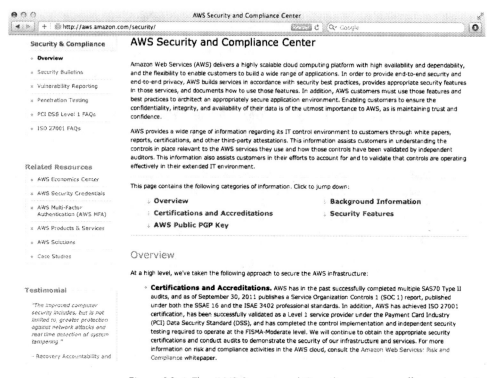

Figure 10-4 The AWS Security and Compliance Center offers a detailed look at Amazon's extensive security practices.[15]

 Note

Many cloud service providers state in their customer agreements that they can and will update the terms of their contracts unilaterally and without notice, and that they will do this simply by posting a new version of the contract on their website. So it is up to you, the customer, to regularly download provider contracts and analyze them for new terms!

Other Contract Terms

Besides an SLA and a security agreement, all cloud providers ask you to agree to other contract terms, usually in the form of Terms of Service (ToS) and Acceptable Use Policy (AUP) documents. These agreements almost always come with a long list of clauses, definitions, and terms, and it is important to understand what these agreements are saying. To that end, the next few sections take you through some of the more important terms in a typical public cloud vendor agreement.

Support

You might go into an agreement with a cloud provider hoping that the service will be perfect for the duration of the contract, but that is not a realistic hope. Problems will always arise, and when they do, you will need to contact the vendor to try to get things fixed as quickly and as efficiently as possible.

With that in mind, you need to make sure the agreement specifies your support options, including the specific steps you need to take when a problem arises or the vendor is in some way failing to live up to the terms of the agreement. You need to know who you can contact and when, and there should be multiple contact modes (phone, email, chat, and so on). You should also know the procedure for escalating a support ticket to a higher level if you feel your problem is not being dealt with properly.

Disaster Recovery

In the context of a public cloud service provider, disaster recovery means getting your public cloud infrastructure, platforms, or applications back online after a failure. Unfortunately, you are unlikely to find any direct mention of disaster recovery provisions in a public cloud vendor agreement. Instead, you need to check to see if the provider offers either data redundancy measures that enable services to remain running if a main system fails, or backups of data or virtual machine images that can be used as part of a recovery process.

The cloud provider's agreement is much more likely to say that *you* are responsible for your own data, which includes keeping that data safe and setting up your own data recovery strategy. In this case, you will need to implement a backup strategy for your data and even your public cloud infrastructure. This will entail placing backup copies of data structures and virtual machine images either in your own data center or in another public cloud. Your IT people will then need to understand the procedures required to restore the data or images from the backup location to the original public cloud (via APIs, for example).

> "[A]sk questions, read the fine print, and make sure you understand your risks going into ANY cloud or SaaS contract." [16]
> —Morgan Hunter

Liability

Most public cloud vendor agreements define the vendor's level of liability, which almost always extends only as far as breaches of the agreement by the vendor and "gross negligence or willful misconduct." The agreement will also specify a maximum liability payment, which is usually the cost of your service fees over six or twelve months, or some maximum dollar amount (typically, a few hundred dollars). These are woefully inadequate amounts, and you should try to negotiate higher liability payments.

Service Suspension

The public cloud agreement will most likely contain a clause or two regarding suspension of your services, and you need to understand under what situations this can happen. In particular, check to see if the public cloud provider can suspend your account due to overdue payments. Many agreements have provisions that they can suspend customer accounts if payments are overdue by as little as 15 days. In such cases, you should negotiate with the cloud provider to guarantee that your account will not be suspended pending the investigation of overdue payments.

It also pays to check the agreement fine print to see if the public cloud vendor will charge you a *reinstatement fee* to return your services after a suspension. If this fee is exorbitant (say, several hundred dollars or more), it is probably worthwhile trying to negotiate the fee out of the agreement.

> "The survey found that some contracts, for instance, have clauses disclaiming responsibility for keeping the user's data secure or intact. Others reserve the right to terminate accounts for apparent lack of use (potentially important if they are used for occasional backup or disaster recovery purposes), for violation of the provider's Acceptable Use Policy, or indeed for any or no reason at all." [17]
>
> —Emma Lowry

Contract Termination

Most public cloud providers offer no notice at all for terminating a contract *for cause* (such as violations of the provider's terms of service or acceptable use policies) and 30 days' notice for terminating a contract *for convenience* (that is, for any other reason than a violation). So, you first need to understand the difference between these two types of termination, and, in particular, what circumstances could initiate a *for cause* termination.

With a *for convenience* termination, you should determine in advance whether 30 days is enough time for you to locate, provision, and configure a replacement service, and to migrate your data and services to that service. If not, see if you can negotiate a longer notice period. Also, make sure you know exactly what rights you have during the post-termination period. For example, it is important that the cloud provider not delete your data until the notice period has expired.

REFERENCES

1   *Amazon Web Services: Overview of Security Processes*, http://d36cz9buwru1tt. cloudfront.net/pdf/AWS_Security_Whitepaper.pdf (May 2011).

2   **Ellen Rubin**, *Is Amazon the Official Cloud Standard?*, CloudSwitch, http:// www.cloudswitch.com/page/is-amazon-the-official-cloud-standard (July 7, 2010).

3   See https://cloudsecurityalliance.org/star-registrant/microsoft-office-365/.

4   **Jerry Archer**, quoted in *Major Cloud Providers to Participate in CSA STAR— CSA Security, Trust and Assurance Registry*, Cloud Security Alliance, https:// cloudsecurityalliance.org/csa-news/major-cloud-providers-to-participate-in-csa-star/ (November 16, 2011).

5   See https://cloudsecurityalliance.org/research/cai/.

6   **Simon Bradshaw, Christopher Millard, and Ian Walden**, *Contracts for Clouds: Comparison and Analysis of the Terms and Conditions of Cloud Computing Services*, Cloud Legal Project, http://papers.ssrn.com/sol3/ papers.cfm?abstract_id=1662374 (September 2, 2010).

7   See http://aws.amazon.com/ec2-sla/.

8   **Judith Hurwitz**, *5 Big Cloud Trends For 2012*, Informationweek, http://www.informationweek.com/news/cloud-computing/ infrastructure/232200551 (December 28, 2011).

9   See http://www.rackspace.com/legal/sla/.

10 See http://sas70.com/index.html.

11 See http://csrc.nist.gov/groups/SMA/fisma/index.html.

12 See http://en.wikipedia.org/wiki/ISO/IEC_27001.

13 See https://www.pcisecuritystandards.org/security_standards/.

14 See http://export.gov/safeharbor/.

15 See http://aws.amazon.com/security/.

16 **Morgan Hunter**, *Amazon Supplement*, Lotus MBA, http://lotusmba. blogspot.com/2011/04/amazon-supplement.html (April 26, 2011).

17 **Emma Lowry**, *The good, the bad and the ugly terms of Cloud Computing*, Queen Mary, University of London, http://www.qmul.ac.uk/media/news/ items/hss/40121.html (November 23, 2010).

11 Migrating to the Cloud

By this point you have learned enough about cloud advantages and disadvantages, service models, deployment models, the business case for cloud, and setting up a cloud strategy that you should already have a pretty strong sense of what goes into a cloud migration plan. You should know, in particular, that any move to the cloud must be done slowly, deliberately, with eyes open to potential pitfalls and traps, with great attention to detail, with a spirit of collaboration, and with an overall goal of creating a better company, when all is said and done.

This chapter is not a step-by-step cloud migration formula that you can follow. Any such generic plan would not be worth the paper it was written on, since every business is unique and must forge its own equally unique path to the cloud. Instead, this chapter takes you through the main ingredients of such a plan, just to make sure you are getting off on the right foot and that you are not missing anything.

Planning Your Cloud Migration

Let's begin with a list of some of the main ideas and actions that should be part of your cloud migration plan:

"Start with a clear plan for your overall IT delivery strategy and avoid a scattershot, uncoordinated approach that can do more harm than good. Start with a comprehensive plan and then use modular building blocks and a step-by-step approach and you will have a better chance of building a fully automated cloud solution."[1]
— Judy Redman

- Analyze your business needs and goals and determine how the advantages of a cloud environment (whether private, public, or hybrid) can help you meet those needs and achieve those goals.

- Make a prioritized list of the objectives you hope to achieve by migrating to the cloud: greater agility, faster time-to-value, reduced costs, greater innovation, and so on.

- Determine your preferred cloud deployment model: private cloud, public cloud, or a hybrid cloud that mixes both types.

- For a private cloud, begin the process of standardizing, virtualizing, automating, and self-provisioning IT resources.

- For a hybrid cloud, begin the creation of a service catalog that includes both private and public services, thus enabling IT to act as a service broker.

- Using your company's compliance restrictions and regulations, determine which data can be safely placed within a public cloud and which must remain on-premises.

- Establish governance procedures and models for evaluating, ordering, deploying, and managing cloud services.

- Assign readiness and value scores to your applications to determine the best candidates for migration to the cloud, and the order in which those applications will be migrated, upgraded, or replaced.

- Based on your needs and objectives, research possible public cloud providers.

- After examining the SLAs, Terms of Service, and Acceptable Use Policies of potential cloud vendors, determine which clauses you want to negotiate to receive terms that are more favorable to your business needs and goals.

- Perform a cost analysis that takes into account all possible public cloud charges beyond the standard service rental fees.

- Establish a set of trial deployments that you can use to evaluate CSPs and their services.

- Create at least one backup plan just in case unforeseen circumstances arise and you must change how the migration is implemented.

Timing Your Move to the Cloud

Assuming you do not want to make a wholesale migration to the cloud (a good idea), how do you decide which resources get moved to the cloud, and in what order? I discussed that in "Chapter 7: Devising a Cloud Strategy," and one of the methods I mentioned involved taking advantage of resource lifecycles and similar timings to trigger cloud moves. Here is a closer look at this strategy:

> "The movement to the cloud is a one-way street."[2]
> —Vivek Kundra

- **Infrastructure replacement** If a server or other piece of hardware is at the end of its lifecycle, consider replacing it with a virtual cloud resource instead of a physical resource. In many scenarios, this will not only save money (since renting virtual infrastructure is usually cheaper in the long run than purchasing physical hardware), but it will also be much faster (since you can provision virtual hardware in minutes, while physical hardware might take weeks or even months).

- **Infrastructure upgrade** If a server or similar hardware requires an upgrade to continue functioning at an acceptable level, it may still be quicker and more cost effective to cancel the upgrade and replace the hardware with its virtual cloud equivalent.

- **Software update** If an application that is used broadly across the company is due for an update, purchasing and then deploying that update can be both expensive and time-consuming. If a SaaS equivalent exists, now would be a good time to switch to the cloud application.

- **New infrastructure or software** If you get a request for new equipment, such as a server or development platform, or for a new application, first assess the request (in terms of security, compliance, governance, and cloud availability) to see if the new hardware or application is suitable for the cloud. If it is, then provision the request via the cloud to avoid new physical infrastructure or software charges.

- **Pilot projects** Tests, trials, and similar pilot projects are an excellent way to try out cloud provisioning. Also, it is usually considerably cheaper to deploy such trials in the cloud, since they tend to be short-term projects; instead of purchasing expensive non-cloud resources, you only pay for what you need, when you need it.

Avoiding Migration Problems

If you have taken the time to put together a detailed cloud strategy, then the migration from traditional data center to private or public cloud environment should be reasonably straightforward. Unfortunately, *straightforward* does not mean *problem-free*. Few cloud migrations come off without a hitch, but you can minimize such problems with a few common-sense precautions:

- **Run tests** The biggest mistake you can make when moving to a cloud environment is to move too fast. Instead of migrating huge chunks of your business into the cloud at once, a better approach is to slow down and begin with a few trial deployments. The first of these could be simple "Hello World" services developed by your IT department, which are good for test-driving the migration without putting any real assets at risk. Next, try migrating real services that have a low priority or importance within the business.

- **More monitoring** Remember that migrating services to the public cloud usually means you need *more* monitoring, not less. Public cloud services are outside the data center and under the control of a third party, so they are inherently more opaque than on-site services. This lack of visibility means that you must either take advantage of the cloud provider's native monitoring tools (such as Amazon's AWS Management Console[3]), or use the provider's APIs to create your own monitoring applications in-house.

- **Consider data retrieval** Data you move to the public cloud should be considered less safe than data that resides in your data center. Therefore, you should have a robust backup plan in place to ensure that data is always safe. However, it is just as important to create a plan to bring that data back in-house whenever you might need it (e.g., for testing, use in another application, legal discovery, and so on).

- **Come up with VM specs** Public cloud makes it easy to provision virtual machines, but in most cases they also offer lots of alternatives in terms of number of CPUs, memory size, storage space, and other specs. If you plan on allowing non-technical users to provision VMs, then your IT team needs to determine what VM specs are required in what circumstances, so that users know what to order and can avoid over- or under-provisioning for their business needs.

- **Encourage collaboration between IT and business** While automation and self-provisioning are cloud hallmarks that can make your business more agile, they also can make it too easy to provision services, resulting in cloud sprawl. To avoid this, IT and business must collaborate on creating a set of cloud-friendly best practices, workflows, and business processes.

- **Beware the uneven handshake** When you sign a contract with a public cloud provider, that contract outlines the vendor's responsibilities, which usually include maintaining the physical infrastructure and security of their data center, exposing interfaces for provisioning virtual resources, and offering basic monitoring and management tools. It is easy to forget that this means everything else is up to you: backups, failovers, data security, authentication, governance, integration, and testing. Forrester Research calls this the *uneven handshake*, and it can become a real problem if you go into your relationship with a public cloud provider expecting them to handle tasks that are not part of the agreement.

> "When the cloud is your IT platform, and it's in the hands of an outside firm, how do you ensure that their technical or business problems won't become yours?"[4]
> —Rick Freedman

> "When you leverage cloud platforms... you continue to incur costs for managing, securing, monitoring, and backing up and recovering your cloud deployments. These costs for any management functions that lie above the service being provided are all yours. We call this operational relationship 'the uneven handshake'."[5]
> —James Staten

Moving Applications to the Cloud

A big part of your migration to the cloud will involve moving applications to (or creating new applications in) the cloud, whether it is an on-premises private cloud or a third-party public SaaS cloud. Here are a few pointers to bear in mind to help make this migration easier:

- **Pick a service model** An application can operate in any cloud service model—SaaS, PaaS, or IaaS—so you need to determine which model best suits your needs. For example, you would most likely choose a PaaS environment if the application is based on a standard server platform, such as Microsoft .NET. You would most likely go with an IaaS environment if you also want to control the virtual infrastructure on which your application runs. Going the SaaS route means you want to replace the application with a SaaS service.

- **Core versus context** Identify your company's keeping-the-lights-on context functions as well as its core functions that differentiate your from your competitors (see "Chapter 7: Devising a Cloud Strategy"). Then, do everything you can to move your core applications to an agile, flexible private cloud. Wherever possible, outsource your context applications to a public SaaS provider.

- **Legacy applications** As a general rule, older applications do not make good cloud candidates. That is because legacy applications tend to be rigidly coded, with outdated programming constructs, lots of references hard-wired into the code, and a reliance on a single (usually massive) database. There is no easy way to transform such an application into a flexible, agile cloud service, so you are most often better off leaving such applications *on the ground*.

- **Modern applications** All things considered, newer applications that use modern programming techniques and architectures are well suited to a cloud migration. This is particularly true of multi-tiered applications that are based on web and Internet standards and that use multiple, distributed databases.

- **Multi-tenant applications** If an application will be accessed by a large number of users, it is best to code that application using the multi-tenant architectural principles used by public SaaS providers, which allows thousands or even millions of users to share the same code base.

- **Application testing** If you will be migrating an application to a public cloud environment, it is crucial to test the application under expected loads to analyze performance, responsiveness, network latency, and other factors that might prevent the application from being implemented with an acceptable level of service quality.

- **New applications** Unless there are security, privacy, or other compliance concerns that require a non-cloud environment, all new applications should be deployed in the cloud. And since it is easier and faster to provision a virtual PaaS development platform rather than a traditional physical platform, you should develop those new applications in the cloud, as well.

Moving Data to the Cloud

All computing resources require data, so an inevitable part of your cloud migration will be the migration of data to the cloud. As you have seen throughout this book, this is not a simple task. First, there may be laws, regulations, and other compliance concerns that restrict what types of data you can migrate to the cloud. Second, it is not always easy to get your data to interoperate with other cloud resources. And third, you need to ensure that your cloud data is integrated with the rest of your IT infrastructure and with the enterprise as a whole. With these potential restrictions in mind, this section runs through a few ideas for migrating data to the cloud.

> "Figuring out which applications to bring into the cloud and which to retain in the traditional data center can be a daunting task for any IT organization. If not done properly, it can bring on "cloud in a corner" syndrome—a condition where new cloud-based solutions are disconnected from existing IT resources."[6]
> —John Treadway

Data Classification

Before you consider moving your data to the cloud, your first step is to classify your company's data. The idea behind data classification is to understand what types of data can be moved to the cloud and what types must remain behind the firewall. There are many approaches to data classification, but if you are going to be using a public cloud environment, then security and compliance issues are paramount. That is, you need to examine your data and decide what the impact would be to your company if that data were inadvertently exposed, lost, or stolen.

To that end, you should classify your data into one of the following sensitivity levels:

- **Public** This level refers to publicly available data that would cause no harm or risk to your organization should it be subject to unauthorized disclosure, loss, or theft. Examples include press releases, public-facing website data, and annual reports. This level requires minimal security, although you still need to exercise some care to ensure the data is not altered without authorization.

- **Internal** This level refers to internal company data that would cause some inconvenience if it were to be disclosed without authorization or lost, but no harm or risk should it be stolen. Examples include internal emails, memos, reports, and meeting minutes. Security at this level is higher than for public documents, but only high enough to ensure some control over the data.

- **Proprietary** This level refers to data that is unique to the company and defines the company's internal operations, and so would cause significant inconvenience if it were to be disclosed, lost, or stolen. Examples include business rules and procedures, operational workflows, project plans, product designs and specifications, and non-identifiable employee and customer data. This level requires high security to prevent access not only from outsiders, but also from non-authorized employees.

- **Confidential** This level refers to highly sensitive data that is critical to the company's operations and so would cause significant harm or risk if it were to be disclosed without authorization, lost, or stolen. Examples include financial information, legal documents, business plans, research results, medical records, and identifiable employee and customer data. This level requires extremely high security to ensure no unauthorized access (both internal and external) and to maintain control over the location of the data.

- **Secret** This level refers to the most sensitive and top-secret company data that would cause long-term or even irreparable harm should it be exposed, lost, or stolen. Examples include trade secrets, merger negotiations, acquisition plans, and investment strategies. This level requires the highest possible security to prevent unauthorized external access, to restrict internal access to a small subset of employees, and to maintain complete control over the location and integrity of the data at all times.

SCENARIO 1 Private Cloud Storage with Public Cloud Access

In this scenario (see Figure 11-1), a virtual private networking (VPN) server is maintained just outside the corporate firewall, and a copy of the public data is stored on that server. The original versions of the public data remain behind the firewall, and the two copies are synchronized. The VPN server uses a secure connection to send data to the public cloud when the application requests it. This model limits exposure to the data because it never resides permanently in the public cloud, but performance might suffer as the data transfer takes place (particularly if you are dealing with large data files).

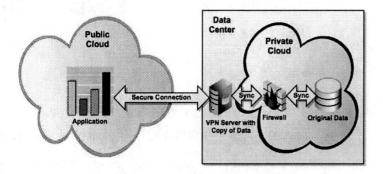

Figure 11-1 Private cloud storage with public cloud access

SCENARIO 2 Duplicate Private/Public Cloud Data with Synchronization

In this scenario (see Figure 11-2), the public data is stored permanently in the public cloud. The original versions of the public data remain in-house, and the two copies are synchronized. The advantages here are improved performance, since the data is always available to public cloud users, and simpler disaster recovery, since there are always two copies of the public data. On the downside, the data's permanent place in the public cloud raises privacy and security concerns (which will need to be dealt with when negotiating the SLA), and it also implies long-term data storage fees. You will also need to develop a mechanism to synchronize the data, as well as policies that determine how often the synchronization occurs.

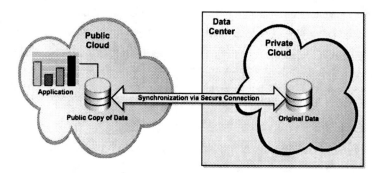

Figure 11-2 Duplicate private and public cloud data with synchronization

SCENARIO 3 Migrate Data from Private to Public Cloud as Needed

In this scenario (see Figure 11-3), the public data remains in-house and is only migrated temporarily to the cloud as it is needed by the user. The main advantages here are that the data is always stored behind the firewall and, since only one copy of the data is required, no complicated synchronization mechanisms are needed. The main disadvantage is the impracticability of moving large data files in a timely manner, so this approach would only work with relatively small data transfers.

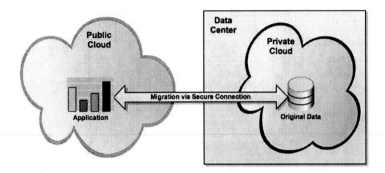

Figure 11-3 Migrating data from private to public cloud as needed

Cloud Provider Migration Tools

You likely noticed that all three of these scenarios had something in common. That is, they all require some movement of data from your on-premises data center to the public cloud environment. Rather than using standard file transfer methods (such as FTP) or custom tools (built using the cloud provider's API), you should check with your public cloud vendor to see if they offer a secure mechanism for migrating your data. Examples include Amazon's AWS Storage Gateway[7] (see Figure 11-4) and Google's Secure Data Connector.[8]

Figure 11-4 Amazon's AWS Storage Gateway gives you a simple and secure method for transferring files to the cloud.

HP's Cloud Migration Tools

If you have not yet got a handle on your cloud migration strategy, there are many tools available that can help. To give you an idea of what is available, I will use the rest of this chapter to take you through a few of the cloud migration tools that are available through HP.

HP Cloud Discovery Workshop

HP offers the HP Cloud Discovery Workshop,[9] a one-day workshop where HP consultants and cloud experts introduce you to the cloud and take you through the most important steps involved in migrating to the cloud, all with an eye on the unique needs and challenges faced by your company. This workshop focuses on the following:

- **Introduction to the cloud** The workshop begins with a discussion of current business and technology trends, an overview of cloud computing, and answers to common questions about cloud computing.

- **Cloud computing concepts** This section of the workshop dives a bit deeper into cloud computing by defining concepts such as cloud providers and cloud consumers, cloud service models, and cloud architectures. You also learn about cloud deployment models and the various types of cloud computing.

- **The journey to the cloud** Here you learn about cloud-related strategic opportunities as well as how to prioritize your cloud migration. You also learn the critical success factors for making the most of cloud computing in your organization.

- **Cloud service catalog and cloudonomics** This section shows you how to set up a cloud service catalog. You also learn the basics of *cloudonomics*, including cloud ROI and delivering business value through the cloud.

- **Cloud infrastructure** Here you learn how to create the cloud infrastructure, with an emphasis on leveraged converged infrastructure.

- **Cloud security and reliability** This section of the workshop focuses on cloud security, including authentication, compliance, data privacy, and user authorization. You also learn about the basic principles for creating highly robust and available cloud services.

- **Cloud management** This part of the workshop shows you various best practices for managing cloud services.

- **Migrating applications and data** Here you learn how to recognize and adapt applications and data for life in the cloud.

- **Governance** This section focuses on cloud governance models as well as integrating cloud services into your organization, including determining staffing needs, implementing change management, and training personnel.

- **Roadmap to the cloud** The workshop ends by helping you define a 30- to 60-day tactical plan for moving to the cloud.

HP Cloud Roadmap Service

HP offers the HP Cloud Roadmap Service,[10] which is an eight- to 12-week program where HP consultants work directly with your IT staff to map out your road to the cloud, including the following:

- **Cloud benefits** Identifying the specific areas of your business where the cloud can help.

- **Architecture** Planning the infrastructure and other resources your company needs to implement a cloud strategy.

- **Analysis and planning** Analyzing your current IT operations, identifying gaps in your IT delivery services, and planning a revised IT program.

- **Strategy** Recommending ideal strategies for cloud services, cloud governance, and cloud operations.

- **Business case** Analyzing infrastructure, staffing, and other costs, as well as economic benefits to determine the cloud return on investment.

- **Roadmap** Creating a step-by-step, project-by-project plan for implementing a cloud.

HP Applications Transformation to Cloud

HP offers the HP Applications Transformation to Cloud[11] service, which helps you determine how suitable your applications are for the cloud, and what actions you need to take, if any, to transform an application to run in the cloud. This consulting service does the following:

- **Analysis** This phase analyzes each application to determine its suitableness for cloud computing. If an application is deemed cloud-suitable, you also learn the best option for sourcing the application (e.g., private cloud or public cloud).

- **Roadmap** This phase creates a plan for transforming each application to make it cloud-ready.

- **Migration** This phase modernizes those applications that need to be updated to run in the cloud, and then migrates the cloud-ready applications.

HP IT Transformation Consulting Services

HP IT Transformation Consulting Services[12] works with your company to come up with a strategic plan for transforming your IT resources and services to best suit the needs of your business. HP's consultants offer four levels of transformation services:

- **IT Strategy and Transformation Planning** Provides you with a big picture strategy for defining what needs to be transformed and the steps required to implement that transformation.

- **IT Governance** Analyzes your current governance state with respect to your industry's best practices and benchmarks, and then creates a governance structure that helps ensure that IT and business work together to reach the company's goals.

- **Enterprise Architecture Planning and Design** Defines and creates a strategy for the structures, processes, methodologies, and other IT architecture that your business requires.

- **Value Management (Benefits Management and Realization)** Helps you define a clear benefits calculation for your new IT investment and shows how this can lead to better decision making with an emphasis on maximizing business value.

HP Cloud Protection Program and Consulting Services

You do not want to even think about implementing either a pure public cloud or a hybrid cloud environment without first taking a long and hard look at the security implications. To help you plan and build the necessary security mechanisms and best practices, HP offers a service called HP Cloud Protection Program and Consulting

Services.[13] This service helps you integrate cloud security across your business by providing three tools:

- **Cloud Protection Consulting Services** A collection of services (including HP Cloud Protection Workshop) that help you create strategies against threats defined by the Cloud Security Alliance.

- **HP Cloud Protection Center of Excellence** A computing lab that enables you to test and integrate HP and partner virtualization, cloud, and security technologies.

- **HP Cloud Protection Reference Architecture** A cloud security framework that combines technical, business, and functional viewpoints into a comprehensive security design for your company.

REFERENCES

1   **Judy Redman**, *5 easy steps to building cloud success*, Grounded in the Cloud, http://h30499.www3.hp.com/t5/Grounded-in-the-Cloud/5-easy-steps-to-building-cloud-success/ba-p/5294483 (August 8, 2011).

2   **Vivek Kundra**, quoted in *Cloud First Buyer's Guide for Government*, TechAmerica Foundation, http://www.cloudbuyersguide.org/wp-content/uploads/2011/07/Cloud_Buyers_Guide_072711.pdf (July 7, 2011).

3   See http://aws.amazon.com/console/.

4   **Rick Freedman**, *Cloud computing migration issues: What you need to know*, TechRepublic, http://www.techrepublic.com/blog/project-management/cloud-computing-migration-issues-what-you-need-to-know/1248 (December 22, 2009).

5   **James Staten**, *The Three Stages of Cloud Economics*, Forrester Research, h20195.www2.hp.com/v2/GetDocument.aspx?docname=4AA3-8122ENW (April 28, 2011).

6   **John Treadway**, *Innoculate Yourself Against "Cloud in a Corner" Syndrome*, Unisys, http://blogs.unisys.com/disruptiveittrends/2011/09/02/innoculate-yourself-against-cloud-in-a-corner-syndrome/ (September 2, 2011).

7   See http://aws.amazon.com/storagegateway/.

8   See https://developers.google.com/secure-data-connector/.

9   See http://www8.hp.com/us/en/business-services/it-services.html?compURI=1077460.

10 See http://www8.hp.com/us/en/business-services/it-services.html?compURI=1077468.

11 See http://www8.hp.com//us/en/business-services/it-services.html?compURI=1079041.

12 See http://www8.hp.com//us/en/business-services/it-services.html?compURI=1079306.

13 See http://www8.hp.com//us/en/business-services/it-services.html?compURI=1077478.

12 Cloud Management

After all your hard work getting your private, public, or hybrid cloud up and running, you might be tempted to rest on your laurels for a time. After all, setting up a cloud is a complex task that requires both IT and business to change the way they think about delivering and using computing resources. Given all that creative destruction (to borrow economist Joseph Schumpeter's evocative phrase[1]), surely a period of calm is in order.

Believe me, I wish it was true. The problem is that a cloud implementation brings with it new responsibilities and challenges. That is because, by definition, the cloud portion of any network is an opaque structure where the details are hidden from view. This is particularly true in any public cloud, where a third party is now responsible for many of the tasks and duties that used to fall to your IT department.

In other words, your big challenge now that your cloud is running is to manage that cloud and its various components, including services, integration, costs, security, and support. How do you do that when portions of your cloud lie outside your data center? What tools can you use to peer inside the cloud? How do you monitor things like performance and costs? This chapter answers these and other cloud management questions.

Network Management versus Cloud Management

In a traditional IT shop, there are many frameworks available for standardizing network management, including the following:

- **FCAPS** The ISO network management model that covers fault, configuration, accounting, performance, and security management.[2]

- **FAB** The Enhanced Telecom Operations Map (eTOM) model that covers fulfillment, assurance, and billing.[3]

- **ITIL** The Information Technology Infrastructure Library, which defines best practices for IT service management.[4]

- **COBIT** Control Objectives for Information and related Technology, this is an Information Systems Audit and Control Association (ISACA) framework for IT management and governance.[5]

These are powerful frameworks, and to a certain extent they contain much that is relevant to a cloud environment. However, there are many aspects of cloud computing that do not fit well within these frameworks, including the following:

- On-demand self-service

- Broad network access using standard Internet and World Wide Web protocols

- Rapid elasticity and scalability

- Resource pooling and converged infrastructure

- Measured service and pay-per-use billing

- Abstracted and virtualized resources

- Automation of resource provisioning and de-provisioning

As you see in the rest of this chapter, resolving these issues requires new approaches to cloud management and a new generation of management tools and techniques.

"It's easy to say "ah, we'll just run some cloud management software on a bunch of machines," but it's a completely different matter to uphold the premise of real-time resource availability."[6]
— Thorsten von Eicken

Cloud Management Responsibilities

Perhaps the biggest difference between traditional network management and cloud management is the fragmentation of managerial responsibilities. In a traditional network model, IT is responsible for managing everything: hardware, operating systems, databases, the network, applications, and the users (including interfaces, authentication, and support). However, in a cloud model, who has these responsibilities depends on the service model used in the cloud implementation. Some responsibilities will remain with IT, but others will be farmed out to one or more CSPs.

In terms of management responsibilities, the closest cloud equivalent to the traditional network model is the on-site private cloud, where the cloud hardware and services are built and maintained in the company data center, so responsibility for all six main management layers—hardware (servers, storage, data center infrastructure, and so on), operating systems, databases, networks, applications, and users—falls with IT.

If you include a public IaaS component in your cloud, then you relinquish responsibility for the hardware management layer to the CSP. Also, since you must now use the Internet to transfer data and services between your company and the cloud vendor, as well as manage your own internal network, IT and the CSP share responsibility for the overall network infrastructure. IT remains responsible for the operating systems, databases, applications, and users.

If you include public PaaS resources in your cloud, the hardware layer remains the responsibility of the CSP, which also takes on the responsibilities associated with the operating systems and databases, which are part of the platform provided by the CSP. The network infrastructure remains a shared responsibility of IT and the CSP. IT remains responsible for the applications and users.

Finally, if you include a public SaaS application in your cloud, the CSP is responsible for the hardware management layer, as well as for the operating system and database management layers that undergird the application. IT and the CSP split responsibility for the network infrastructure and the application (the CSP deploys the application, creates interfaces for the users, monitors performance, and manages

> "When enterprises move to a cloud solution, there is a shift in the organizational structure that can have significant consequences on how accountabilities and responsibilities are implemented."[7]
> —ISACA

upgrades; IT provisions users, configures the application, and monitors costs). IT remains responsible for the users.

Table 12-1 summarizes these cloud management responsibilities.

Table 12-1 Who is responsible for what in various cloud service models

| Model | Cloud Management Responsibility Layers | | | | | |
	Hardware	OS	Database	Network	Application	User
On-Site Private	IT	IT	IT	IT	IT	IT
Public IaaS	CSP	IT	IT	CSP/IT	IT	IT
Public PaaS	CSP	CSP	CSP	CSP/IT	IT	IT
Public SaaS	CSP	CSP	CSP	CSP/IT	CSP/IT	IT

Managing the Cloud

Some people (particularly cloud vendors) might give you the impression that cloud computing is a provision-it-and-forget-it operation. That is, once you have set up your private cloud or established relationships with one or more cloud service providers, then all that is left is for business and IT to provision what they need, when they need it. Of course, nothing could be further from the truth. Cloud environments still require extensive management time and effort. To give you an idea of how extensive these responsibilities are, the next few sections take you through seven key cloud management tasks.

Managing Multiple IT Platforms

It is possible that your company is a start-up enterprise that decided to go all-in with public cloud services from the beginning. In that case, then you only have a single IT platform to manage: the public cloud (albeit probably with multiple CSPs—particularly multiple PaaS platforms—within that environment).

However, it is more likely that you have an existing IT environment that consists of one or more platforms, such as Windows or Linux, and perhaps a mainframe. Throw in a private cloud and one or more public IaaS or PaaS environments, and suddenly you have quite a few platforms in your IT stable. Even if your long-term goal is to eventually end up with an all-cloud infrastructure, that will take some time to implement, so you will have to deal with the increased management complexity of multiple cloud and non-cloud platforms for some time.

This means dealing with the following questions:

- Which applications or services go with which platform?

- When creating a new application, which platform will you use to build the application and which platform will you use to deploy it?

- When a resource in a physical platform reaches the end of its lifecycle, which platform do you use to replace it?

- How do you integrate each platform into your larger enterprise?

- How do you move data from one platform to another?

- What guidelines can you give to end users regarding which platforms they should use when they need to provision particular types of resources?

> "Managing and measuring complex IT sourcing environments in terms meaningful to the business has become a pressing need for the CIO, particularly with the recent and rapid adoption of cloud computing."[8]
> —Will Cappelli

Managing Services

Whether you have a pure cloud environment (public, private, or hybrid) or a mixture of cloud and non-cloud platforms, your long-term goal for IT should always be to transition from delivering products to delivering services. This means that the main task for IT will become the management of those services, which includes the following:

- Deciding on what mix of services best helps the company meet its needs and objectives

- Using laws, rules, and similar compliance restrictions to decide which services must remain behind the firewall and which can be outsourced to one or more public cloud providers

- Planning, architecting, and overseeing the coding and deployment of in-house services

- Researching and negotiating public cloud services

- Setting up and maintaining a service catalog that combines all in-house and public cloud services

- Transitioning existing non-cloud applications to cloud services

- Evaluating existing services to decide when a service should be replaced or retired

> "With the delivery of infrastructure, platforms and software as a service, it's not all that surprising to discover that IT organizations are struggling a bit to keep pace with who is using what service when and for what."[9]
> —Michael Vizard

Managing Integration

In a multi-platform IT setup, one of the most crucial management tasks is overseeing the integration of data and services from all of the platforms. Business intelligence and insight are often derived by combining data and results from multiple applications, services, and databases. This is usually not much of a problem when you are dealing with a single IT platform, but it becomes a major challenge when you have multiple in-house and public cloud environments to deal with.

You need to develop a custom integration service, hire an integration consultant (such as HP Service Integration and Management Services[10]; see Figure 12-1) or purchase third-party integration software (such as Pervasive,[11] shown in Figure 12-2, or CloudSwitch[12]) that enables your team to manage the integration.

Figure 12-1 HP Service Integration and Management Services is a consulting service that can help you set up a multi-platform integration management strategy.

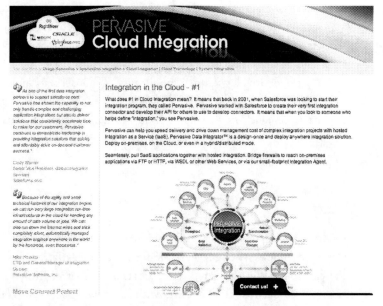

Figure 12-2 Pervasive offers cloud integration technology that enables you to integrate data between multiple public cloud environments and your in-house IT platforms.

Managing Costs

I have mentioned several times in this book that making the move to the cloud should be more about increasing business agility in a complex, globalized, fast-paced world, and less about saving money. Having said that, however, it does not follow that cloud computing costs should be ignored. On the contrary, although it is often better to replace a fixed capital expense model with a variable pay-per-use model, pay-per-use is only cost effective because you do not pay for a resource when you are not using it. If, for some reason, a particular rented resource is not de-provisioned when it is no longer needed, then its *use* effectively becomes 24/7, and you will *pay* accordingly.

To avoid such a scenario, you need to set up a management model that tracks cloud costs and can spot anomalies such as over-provisioning and excessive pay-per-use charges.

Managing Security

Once you have decided which data and services can reside outside of the firewall, your security responsibilities are only just beginning. Management of public cloud security means aligning your company's security requirements and best practices with the security technologies and techniques used by each public cloud provider. It means auditing cloud provider security, monitoring vendor security and privacy policies for changes, and keeping abreast of third-party security organizations (such as the Cloud Security Alliance[14]) for the latest news on threats as well as initiatives such as STAR[15] (see "Chapter 10: Selecting a Public Cloud Provider").

Managing Support

Another consequence of a multi-platform IT environment is the increased complexity of end-user support. In a single-platform setup (for example, a Windows shop), support is relatively straightforward. That is, you need to handle issues with Windows itself, your company's authorized Windows applications, and network problems. That is a significant challenge, but now multiply that challenge by the number of platforms you have once cloud comes into the picture.

One way to ease this challenge is to standardize on a particular platform type. For example, if your traditional IT environment ran on a Windows platform, then you would include as part of your cloud strategy and planning a directive to implement only Windows platforms in your private cloud and any IaaS or PaaS platforms you provision in the public cloud.

It is also important to implement a policy of initiating all public cloud support requests with IT. That is, you do not want end users contacting the public cloud provider directly to resolve issues. That would mean having support tickets scattered among multiple vendors, which is bad enough, but it also means that IT almost certainly has no idea that those tickets are even outstanding, so it does not get the required feedback that might point to larger problems with a particular cloud provider.

Managing Lifecycles

Despite being virtual, cloud services are not immune to the normal processes that define the lifecycle of traditional IT resources. This should come as no surprise, since the specifications, functions, and purpose of a cloud service might work well today, but cannot be guaranteed to remain applicable or relevant in the future.

Because of this, you need to manage the lifecycle of your cloud resources, a task that roughly breaks down into the following half dozen areas:

- **Specification/Development** This phase covers the detailing of specifications for a cloud resource, including specs such as number of CPUs and total memory for a virtual machine image. This phase also covers the development of services, applications, and interfaces.

- **Testing** This phase covers testing and quality assurance of the cloud resource to show that it performs to its specifications and meets the needs it was designed to address.

- **Deployment** In this phase, the cloud resource is deployed and configured, and any interfaces for provisioning and configuring the resources are put into place.

- **Monitoring** This phase involves using monitoring tools to examine the resource's performance, latency, health, storage needs, bandwidth usage, and user feedback.

- **Upgrade** In this phase, the resource gets any upgrades that are deemed necessary to maintain performance, fix security holes, and implement user suggestions.

- **Retirement** When the cloud resource reaches the end of its usefulness, it is retired to make way for new resources.

Cloud Management Tools

In the same way that it is possible to tell at least something about the weather by licking your finger and holding it up to the wind, you could manage (if that is the word) your cloud by checking to see if your virtual server is running.

Clearly that is a bit *too* rudimentary, and fortunately the available cloud management tools are much more sophisticated than that. Here are just a few of the tasks a typical cloud management service allows you to perform:

- Provision, pause, reboot, and de-provision virtual servers

- See the number of virtual servers you currently have provisioned

- See the current status of each virtual server

- Monitor virtual server data such as CPU utilization, hard disk usage, hard disk throughput, and network bandwidth

- Create and restore image backups

- Launch, restart, upgrade, and terminate virtual applications

- View the status of virtual applications

- View activity and error logs

Cloud management tools fall into four broad categories: native provider tools, third-party public cloud tools, third-party private cloud tools, and in-house tools.

Native Tools

Almost all major cloud service providers offer web-based management applications that you can run on the provider's site to manage your virtual environment (see Figure 12-3). The tools available depend on the services you are using. For example, a public IaaS vendor will provide you with tools for provisioning and managing virtual servers, while a public PaaS vendor will gear its tools more toward creating and managing applications.

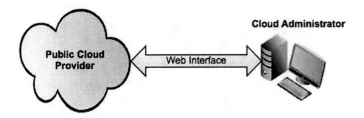

Figure 12-3 You use a web interface to access a cloud vendor's native management tools.

Larger vendors that offer multiple services will provide you with more comprehensive management tools. One of the best of these is

Amazon's AWS Management Console,[16] which offers tabs for a number of AWS tools, including EC2 (see Figure 12-4), S3, and Elastic Beanstalk.

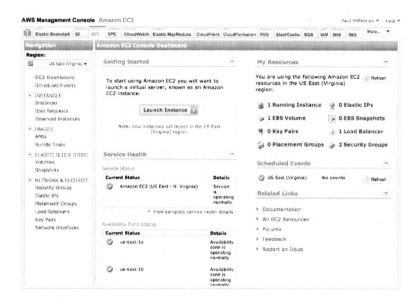

Figure 12-4 Amazon's AWS Management Console offers tabs for all AWS tools, including Elastic Compute Cloud (EC2).

Third-Party Public Cloud Tools

The problem with native cloud management tools is that they tend to be on the basic side, although some CSPs offer beefed-up management suites for an extra charge. However, it is likely you can also find many third-party vendors that offer management tools for public cloud providers. How can they do this? By taking advantage of the *application programming interface* (API) made available by the CSP.

An API is a set of prefabricated programming functions that are made available to anyone who knows how to code. When a vendor publishes an API, what they are really doing is offering a set of instructions for using these programming functions in third-party code. For a public cloud vendor, these functions all relate to managing and controlling cloud services. For example, there might be a Reboot function that enables a programmer to reboot a virtual machine using programming code. The programmer does not need to know the specifics of the underlying code, just how to incorporate the function, which usually means passing one or more parameters to the function that specify exactly what the programmer wants to happen. (In programming lingo, this is known as *calling* the function.) For example, to use our hypothetical Reboot function properly, the programmer's code would have to specify exactly which virtual server is to be rebooted. When an API receives such a call, it carries out the requested action and then returns the result to the calling program.

Many CSPs offer APIs, but the most commonly used is the Amazon Web Services API,[18] which offers hundreds of functions that cover almost every aspect of its cloud services.

The bottom line is that an API enables one program to communicate with another without human intervention. This enables third-party software developers to build management tools that use these functions in the background to communicate with and control the cloud vendor's services, as shown in Figure 12-5. You can then contract with the developer to use their management tools over the web.

 Note

If you are interested, you can find a more or less complete list of available web APIs (more than 5,000 as I write this!) at the Programmable Web site.[17]

 Note

For an extensive list of cloud management software, see the Infrastructure Management category in OpenCrowd's Cloud Computing Vendors Taxonomy.[19]

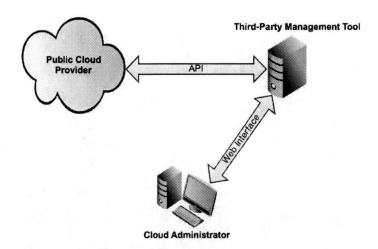

Figure 12-5 Third-party developers can use a cloud vendor's published API to create tools for managing the vendor's services, which you then access over the web.

Third-Party Private Cloud Tools

If you are running a private cloud, there are third-party management tools available that can help you keep an eye on your cloud. Most of these tools install on a network computer, and you usually need to install a separate monitoring program on each client computer. However, some tools, such as Windows Intune,[20] shown in Figure 12-6, offer a web interface, which allows for more monitoring flexibility (since, theoretically, you can manage and monitor your private cloud from any Internet-enabled location).

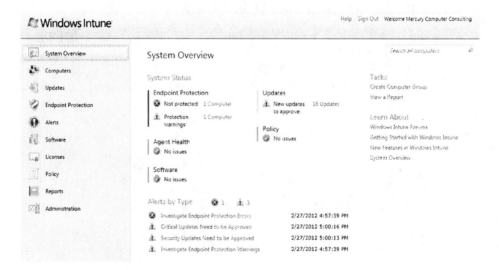

Figure 12-6 You can use a program such as Windows Intune to manage a private cloud.

In-House Tools

The main problem with the management programs provided by CSPs and third-party developers is that they tend to offer a generic set of tools, services, and metrics. That is fine if you just plan on performing basic management chores. However, if you have specific or unique requirements or needs when it comes to cloud management, then you need to roll your own management software.

You do that by taking advantage of the APIs provided by public cloud vendors. In this case, however, your management applications can interact directly with the CSP API, as shown in Figure 12-7.

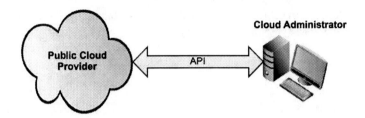

Figure 12-7 Your in-house developers can take advantage of the cloud vendor's API to create a custom management tool that suits your business requirements.

Monitoring Your Cloud

One of the main planks of your cloud management platform should be monitoring your cloud resources. Monitoring services is one of the best ways (indeed, in many cases the *only* way) to break through the natural opacity of a public cloud environment and see what is actually happening inside the cloud.

For example, if you have provisioned a server from a public IaaS provider, you need to monitor the server's performance use metrics such as the following:

- CPU utilization

- Hard disk reads and writes

- Bandwidth usage for uploads and downloads

- Idle time

- Network latency

Similarly, you would want to monitor an application running on a PaaS instance using metrics such as bandwidth in and out, total users, storage, and memory utilization.

As with cloud management tools, cloud monitoring tools come in four flavors. You can use the cloud provider's native tools, such as Amazon Web Services' CloudWatch tool (see Figure 12-8); you can use third-party public cloud tools, such as Unified Monitoring[21] and Cloudability[22]; you can use third-party private cloud tools, such as VMware's vFabric[23]; and your IT team can take advantage of cloud vendor APIs to create custom, in-house monitoring tools.

Figure 12-8 Amazon Web Services' CloudWatch tool enables you to monitor your EC2 instances, EBS storage, and much more.

REFERENCES

1   "This process of Creative Destruction is the essential fact about capitalism."
    See http://www.econlib.org/library/Enc/CreativeDestruction.html.

2   See http://www.itu.int/rec/dologin_pub.
    asp?lang=e&id=T-REC-M.3400-200002-I!!PDF-E&type=items.

3   See http://www.tmforum.org/BestPracticesStandards/
    BusinessProcessFramework/1647/Home.html.

4   See http://www.itil-officialsite.com/home/home.asp.

5   See http://www.isaca.org/Knowledge-Center/cobit/Pages/Overview.aspx.

6   **Thorsten von Eicken,** *Cloud Computing vs. Grid Computing,* RightScale
    Blog, http://blog.rightscale.com/2008/07/07/cloud-computing-vs-grid-
    computing/ (July 7, 2008).

7   *Guiding Principles for Cloud Computing Adoption and Use,* Information
    Systems Audit and Control Association, http://www.isaca.org/Knowledge-
    Center/Research/Documents/VS-Guiding-Principles-Cloud-WP-
    10Feb2012.pdf (February, 2012).

8   **Will Cappelli,** quoted in Manda Banda, *HP services target rapid cloud
    growth,* ITP.net, http://www.itp.net/588000-hp-services-target-rapid-
    cloud-growth (February 21, 2012).

9   **Michael Vizard,** *Putting a Stop to Cloud Services Sprawl,* ITBusinessEdge,
    http://www.itbusinessedge.com/cm/blogs/vizard/putting-a-stop-to-cloud-
    services-sprawl/?cs=49868 (February 27, 2012).

10 See http://www8.hp.com/us/en/software/software-product.
    html?compURI=tcm:245-953809.

11 See http://integration.pervasive.com/.

12 See http://www.cloudswitch.com/.

13 **Alex Williams,** *Managing the Costs and Complexities of a Cloud-
    Based Infrastructure,* ReadWriteWeb, http://www.readwriteweb.com/
    cloud/2010/05/managing-the-costs-and-complex.php (May 14, 2010).

14 See https://cloudsecurityalliance.org/.

15 See https://cloudsecurityalliance.org/star/.

16 See http://aws.amazon.com/console/.

17 See http://www.programmableweb.com/.

18 See http://aws.amazon.com/documentation/.

19 See http://cloudtaxonomy.opencrowd.com/taxonomy/cloud-software/cloud-management/.

20 See http://www.microsoft.com/en-ca/windows/windowsintune/pc-management.aspx.

21 See http://unifiedmonitoring.com/.

22 See https://www.cloudability.com/.

23 See http://www.vmware.com/products/application-platform/vfabric-hyperic.html.

13 Cloud Security Issues

A non-cloud environment has one key advantage over a cloud setup: the hardware, software, and services are well-known, physical components that can be configured and protected using time-tested strategies and techniques. Non-cloud security is not perfect (no security system is), but it lacks surprises and is easily patched to thwart any new vulnerabilities that come along.

The cloud, on the other hand, offers virtual resources that are in many ways harder to protect. This is due in part to its inherently amorphous (and in the case of public cloud, opaque) environment, but the cloud also seems to be a place of *unknown unknowns* (to quote from former Defense Secretary Donald Rumsfeld's famous phrase[1]) where you cannot predict where danger will strike. According to Terry Woloszyn, founder and chief technical officer of PerspecSys, a cloud security company,

> The cloud security landscape is growing ever more dangerous—SSL has been compromised, insecure technologies are introduced daily, and even more highly sophisticated attacks are directly targeting private and public cloud environments. Enterprise adoption of cloud computing is more challenging than ever.[2]

Note that he mentions both public *and* private clouds. Yes, even that seemingly secure cloud behind your firewall is vulnerable.

The Privacy Rights Clearinghouse tracks data breaches[3] caused by unintended disclosures, malicious hackers or malware, payment card fraud, malicious insiders, and theft. In 2011 alone, the PRC logged 590 breaches involving more than 31 million data records, and those are just the breaches that were made public.

So, yes, cloud security is a problem. However, that should not stop you from adopting cloud computing in your business, because keeping your company safe in the cloud is largely a matter of knowing the issues involved. This chapter takes you through the most important of those issues.

Public Cloud Security Issues

I could spend an entire chapter just going through the results of surveys that show time and again that the biggest concern CIOs, CTOs, and other IT professionals have with public cloud environments is security. It must be said that some of these concerns are really about the unpalatable (to an IT person) decision to relinquish some control over platforms and data that is part of the move to the public cloud. These concerns are also related to the opaque nature of public clouds and the inherent difficulty in knowing just what security precautions and procedures a cloud service provider is implementing.

Having said that, however, I do not mean to discourage you from using public cloud services. Public cloud vendors are constantly battening their security hatches, an increasing number of third-party tools are available to help you lock down your public assets, and there are plenty of steps you and your company can take to bolster public cloud security. The first step is knowing the challenges that you face, and that is what this section is all about.

"When wireless came along, we didn't really know a lot about how to protect it, but we developed that understanding as we went forward, and now we do a pretty good job of protecting wireless."[4]
—Ron Ross

Compliance

Assessing your public cloud security needs should always begin with your compliance needs. That is, what regulations and laws are applicable to your company when it comes to the storage and use of data? Depending on your country of operation (and even your state or province within that country), there may be a long list of potential regulations out there. In the U.S., for example, such regulations include the Federal Information Security Management Act (FISMA),[5] the Health Insurance Portability and Accountability Act (HIPAA),[6] the Sarbanes-Oxley Act,[7] and the Payment Card Industry Data Security Standard (PCI DSS).[8] You may also have to follow internal company regulations, industry rules and best practices, contract stipulations, corporate social responsibility practices, and ethical guidelines.

Many of these regulatory standards also offer certifications to cloud providers that can demonstrate they operate their cloud environments in accordance with the standards. For example, FISMA offers low-impact, moderate-impact, and high-impact security categorizations.[9]

> "By 2016, 40 percent of enterprises will make proof of independent security testing a precondition for using any type of cloud service."[10]
> —Gartner

The data security and privacy aspects of these regulations usually require specific knowledge of where data resides, how it is protected, and how it can be accessed. Unfortunately, public cloud environments do not do well on all these fronts. For example, if a cloud provider uses multiple, geographically-diverse data centers (as any decent large CSP should), then data location becomes a problem if your compliance needs require your data to remain in the country, or even in a particular state or province. Similarly, the inherently virtual and multi-tenant environment of public cloud is problematic for many compliance rules, unless the public cloud provider can demonstrate that its virtual machines are completely and inviolably isolated from one another. (See "Multi-tenant Issues," later in this chapter, for more information on multi-tenancy and its effect on public cloud security.)

Many of these compliance needs require regular reports and trails for auditors (both internal and external). A good public cloud provider will help you to comply with these rules and regulations by offering the following:

- Management tools that enable you to implement compliance policies

- Monitoring tools that enable you to check your compliance policies

- Reporting tools for compliance-related data.

- Auditing tools for compliance checking

> "The real truth about public cloud services is that the biggest barrier to entry isn't security. The biggest barrier is compliance."[11]
> —Christofer Hoff

Access Control

In the pre-cloud days, access control to a network was a relatively simple affair. That is, each user was assigned an account that consisted of (at least) a username, password, and associated security rights and privileges, all of which was stored in a central database. Logging on to the network gave the user access to those resources for which he or she had access, and determined what he or she could do with those resources (view them, read them, edit them, and so on).

The cloud—particularly the public cloud—changes all that because it alters how we look at access control:

- Internal users may need to access resources outside of your local network (that is, in the public cloud environment).

- External users may need to access your public cloud resources.

For the internal users, one solution would be to extend the internal security privileges to include the public cloud environment. This is slow and unwieldy, however, and so it does not scale with the speed and elasticity that is the hallmark of cloud computing.

Similarly, one solution for external users is to offer each one an internal user account that has extremely limited privileges. However, again, this is a solution that does not scale very well.

Many public cloud providers implement their own authentication schemes, which means providing users with their own accounts. This is relatively simple to implement, but if the CSP does not encrypt the login, the user's credentials are vulnerable to packet sniffers and other malicious users. Also, when users must create and manage a large number of cloud accounts, they tend to repeat the same credentials across multiple accounts, thus creating a larger security concern if one set of credentials is compromised.

A step up from this one-account-per-user approach is a system called *single sign-on* (SSO), which involves logging in once with a single set of credentials that provides access to multiple cloud environments without having to log in to each one individually. This solves some of the problems with access control, particularly since the initial log-ins are encrypted, but it raises other security issues. For example, if a user's SSO credentials are stolen in some other manner (say, by shoulder surfing or by guessing an obvious password), then the thief automatically gains access to multiple cloud environments.

The latest form of access control is called *federated identity*. This approach combines elements of both the enterprise login model and the SSO model to create one or more trusted authorities for authenticating digital identities across multiple cloud providers. Those providers use standard mechanisms to share identity attributes, and thus make it easier for each provider to authenticate and provide the appropriate level of access to each user. We are only just starting to see public cloud vendors adopt federated identity.

Data Loss or Disclosure

There are many ways to store data in the public cloud: as part of some IaaS virtual machines; using IaaS virtual storage (for backups, for example); as part of a PaaS platform; or within a SaaS application. If you have compliance regulations to follow, or if you are just rightfully paranoid about your data, then you probably do not have sensitive, secret, or private data in the public cloud, but have stored it safely within your own data center.

However, what if you do not have a data center and instead are relying on a pure public cloud environment for your infrastructure, platforms, and applications? In that scenario, you necessarily have all your business data within the public cloud, so it becomes vulnerable to both data loss and data disclosure.

Data loss means that you can no longer access your data, and it can happen in many ways:

- Deletion of data without a backup

- Alteration of data so that the original content no longer exists

- Overwriting of an existing data file with a different file of the same name

- A hard disk (or similar media) error that corrupts the data

- A lost encryption key that renders the data unreadable

- Malicious destruction of data by an insider or unauthorized user

To prevent this, make sure you retain multiple backups of your data. Check with your cloud vendor to see if they perform backups internally. You should also implement your own backup strategy, where you store backups in your own data center (if you have one), on a separate virtual machine within your cloud provider's data center (ideally, on a different physical server, if possible), or using a different public cloud provider entirely. Also, if you use encryption, set up policies for generating and managing the associated keys.

The other potential data problem inherent in a public cloud environment is data disclosure, which is the accidental or malicious exposure of data to a non-authorized user. As with data loss, data disclosure can occur in a distressingly large number of ways:

- A malicious user can use a packet sniffer to read unencrypted data as it travels between your company and the public cloud.

- If the CSP does not erase a virtual storage block after you are done with it, the next user could see your data.

- Inadvertently emailing data to a non-authorized user

- Storing company data in a non-secure cloud

- Not implementing strong access control policies (for users, API-based services, or both), and thus enabling a nefarious user to gain access to your data

To help prevent data disclosure, make sure the pipe between your company and the public cloud is encrypted, and make sure your use an encrypted file system on your virtual machines. Make sure you use strong access controls, both at the user interface level and at the API authentication level. Only deal with CSPs that routinely wipe data storage blocks before releasing them back into the storage pool.

Physical Resource Loss

You might be asking yourself, "If a public cloud consists of nothing but virtualized resources, why is *physical resource loss* a potential security problem?" In this context, when I am talking about the loss of physical resources, I am talking about actual servers and hard drives that reside within the cloud provider's data center. What I am not talking about, however, is the inevitable failure of a server or other component. That kind of thing happens all the time in any reasonably large data center, and a good cloud service provider will have mechanisms in place—data redundancy, failover systems, and so on—to take the dead device offline and resume operations without a hiccup.

The real concern here is the physical seizure of a working server or hard drive from the cloud vendor's data center. Outright theft is one possibility, but the more likely (and increasingly more common) scenario is the seizure of physical cloud vendor assets by law enforcement agencies. Perhaps the most famous such incident occurred on June 21, 2011, when the F.B.I. raided the data center of the service provider DigitalOne, looking for a particular server used by the digital activist group Lulz Security. However, instead of taking just a single server, the F.B.I. agents took three entire *racks* of servers, several dozen in all. The result was that a number of websites completely unrelated to Lulz Security went dark, while others had to switch to backup servers.

That all sounds bad enough, but a bit of luck was involved or things could have been much worse. It is possible that if DigitalOne had been unable to pinpoint the servers used by Lulz Security, the F.B.I. could conceivably have designated the *entire* data center a crime scene and confiscated every server in the place!

> "Cloud security only happens through a combination of vigilance, best practices, and technology, including encryption, patching, and monitoring."[12]
> —J. Nicholas Hoover

> "The F.B.I. seized Web servers in a raid on a data center early Tuesday, causing several Web sites, including those run by the New York publisher Curbed Network, to go offline."[13]
> —Verne G. Kopytoff

So the seizing of physical resources from a cloud data center is a real possibility, but having your public cloud infrastructure go down is just one of the problems it can cause. If your virtual resources reside on a seized physical server, it also means that your data, code, and other proprietary information also reside on that server. So, against your will, you could end up with your data in the hands of the authorities, with all sorts of compliance ramifications, none of them good.

This means that the loss of physical cloud provider resources is something that you should incorporate into your risk management strategy. For example, you might consider mirroring your entire public cloud environment in a second data center, or in your private cloud. There is not much you can do about a law enforcement agency ending up with your data, except to ensure that no sensitive or secret data resides permanently in the cloud provider's data center.

Insecure APIs

As you have seen in several places in this book (particularly in "Chapter 12: Cloud Management"), cloud vendors provide application programming interfaces (APIs) to allow software-based interaction with cloud services. Using the functions exposed by these APIs, coders can create scripts, services, interfaces, and applications that can be used for both automated and user-controlled provisioning, management, and monitoring.

> "Security has been completely left out or poorly implemented in many of the applications and mashups built on these Web APIs. What's more, in many cases, the core Web API itself is vulnerable."[14]
> — Stephan Chenette

This is convenient and efficient, but in the race to become even easier to use, many cloud APIs turn a blind eye to security. They do this by allowing unauthenticated access, unencrypted transmission of credentials or data, and weak forms of authentication. In some cases, an API (particularly one implemented by a mashup of two or more cloud services) depends on other APIs to function, which just adds another layer of insecure authentication and data transfer.

As a result, some APIs are vulnerable to the following exploits:

- **Man in the middle attack** A malicious user intercepts—and possibly alters—data traveling between a public cloud service and your business. To prevent such an attack, your CSP should implement SSL (Secure Sockets Layer; a powerful security protocol) protected API endpoints that provide server authentication and allow SSL-based communications that cannot be intercepted.

- **IP spoofing** A malicious user sends data to your business that appears to come from a virtual server maintained by the public cloud provider. An IP (Internet Protocol) address is a numeric value that uniquely identifies every computer connected to the Internet to enable data to find its destination. A malicious user could use a virtual server on the public cloud to send data to your business using the IP address of a trusted virtual server in the same public cloud. A properly secured public cloud will configure its firewall to prevent a virtual server from sending data with an IP address other than its own.

- **Distributed denial of service (DDoS)** A malicious user attempts to disable a public cloud virtual server by inundating it with massive amounts of meaningless data. The CSP should deploy techniques that enable its API endpoints to either fight off such attacks, or switch the workload to a different network to bypass the attack completely.

Data Center Security

One of the biggest concerns with using a public cloud environment is that services, applications, and data reside within a third-party's data center, and it is not always clear just how secure that data center is. Specifically, it is usually very difficult to know how the vendor distributes security clearances for its employees to gain physical access to the inside of the data center, and then what those who are given access are allowed to do within the data center. Even more problematic are the CSP's contractors—that is, outside agencies who might provide services such as cleaning, maintenance, and repair—and the amount of access they are given within the data center and how much supervision they are given once inside.

Access to the public cloud provider's data center should be restricted to company personnel and contactors who actually require such access. The best-case scenario is a data center that is staffed 24 hours a day, seven days a week, 365 days a year. Access to the data center should require special authorization technology, which means security codes at the least, or, ideally, biometric authentication technology such as fingerprint or hand scanners. The CSP should also have an identified policy for revoking access when it is no longer required by an employee or contractor.

Bad Operators

When you recruit employees for your IT department, you probably perform thorough background checks and other tests to ensure that you are hiring upstanding individuals who can be trusted. Not only that, but you can also build company loyalty by treating employees with respect and trust. (Having said all that, see my look at private cloud insider threats, later in this chapter.)

When it comes to the public cloud, however, you likely have no way of knowing a CSP's hiring practices and job qualifications, and you certainly won't know how (or even whether) the company inspires loyalty among its employees. In the absence of such information, you must assume that your public cloud component is vulnerable to attacks from CSP insiders.

When researching public cloud providers, examine their security protocols to see if they discuss employee hiring. For example, Amazon Web Services explicitly states that it requires that "staff with potential access to customer data undergo an extensive background check (as permitted by law) commensurate with their position and level of data access."[15] A good cloud vendor will also detail the lifecycle of employee security access, including how security accounts are handed out, how often they are reviewed, what password policies are used, and when and how security accounts are revoked.

Multi-tenant Issues

A public cloud environment is, by definition, a multi-tenant environment. (The exception would be a hosted private cloud, which is a single-tenant environment within a third-party vendor's data center; see "Chapter 4: Cloud Deployment Models.") Multi-tenant means, essentially, that multiple customers share a single physical machine within the cloud provider's data center. Each customer has its own virtual server running in that physical server, and the hypervisor's job is to ensure that all those virtual servers are isolated from each other.

Modern central processing units (CPUs) are designed to allow for separate, isolated virtual machines within a single server, but other physical structures shared by the VMs within that server are not as good at isolating workloads. These structures include the graphics processing unit (GPU), which handles graphical tasks that bypass the CPU, and the CPU caches, which are on-chip memory areas that the CPU uses to store frequently accessed bits of code and data.

Modern hypervisors are designed to work around the sharing limitations of these physical structures, but malicious hackers continue to find ways to exploit these weaknesses to use one virtual machine to attack another.

Check with your public cloud provider to see what steps they are taking to ensure VMs remain isolated from one another. For example, the CSP might implement a firewall between the hypervisor and the server's physical resources (see Figure 13-1). Another example (used by Amazon's AWS and others) is to use only virtualized disks, which not only ensures that VMs have no access to the physical disks, but also allows the CSP to reset storage blocks before they get reallocated, thus ensuring that the previous customer's data is never exposed to the next customer. If you store important data in the public cloud, be sure that the CSP stores that information in a single, encrypted database *not* in a database shared with many other customers. Finally, your company also needs to be proactive when it comes to multi-tenant defenses. For example, you could configure your VMs to use an encrypted file system.

> "The vulnerability could allow denial of service if a malformed sequence of machine instructions is run by an authenticated user in one of the guest virtual machines hosted by the Hyper-V server."[16]
> —Microsoft

> "Let's say a hacker is able to break the encryption of a database operated by a cloud service provider. If it's a multitenant service, chances are he or she will be able to steal the data of dozens or hundreds of different business customers all stored on that database."[17]
> —Eric Lai

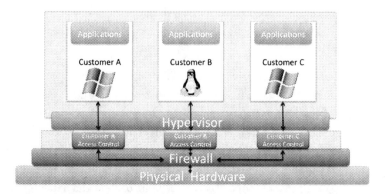

Figure 13-1 Placing a firewall between the physical layer and the virtualization layer can help the hypervisor isolate the VM instances.

Disaster Recovery

In the context of a public cloud service provider, disaster recovery means getting your public cloud infrastructure, platforms, or applications back online after a failure. Although it is generally the case that you are responsible for your own data in the public cloud, that does not mean the CSP is exempt from even trying to keep your data safe. Check your cloud vendor's terms and conditions or security features to see if they offer one or more of the following:

■ Multiple data centers in geographically diverse locations, so that if one center goes down, workloads can be moved to another data center to ensure continuity

■ Uninterruptible power supplies and onsite backup generators, so in the event of a power failure, you have enough warning time to move VMs and data to a different location

■ Data redundancy measures that enable services to remain running if a main system fails

■ Backups of data or virtual machine images that can be used as part of a recovery process

■ A clear incident response strategy, which involves not only 24-hour-a-day monitoring to detect incidents, but also measures to reduce the impact of any incident, steps to resolve the problem, and a mechanism that quickly alerts you that something is amiss

- For customers, the capability of running virtual machines and storing data in multiple geographic regions

- For customers, independent failure zones within a geographic region, which means that if one zone fails, the other zones in the same region remain operational

In the two-way street that is public cloud disaster recovery, you need to do your part, which means setting up your own data recovery strategy. This generally includes the following:

- Implementing a backup strategy for your data. This entails placing backup copies of databases, data structures, and unstructured data either in your own data center or in another public cloud

- Implementing a backup strategy for your public cloud infrastructure. For each virtual machine, this entails storing copies of the original VM image (if you have access to it) and one or more VM snapshots (each of which holds the current state of the VM, including running applications) in your data center or another public cloud

- Implementing the procedures required to restore the data or images from the backup location to the original public cloud (via the cloud vendor's API, for example)

Private Cloud Security Issues

There are so many potential security risks associated with the public cloud, that by this point you might be tempted to throw up your hands and just go all-in with a private cloud. To be sure, a private cloud is an excellent way to get started in cloud computing, and you might have legal or regulatory issues that require you to keep certain data or services in-house anyway. But you should not go into a private cloud project under the assumption that this on-site cloud is going to be *ipso facto* secure, just because it lies behind your firewall. Private clouds have their own vulnerabilities, as the next few sections show.

> "The burgeoning field of cloud insurance looks even better than ever. A well-thought-out insurance model will address the actual costs and risks of cloud outages or security breaches, for both customers and providers."[18]
> —Derek Harris

Virtualization

Virtualization is one of the key components of a private cloud, because it enables the simulation of computing resources via software. This means that a small number of physical resources can support a large number of virtual resources, so your data center becomes more efficient (in terms of costs and energy use) and more agile (since new virtual resources can be provisioned in minutes).

Unfortunately, virtualization also opens up a fairly large security hole. To understand why, you first need to know that one of the main ways that IT security personnel keep your network safe is to monitor network traffic for unusual patterns. This is usually accomplished by installing traffic-scanning devices at strategic points within the physical network infrastructure.

The problem is that virtual machines often do not use the physical network to transfer data. For example, if two VMs are managed by the same hypervisor on a single physical server, data exchanges between those VMs occur within the physical server. This makes for faster communication between the VMs, but it also means that the traffic between these VMs does not go through the physical network, so that traffic cannot be monitored for malicious or suspicious patterns.

In short, if a VM gets compromised, it can begin sending malicious data and instructions to other VMs on the same physical server, and no one in IT will be the wiser, since none of that traffic gets picked up by the security devices that guard the physical network.

What is the solution? Fortunately, enterprising software developers have come up with ways to monitor so-called *inter-VM* network traffic. An example is Phantom Virtual Tap[20] (see Figure 13-2), which monitors traffic in VMware environments.

"Given the privileged level that the hypervisor/VMM holds in the stack, hackers have already begun targeting this layer to potentially compromise all the workloads hosted above it."[19]

—Gartner

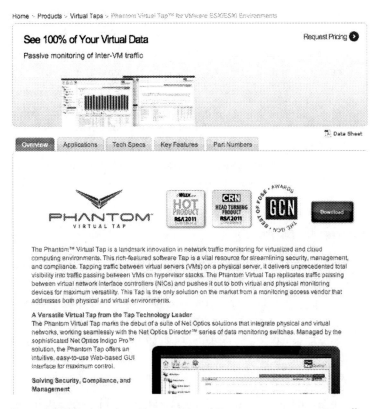

Figure 13-2 Tools such as Phantom Virtual Tap can monitor inter-VM traffic to look for suspicious patterns.

Automation

As you have learned in this book, one of the main benefits to having standardized, virtualized resources is *automation*, which means that those resources can be controlled and configured via software instead of via human intervention. For example, IT can set up virtual machine images and an interface that allows end users to provision an image. Automation means that not only does the new VM come online within minutes, but that it is also fully configured with an operating system, software, databases, and anything else the user needs to operate the machine.

> "On the virtualization side, security needs to be more than just antivirus."[21]
> —Sergi Isasi

Unfortunately, the one thing that many virtual machine images lack is security software. That is because many IT shops prefer to install and configure security tools by hand after the virtual machine has been provisioned. This ensures that the virtual machine is fully locked down, but it is not very efficient. If IT personnel cannot get to a new VM right away, then you end up with the highly undesirable situation of an insecure VM sitting within your private cloud. Throw in the rapid elasticity and easy self-provisioning of virtual resources in a private cloud, and having non-automated security procedures becomes a huge security problem.

Insider Threats

> "If you work with a company long enough, eventually you will have access to everything, and no one will know it."[23]
> —Steve Katz

While nefarious hackers have been known to penetrate corporate firewalls, a more insidious problem is the risk of insider attacks or employee data theft. In a 2011 survey by Application Security, Unisphere Research, and the International Sybase Users Group (ISUG), called *2011 ISUG Report On Data Security Management Challenges*,[22] a full 20% of respondents cited insider attacks as the root cause of data breaches over the previous twelve months.

> "A majority of respondents, 53%, cite security concerns regarding public cloud-based configurations. Another 37% say they are concerned about the security within private cloud or virtualized database environments."[24]
> —Joseph McKendrick

Having to worry about malicious insiders is bad enough, but a much more common concern is the otherwise-model employee who unintentionally or accidentally creates a security threat. For example, if an employee leaves his or her desk without logging off the network, another person can access data and network resources just by sitting down at the unattended computer. Similarly, an employee who needs to take sensitive corporate data home might email it to a personal address, upload it to an online storage site, or copy it to a USB thumb drive, all of which make the data vulnerable to theft. (In that same ISUG survey, 46% of respondents identified human error as the root cause of data breaches, while another 17% cited accidental loss of a device or storage media containing sensitive data.) These threats are magnified if any employees have been given network security privileges that far exceed what they require to perform their jobs, which is a not uncommon scenario.

Consumerization and Shadow IT

One of the realities of the twenty-first century workplace is that it places tremendous pressure on employees to raise their productivity and to make themselves available outside of the office. One of the main ways that workers are coping with this pressure is to consumerize IT. For example, if IT cannot provide them with the tools they need, workers are attempting to boost their productivity by turning to consumer-focused websites such as LinkedIn and Google Docs (these are examples of the shadow IT that I talked about in "Chapter 1: Introducing Cloud Computing"). Similarly, business users are staying connected and working in non-office locations by using their own devices, such as smartphones, tablets, and notebooks, a phenomenon known as BYOD—bring your own devices.

Consumerization is important enough to workers and to managers (who, after all, *want* their employees to be more productive and connected) that it is likely to become entrenched, if it is not already. Unfortunately, the benefits of consumerization are somewhat outweighed by the significant security holes that it brings to the business:

- As a general security strategy, IT configures company-owned devices to match company security policies, and upgrades device firmware and software as needed when security-related patches become available. IT has no such control over employee-owned devices.

- Your company may have compliance regulations or audit concerns that require certain security standards for devices. It is extremely difficult, if not impossible, to enforce such regulations on employee-owned devices.

- Consumer-focused websites almost certainly do not offer security controls or standards that match (or even come close to) those required by your business (either through company policies or compliance rules).

These holes make the company's IT structure vulnerable in a couple of ways. First, any corporate data that ends up on an employee's device is vulnerable to theft, literally by stealing the device, or less directly, either by using an unattended (but logged-in) device or by tapping into a non-secure transmission signal. Second, employee-owned devices that are not maximally secure or patched can be hacked, which can lead to unauthorized access of the corporate network.

"As more and more people bring their own smartphone and/or tablet into the office, it gets to be quite difficult and costly for IT managers to control access to company data and information."[25]
—Matthew Miller

REFERENCES

1 The full quote is "Reports that say that something hasn't happened are always interesting to me, because as we know, there are known knowns; there are things we know we know. We also know there are known unknowns; that is to say we know there are some things we do not know. But there are also unknown unknowns—the ones we don't know we don't know." See Donald Rumsfeld, DoD News Briefing, U.S. Department of Defense, http://www.defense.gov/transcripts/transcript. aspx?transcriptid=2636 (February 12, 2002).

2 **Terry Woloszyn,** *Cloud Security Reaches Enterprise Scale for the First Time with PerspecSys PRS*, BusinessWire, http://www.businesswire.com/news/home/20111109005165/en/Cloud-Security-Reaches-Enterprise-Scale-Time-PerspecSys (November 9, 2011).

3 See http://www.privacyrights.org/data-breach/.

4 **Ron Ross,** quoted in Doug Beizer, *NIST creates cloud-computing team*, Federal Computer Week, http://fcw.com/Articles/2009/02/25/NIST-cloud-computing.aspx (February 25, 2009).

5 See http://csrc.nist.gov/groups/SMA/fisma/index.html.

6 See http://www.cms.gov/HIPAAGenInfo/.

7 See http://www.sec.gov/about/laws.shtml#sox2002.

8 See https://www.pcisecuritystandards.org/security_standards/index.php.

9 See http://csrc.nist.gov/publications/nistpubs/800-53-Rev3/sp800-53-rev3-final_updated-errata_05-01-2010.pdf.

10 *Gartner Reveals Top Predictions for IT Organizations and Users for 2012 and Beyond*, Business Wire, http://www.businesswire.com/news/home/20111201005541/en/Gartner-Reveals-Top-Predictions-Organizations-Users-2012 (December 1, 2012).

11 **Christofer Hoff,** quoted in Bill Bulkeley, *Cloud Providers are Stepping up Compliance*, The Network, http://newsroom.cisco.com/feature-content?type=webcontent&articleId=5870793 (January 18, 2011).

12 **J. Nicholas Hoover,** *Cloud Security: Better Than We Think?*, Informationweek, http://www.informationweek.com/news/government/cloud-saas/231902850 (November 14, 2011).

13 **Verne G. Kopytoff,** *F.B.I. Seizes Web Servers, Knocking Sites Offline*, The New York Times, http://bits.blogs.nytimes.com/2011/06/21/f-b-i-seizes-web-servers-knocking-sites-offline/ (June 21, 2011).

14 **Stephan Chenette,** *AusCert 2009—POwning The Programmable Web*, Security Labs Blog, http://securitylabs.websense.com/content/Blogs/3402.aspx (May 22, 2009).

15 *Amazon Web Services Overview of Security Processes whitepaper*, Amazon Web Services, http://aws.amazon.com/security/ (May 2011).

16 *Microsoft Security Bulletin MS10-010- Important: Vulnerability in Windows Server 2008 Hyper-V Could Allow Denial of Service (977894)*, Microsoft, http://technet.microsoft.com/en-us/security/bulletin/MS10-010 (February 10, 2010).

17 **Eric Lai**, *Multitenancy and Cloud Platforms: Four Big Problems*, Wired Cloudline, http://www.wired.com/cloudline/2012/02/multitenancy-and-cloud-problems/ (February 18, 2012).

18 **Derek Harris**, *After power outages, cloud insurance looks even better*, GigaOM, http://gigaom.com/cloud/a-week-after-clouds-fall-cloud-insurance-looks-even-better/ (August 15, 2011).

19 *Gartner Says 60 Percent of Virtualized Servers Will Be Less Secure Than the Physical Servers They Replace Through 2012*, Gartner, http://www.gartner.com/it/page.jsp?id=1322414 (March 15, 2010).

20 See http://netoptics.com/products/virtual-taps/phantom-virtual-tap%E2%84%A2-vmware-esxesxi-environments.

21 **Sergi Isasi,** quoted in Jennifer LeClaire, Symantec, *VMware Hook Up for Virtual Security*, CIO Today, http://www.cio-today.com/news/Symantec--VMware-Team-on-Security/story.xhtml?story_id=00100018P9Y6 (March 1, 2012).

22 **Joseph McKendrick,** *2011 ISUG Report On Data Security Management Challenges*, Application Security, http://www.appsecinc.com/news/casts/11-0503-2011-ISUG-REPORT-ON-DATA-SECURITY-MANAGEMENT-CHALLENGES/ISUG-DataSec-FINAL.pdf (April 2011).

23 **Steve Katz**, *Tackling the Insider Threat*, BankInfoSecurity, http://www.bankinfosecurity.com/blogs.php?postID=140 (February 17, 2009).

24 **McKendrick**, 17.

25 **Matthew Miller**, *BYOD security problem: Less than 10% of tablet owners use auto-lock*, ZDNet, http://www.zdnet.com/blog/mobile-gadgeteer/byod-security-problem-less-than-10-of-tablet-owners-use-auto-lock/5536 (March 1, 2012).

Index